Acclaim for *Married Catholic Priests*

"Anthony Kowalski writes from a lifelong commitment to the Church. In *Married Catholic Priests* he bears witness to this commitment and to his deep hope for the renewal of the Church he loves."

— Donald Cozzens, author of *The Changing Face of the Priesthood* and *Sacred Silence: Denial and Crisis in the Church*

"Wonderfully instructive about married popes, bishops, and priests of the first millennium, Kowalski traces the moves toward a celibate clergy in the West before he turns to the pre- and post-conciliar period. Perhaps the most interesting part reports the shame and humiliation visited on married priests and their wives balanced by accounts of those who have continued active in church life, some on the national scene. The book makes one ask how and when the Roman See will set up vicariates like those of Opus Dei and the military chaplaincies to reinstate the active service in any diocese those who wish to resume priestly ministry."

— Gerard S. Sloyan, author of *Preaching from the Lectionary*

"Anthony Kowalski puts a human face on married Catholic priests. Through descriptions of real-life experiences he shows their joys and their struggles and their ongoing commitment to their faith. If theology starts by reading 'the signs of the times,' then this biographical work helps shape theology in the new millennium."

— Anthony J. Tambasco, Professor of Theology, Georgetown University

"I recommend Anthony Kowalski's insightful, fair, and literate account of the married priest movement. The history of our effort and our time has found an eloquent voice in the language and testimony of this book."

— Anthony Padovano, Professor of Theology, Ramapo College of New Jersey

Married Catholic Priests

Married Catholic Priests

Their History, Their Journeys, Their Reflections

Anthony P. Kowalski

A Crossroad Book
The Crossroad Publishing Company
New York

Cover icon *Peter and His Wife* by Eileen McCabe. Used with permission. Copies of *Peter and His Wife* are available from Eileen McCabe at 12 Moorea Court, Garnerville, NY 10923; tel.: 845-354-5434.

The Crossroad Publishing Company
16 Penn Plaza – 481 Eighth Avenue, Suite 1550
New York, NY 10001

Printed in the United States of America

The text of this book is set in 11/15 Sabon.
The display face is Goudy Sans.

Library of Congress Cataloging-in-Publication Data
Kowalski, Anthony P.
    Married Catholic priests : their history, their journey, their reflections / Anthony P. Kowalski.
        p.   cm.
    Includes bibliographical references and index.
    ISBN 0-8245-2349-0 (alk. paper)
    1. Catholic Church – Clergy. 2. Celibacy – Catholic Church.
3. Marriage – Religious aspects – Catholic Church.   I. Title.
BX1912.85.K69 2005
262′.14208655 – dc22

                                                            2005025673

1   2   3   4   5   6   7   8   9   10   10   09   08   07   06   05

To my beloved wife
Joan
and our dear son
John

Contents

Preface

BEFORE 1965, release from the law of priestly celibacy in the Roman Catholic Church was not possible. A priest who fell in love had few options — abandon the woman, maintain a secret affair, face censure and expulsion. Each option brought pain.

Pope John XXIII (1958–63) grieved over this. As papal nuncio in Sofia, Bulgaria, he had befriended Orthodox married priests and respected them. As papal nuncio in Paris, France, he dealt with worker-priests and admired their efforts. These experiences led to greater compassion toward priests. His friend, the German theologian Bernard Häring, wrote that John XXIII on his deathbed expressed regret for not resolving the matter of priests who marry.[1]

Pope Paul VI (1963–78), aware of his predecessor's concerns, resolved to do something about them. Although opposed to discussing celibacy at the Second Vatican Council, he put in place in 1964 a judicial procedure for dispensing priests and allowing them to marry. Roman officials handled these matters privately until 1972, when the norms were made public. A major exodus followed. Requests for dispensation flooded to Rome from parish curates and high dignitaries, from remote mission territories and major urban areas, and from every diocese and religious congregation in the world. At a press conference in June 1991 the undersecretary of the Congregation of the Clergy in Rome estimated that the Vatican had granted sixty thousand dispensations.

Pope John Paul II, upon taking office in 1978, halted the process. But he then authorized the ordination of married Episcopal, Lutheran, and other Christian ministers who converted to Catholicism. This happened when ordained Catholic priests were marrying and being accepted as pastors and bishops in Protestant churches.

Never before has the Roman Catholic Church witnessed anything like this. First, former Protestant clergy are working as married priests in Roman Catholic parishes. Second, ordained Roman Catholic priests are accepted as married pastors in Protestant Churches. Third, ordained Roman Catholic priests are working as married laymen in Roman Catholic institutions. Fourth, Roman Catholic clerics, denied a dispensation, marry and continue sacramental ministry without church sanction. Fifth, the ordination of women a generation ago by a Roman Catholic bishop in the underground church of Czechoslovakia and the ordination of seven Catholic women by Old Catholic bishops in Austria have been verified.

A further dilemma arises from the dwindling number of celibate priests. Catholics and other Christians in need of pastoral care are requesting sacramental ministry from former clerics, who are eager to respond — preaching the Gospel, celebrating the Eucharist, and performing baptisms, weddings, and funerals. With Christ they say, "What man among you, if his son asks him for bread, will give him a stone? Or if he asks for a fish, will give him a serpent?" (Matt. 7:9–10).

Where is this heading? What does it portend for the future of the Roman Catholic Church?

My wanderings around the country these past twenty-seven years have acquainted me with hundreds of Catholic married priests and their wives and children. Their stories tug at the heart. Most married priests openly show an enduring dedication to the Living God and a persevering fidelity to the message of Christ. The following pages describe their journeys.

Part I presents a historical overview. It begins with the history of a married priesthood in the Catholic Church, including statements of past and present-day bishops (chapter 1). The corresponding tragic stories of priests' wives follow (chapter 2). A new phase began in the late 1960s with the organizing of priests and their advocacy of a married priesthood (chapter 3).

Part II depicts the journeys of many who have left the clerical state: priests reacting to the promulgation of *Humanae Vitae* (chapter 4); couples working as lay people in the Catholic Church (chapter 5);

married priests reflecting the full spectrum from arch-conservative to arch-liberal views (chapter 6); prominent former clergy continuing their professional careers (chapter 7); Catholic clergy transferring to Protestant churches, and Protestant clergy serving as married priests in Catholic churches (chapter 8); and an analysis of the spirituality of priests who marry (chapter 9).

Part III contains personal reflections on a married priesthood, including the specifics of my journey (chapter 10), efforts to help those transitioning (chapter 11), married priest involvement in a vibrant Catholic community (chapter 12), bigoted assaults on married priests (chapter 13), and final perspectives on a married priesthood (chapter 14).

Many have shared their stories. Theologians, religious educators, celibate and married men and women have reviewed this text and offered advice. They are not identified for fear of forgetting some, or betraying the preferred anonymity of others. All deserve gratitude. In narrating these stories, the author has changed the names of some, as requested, but has kept the specific details of their lives in every instance.

This book documents the experience of Roman Catholic priests who marry and give unique witness to the Christian message. The new Pentecost heralded by the Second Vatican Council has begun to bear fruit. Surprises of the Spirit abound. A renewed priesthood is emerging.

Part One

Historical Background

Chapter 1

The Other Tradition

THE TRADITION OF a celibate priesthood in the Catholic Church is well known. Not as obvious to Roman Catholics is the tradition of a married priesthood — ancient, apostolic, and uninterrupted. From the early days of the apostles including the first Popes, throughout the entire history of Eastern Christianity, and amid the changing discipline of Western Christianity, a married priesthood has endured. Today it flourishes.

Biblical Testimony

The Scriptures bear witness to the apostles being married. Paul writes in 1 Corinthians 9:5, "Do we not have the right to be accompanied by a wife, as the other apostles and the brethren of the Lord and Cephas?" (Revised Standard Version/Catholic Edition). The phrase used in the Greek is *gynaika periagein. The Jerome Biblical Commentary,* the work of America's foremost Catholic biblical scholars, notes that even in Classical Greek usage the phrase means "to have a wife," not "to take a woman about with me."[1] Many have translated this text in a way that suggests Paul took a woman along as a servant or secretary. Besides being anachronistic, such translations obfuscate the obvious.

Jerome chose to translate the Greek word *gynē* in that passage using not *uxor,* meaning wife, but *mulier,* meaning woman. After his Latin Vulgate edition became the official Scripture for Roman Catholics, all later vernacular translations in the Catholic Church were based on the Vulgate alone. Only recently has that changed. The word "wife," therefore, is not found in most Catholic Bibles. Moreover, in the Western Church the term "wife" is absent in sermons

3

about apostles from the days of the Church Fathers to the present. The average Christian for many centuries never conceived of apostles as married men.

The distinguished Catholic biblical scholar Raymond E. Brown, reflecting the view of most Scripture scholars today, writes in a footnote to the text in First Corinthians, "From 9:4–6 we learn that other apostles (for Paul this need not mean the Twelve), the brothers of the Lord (including James?) and Cephas (Peter) were accompanied by Christian wives...."[2]

The Jerome Biblical Commentary further concludes, "Peter was a married man when Jesus called him (Mark 1:17); probably all the Twelve were married except John, whom tradition called 'the virgin youth.'"[3] Peter's marital status is clear not only from that text, but also from Mark 1:30–31, "Simon's mother-in-law lay sick with a fever, and immediately they told him [Jesus] of her. And he came and took her by the hand and lifted her up, and the fever left her; and she served them." These passages allow no other interpretation. Jesus cured Peter's mother-in-law. Peter was married. Noted Scripture scholar John L. McKenzie, S.J., further observes, "I Co 9:5 suggests that his wife was still living at the time the letter was written."[4] Scripture scholars usually ascribe that epistle to the years 54 to 57, and put Peter's death a decade later.

The Apostle Paul states that he knows of no saying of the Lord about celibacy. He can only offer his personal opinion in the matter: "Now concerning the unmarried, I have no command of the Lord, but I give my opinion as one who by the Lord's mercy is trustworthy. I think that in view of the impending distress it is well for a person to remain as he is. Are you bound to a wife? Do not seek to be free. Are you free from a wife? Do not seek marriage" (1 Cor. 7:25–27). In the light of "impending distress" — presumed to be the expected and imminent end of the world — Paul advocates neither marriage nor freedom from marriage. He denies knowledge of a command from Christ in this matter.[5]

During his apostolic journeys, Paul planted the seed of the Gospel in communities throughout Asia Minor and set in place leaders to guide them. The author of the Pastoral Epistles, reflecting the Apostle

Paul, gives guidelines for the selection of such leaders. In a long list of qualities to look for in a church overseer (bishop), he insisted first that the person be "above reproach," and second "the husband of one wife." Then followed a list of other qualities or behaviors (1 Tim. 3:1–7). A similar listing is found in Titus 1:5–9. To further clarify the matter, the author adds that the person "must manage his household well, keeping his children submissive and respectful in every way; for if a man does not know how to manage his household, how can he care for God's church?" (1 Tim. 3:4–5).

Catholic biblical scholars point out that marriage is not presented as a requirement for the office of bishop. They are correct. But Protestant biblical scholars note that marriage with children is portrayed as an asset for such office. They are also correct. If a man has not managed well his household, the Pastoral Epistles question whether he can properly manage the Church.

Jean-Paul Audet gives a perceptive commentary on these texts when he notes:

> The Pauline recommendations as to the choice of *episkopoi*, presbyters and deacons seem to be absolutely unambiguous. They make it clear that in Paul's view the framework of a home, with its living mesh of human relationships, with its wonderfully rich and strong customs of hospitality along with the marriage, which constituted its essential and permanent reality, was a veritable education in the governing and serving of small groups and at that time represented the only concrete and tangible possibility for the *ekklesia* — for the local service of the word, for the frequent service of the Eucharist, and for the continual sense of fraternal charity in all its various forms.[6]

Early Christian Witness

Clearly, the early Church chose worthy men from the Christian community — most frequently respected married men — to serve as overseers, *episkopoi*. The practice continued for many generations. Writings in the early church attest to it.

Eusebius in his *Historia Ecclesiastica* reproduces part of a letter sent by Polycrates, a bishop in Ephesus at the end of the second century, to Pope Victor in Rome. In that letter, Polycrates at sixty-five boasts of his being the eighth in a line of bishops that goes back to the turn of the century. He mentions in passing his descent in a direct family line from several of them. No hint of embarrassment here, only pride in the stability and continuity of this great church.[7]

A generation later (c. 220) Hippolytus scolded Pope Callistus for allowing clergy who married to continue in their priestly role. Callistus made no apology for this. He had the support of the community in Rome.[8]

In the 240s, a married Carthaginian priest named Caecilius was responsible for bringing the great Cyprian into the Christian faith. A close friendship developed between the two. The *Vita Cypriani* records that, before dying, Caecilius entrusted his wife and children to the care of Cyprian.[9] The practice seems normal.

In the same period, Clement of Alexandria tells us that "Peter and Philip had children and Philip married his daughters to men."[10] Clement also defended married priests when he wrote, "the husband of one wife is acceptable, be he priest, deacon, or layman, as long as he uses marriage without blame. He will be saved through raising children."[11]

Eusebius bears witness to the persecutions of the third century. In his monumental history, he refers to Chaeremon, bishop of Nilopolis, forced to flee with his wife to the Arabian mountains,[12] and Phileas, a married bishop of Thmuis, martyred during the persecution of Maximinius.[13] No alarm or criticism of their marital status is given.

The author of the *Apostolic Constitutions* at the end of the third century reflects the practice of his day regarding ordinations:

When receiving ordination and being placed in the episcopacy, the man should be examined: whether he is respectful, faithful, and honest; whether he has or has had a modest and faithful wife; whether he has educated his children devoutly, brought them up in the discipline of the Lord, and led them to virtue.[14]

And the *Didascalia,* originating in Syria in the same period, takes for granted that marriage is the normal status for a bishop:

> It is fitting that the bishop be a man of one wife, and a good care-taker of his household. When he receives the imposition of hands and is ordained to the episcopacy, let him be examined: whether he is chaste, and has or has had a faithful and chaste wife; whether he has educated and admonished his children wisely; and whether members of his household revere, honor and obey him. For if his own children plot against him and disobey, what of those outside his household?[15]

The evidence is unmistakable. After more than two centuries of Christian practice, the *Apostolic Constitutions* and the *Didascalia* bear witness in every detail to observance of the admonitions to Timothy and Titus. Married bishops were common in the early church. The same is affirmed by John W. O'Malley, S.J., professor of church history at the Weston Jesuit School of Theology in Cambridge, Massachusetts, who wrote:

> Beginning with the third century there is indisputable evidence that even in the West many priests and bishops in good standing were married. The following list of bishops is but a small sample that I have randomly selected: Passivus, bishop of Fermo; Cassius, bishop of Narni; Aetherius, bishop of Vienne; Aquilinus, bishop of Evroux; Faron, bishop of Meaux; Magnus, bishop of Avignon; Filibaud, bishop of Aire-sur L'Adour was the father of St. Philibert de Jumiages, and Sigilaicus, bishop of Tours, was the father of St. Cyran of Brene.[16]

We know little about the first popes, sometimes nothing more than a name. But a few details survive. Pope Sixtus I (116–25), for example, was the son of a priest. So also in those first five centuries were Pope St. Damasus I (366–84), Pope St. Innocent I (401–17), Pope Boniface I (418–22), Pope Sixtus III (432–40), Pope St. Felix III (483–92), and Pope Anastasius II (496–98). More intriguing, Pope St. Innocent I (401–17) succeeded his father, Pope Anastasius I (399–401).

The First Millennium

Nevertheless, a body of literature arose, featuring enthusiastic praise of virginity, an impassioned defense of widowhood, and fervent exhortations to chastity. The apostolic origins of these texts must also be recognized. Some reasons can be given for this evolution.

First, the ascetic lifestyles of celibate monks captured the imagination of early Christians. Much as Eastern gurus and mystics today attract many followers, so too did monks in the desert in those early centuries. Stories of heroic battles with the devil (in the manner of St. Anthony the Hermit), coupled with the ascetic lifestyle of these men (following the pattern of St. John the Baptist in the desert) and the Christ-centeredness of their teachings, inspired many to follow their example.

Second, in studying the Scriptures early Christians became aware that priests in Old Testament times abstained from sexual relations with their wives on the eve of offering Temple sacrifice. Followers of Christ concluded that New Testament priests should at least do the same before presuming to offer the Holy Sacrifice. Because *daily* Eucharist never caught on in the Eastern Church of Constantinople, clerics there kept abstinent only before their weekly celebrations. In the Western Church of Rome, however, when daily Eucharist became the norm, total abstinence followed.

Third, as time went by, bishops came to be chosen increasingly from the monastic community. Often these men had come from propertied classes and had renounced their wealth. Their celibate state and commitment to poverty prevented nepotism, the passing on of church property to their children or to other members of their family. The Christian community benefited from that.

A fourth and strong influence on the Church in those early centuries was the philosophies of the day, especially Gnosticism and Manichaeism. Rooted in Plato, they taught a clear distinction between matter and spirit. Evil was thought to come from matter, which includes the human body in common with animals and plants. Goodness, however, relates to the spirit, shared with the angels. Such ideas led to a disdain for the human body and reverence for things spiritual.

In extreme form, such thinking also provoked contempt for women and marriage.

Many Christians in those early centuries succumbed to the lure of Gnostic and Manichaean teaching. According to Eusebius, the great early theologian Origen undertook castration at the age of eighteen. St. Jerome, moreover, was led to conclude that all sexual intercourse is impure.[17] And St. John Chrysostom taught, "Matrimony is of much use to those still caught up in their passions, who desire to live the lives of swine and be ruined in brothels."[18] Each reflects the influence of pagan thought.

The Catholic Church in time rejected these teachings because they contradict the first page of the Bible, with its continual refrain after every creative act, "God saw that it was good." And after creating the entire material world, "God saw everything that he had made, and behold, it was very good" [Gen. 1:31]. Christians throughout history are exhorted to praise God for the gifts of creation.

The earliest legislation on sexual matters did not demand celibacy but abstinence in marriage. As Edward Schillebeeckx, the contemporary Dutch theologian, points out, the Eastern and Western Churches throughout the first millennium never considered making celibacy a condition for entering into priestly ministry. Instead, prompted by a concern for ritual purity, they enacted laws of abstinence.[19]

The first recorded law came from the regional Council of Elvira, Spain, in 306, when the assembled nineteen bishops declared in Canon 33 that "bishops, priests, deacons and all other clerics having a position in the ministry are ordered to abstain from their wives and not to have children. Whoever does this, shall be expelled from the dignity of the clerical state." This regulation enunciates the *lex continentiae,* the liturgical law forbidding sexual intercourse the night before approaching the Eucharistic Table. Similar pronouncements arose in succeeding years from many other regional councils of bishops — Arles in 314, Rome in 386, Carthage in 390, Hippo in 397, Turin in 398, and Toledo in 400. These rulings did not forbid priests to marry, but banned sexual union with their wives. The law demanded continence.

One can only surmise the human anguish such rules generated in families of married priests. The father of a household became stigmatized as an immoral person in contrast to the ascetic monk. As a result, communities were led to separate forcibly married priests from their wives and children. To isolate further those who resisted, some bishops enacted laws that forbade the faithful to take part in services celebrated by them.

Yet contradictory rulings vied for many centuries. The Synod of Ancyra in 314 decreed in Canon X that deacons could marry after ordination.[20] The Council of Gangra in 345 declared in Canon IV, "If any one shall maintain, concerning a [married] priest, that it is not lawful to partake of the oblation when he offers it, let him be anathema."[21] In its twenty-one canons that council looked for a balance between celibacy and marriage. It concluded, "We admire the state of virginity; we approve of continence and of separation from the world; if only those states of life be accompanied by humility and modesty; but we also honor marriage."[22]

And contradictory practices can also be found. Gregory the Illuminator (d. 337), venerated by the Armenians as apostle and patron, was a married bishop. Sent as Catholicos, the prime church leader, to Armenia at the end of the third century, he later ordained his two sons as bishops. The title of Catholicos remained in their family over a century. And the revered Doctor of the Church St. Hilary of Poitiers (315–68) was married and had a daughter named Apra.

The three great Cappadocian Fathers also witness to their times. The first, St. Gregory Nazianzen, was the son of Gregory the Elder, a married bishop. The second, St. Gregory of Nyssa, married Theosebea in 365; he was then ordained bishop by his brother Basil in 371. The third, St. Basil the Great, with his older sister Macrina, his younger brothers Gregory and Peter, his parents Basil and Emmelia, and his grandmother Macrina, are all venerated as saints in the Eastern Orthodox and Roman Catholic Churches.

No written defense of clerical marriage in the fourth century has survived. Yet such treatises were written by Jovinian, Vigilantius, and Synesius. Their arguments come down to us only through references by their chief adversaries, Jerome and Augustine, whose texts have survived. Noteworthy is the behavior of the same Synesius, bishop of Ptolemis in Egypt, who in A.D. 400 refused to repudiate his wife and expressed the fond hope of having more children.[23]

The Greek historian Socrates in his famous *Historia Ecclesiastica,* Book V, Chapter XI, records the touching account of an incident that supposedly happened during the deliberations of the Ecumenical Council of Nicaea in A.D. 325. Attending was the elderly Paphnutius, a bishop in Upper Thebes who, during the persecutions, lost his eye. Emperor Constantine had such great respect for this man that when Paphnutius visited the imperial palace, the ruler would kiss the crevice of the bishop's torn-out eye. During deliberations at the Council of Nicaea, a new law was being introduced requiring all clergy to abstain from intercourse with their wives. A startling intervention then occurred:

> Paphnutius, rising up in the middle of the gathering of bishops, protested vehemently that this heavy yoke should not be placed on the clergy: [for] marriage is honorable and intercourse is pure, he said, [and] out of an excessive severity injury should not be inflicted on the Church, because not all are able to follow the discipline of such a strict continence, and possibly from that it could happen that the chastity of the wife of each of them would not be preserved. [Also] he called the coming together of a husband and of a legitimate wife chastity.[24]

Paphnutius was a celibate monk who never married. Assembled clergy assented to his speech by terminating discussion and leaving the practice of abstention from intercourse to the discretion of clerics. The same story is also found in Sozomen's *Historia Ecclesiastica* I, 23.

Schillebeeckx, however, like many Western theologians, denies the authenticity of this story. He argues that in all the records of the Council of Nicaea there is no evidence of a discussion of priestly abstinence. He writes, "This is a legend which came into being in the middle of the fifth century as a reaction from the East against the law of abstinence which had meanwhile been introduced in the West."[25] Legend or not, this narrative even in the fifth century witnesses to strong conviction in the Eastern Church about sexual abstinence of the clergy.

Such evidence is not limited to the Eastern Churches. In a letter to Oceanus in A.D. 359, Jerome writes:

> The Spanish bishop Carterius, a man advanced in years and in priesthood, married once before baptism and, she having died, again after baptism. And you think he went against the judgment of the Apostle who in his list of virtues (1 Tim. 3:2) prescribed that the husband of only one woman shall be ordained bishop. I am amazed, however, that you set forth this one case when the world is full of such ordinations. I am not speaking of priests, not of lower clergy, but of bishops who, if I were to name them individually, would number more than the crowd at the Synod of Rimini.[26]

That Synod brought together roughly four hundred bishops.

Despite a growing disparagement of clerical marriage in the Western Church, sons of priests and bishops continued to be chosen as bishops of Rome. They include the following sons of priests: Pope St. Agapitus I (535–36), Pope Marinus I (882–84), Pope Boniface VI (896), and Pope John XV (985–96); the son of a bishop: Pope Theodore I (642–49); and sons of Popes: the martyred Pope St. Silverius (536–37) son of Pope Hormisdas (514–23), and Pope John XI (931–35) son of Pope Sergius III (904–11).

Moreover, the Byzantine or Eastern Branch of the Catholic Church did not agree with the growing mandates of the Roman or Western Branch of the Catholic Church against combining marriage and priesthood. At the Council in Trullo II in 692, bishops criticized Western practices. Canon XIII of that Council decrees:

> Since we know it to be handed down as a rule of the Roman Church that those deemed worthy to be advanced to the diaconate or presbyterate should promise no longer to cohabit with their wives, we, preserving the ancient rule and apostolic perfection and order, will that the lawful marriages of men who are in holy orders be from this time forward firm, by no means

dissolving their union with their wives, nor depriving them of mutual intercourse at convenient times. . . . If, therefore, anyone shall have dared, contrary to the apostolic canons, to deprive any of those in sacred orders, presbyter or deacon or subdeacon, of cohabitation and intercourse with his lawful wife, let him be deposed. In like manner also if any presbyter or deacon on pretense of piety has dismissed his wife, let him be excluded from communion, and if he persevere in this, let him be deposed.[27]

The Orthodox Church maintains that the Trullian Council was an ecumenical council whose rulings are binding on all Christendom. They have become normative throughout the Byzantine, Orthodox Church and endure to this day.

Many examples of married priests and married bishops can be cited. The Nestorian metropolitan (archbishop) of Nisibis in A.D. 480 married a nun. Descendants of this community are found today on the coast of Malabar in India. The Copts in Egypt and Ethiopia, dating back to the earliest centuries of the Church, allow their bishops to live with their wives after episcopal consecration. Moreover, in all Orthodox Churches today a member of the clergy can get a dispensation to return to the lay state and marry. Such diverse disciplines have survived in Christian communities from the earliest to current times.

The Second Millennium

During the first millennium of the Church, no universal rule of celibacy is found. The Eastern and Western Churches followed different disciplines. Not always did one Church respect the practices of the other.

Cardinal Humbert, the papal legate to Byzantium at the time of separation of the Eastern and Western Churches in 1054, reflects a prevailing attitude. He could hardly hide his disdain for clerical marriage as observed in the Eastern Church: "Young husbands, exhausted from carnal lust, serve the altar. And immediately afterward they again embrace their wives with hands that have been hallowed by the immaculate Body of Christ. That is not a mark of the true faith, but an invention of Satan."[28]

After the separation, the Eastern Church continued its ancient tradition of celibate and married priests. Shortly afterwards the Western Church adopted sterner measures. Attacks on clerical marriages grew in intensity in the eleventh century, reaching their height during the pontificate of Gregory VII (1073–85). A former monk known as Hildebrand, this descendant of a pope decreed that no one from then on could be ordained without a vow of celibacy, and that laity were forbidden to attend services of a married priest, deacon, or subdeacon.

The Gregorian initiatives aroused great hostility to married clergy. As Anne Barstow records:

> The common people, all too ready to heap abuses on the clergy, acted with uncontrolled fury now that they were enjoined to do so. Married priests were ridiculed in public, beaten, deprived of their livings. While some fled, becoming destitute paupers, unable to face the people among whom they had once lived in honor, others attempted to stand their ground and met a worse fate, their bodies mutilated, their only vindication their fists.[29]

A few bishops objected. Bishop Otto of Constance, for example, not only allowed priests to remain married, he also gave permission for unmarried priests to marry. In 1060 (before the Gregorian initiatives) Bishop Ulrich of Imola in Italy responded to Pope Nicholas II's decree on celibacy, arguing from Scripture that the clergy have been permitted wives from the beginning. He wrote, "Can't you see, as the common judgment of all sensible people holds, that this is violence, when one is compelled to enforce special decrees on a person against the evangelical customs and dictates of the Holy Spirit?"[30]

The lines of development in this matter are clear, as outlined by Schillebeeckx.[31] From the fifth to the tenth centuries, rules of sexual abstention by clerics were repeatedly affirmed by regional church councils. These rules were observed only superficially by married priests, as reflected in efforts to impose stricter penalties and more severe economic sanctions. The futility of imposing that discipline on married clergy led to the most drastic measure of all, an absolute ban on clerical marriage.

With the Second Lateran Council in 1139, eleven centuries of an officially recognized married priesthood in the Western, Catholic Church ended. That council decreed in Canon 6 that "deacons, priests and bishops who contracted marriage or have concubines, be deprived of their office and church benefice." And Canon 7 further ordered that "bishops, priests, deacons... who, transgressing the holy precept, have dared to contract marriage, shall be separated. Such a union, contracted in violation of church law, we do not regard as matrimony."

The new universal celibacy law met with resistance in all European countries. Such opposition is reflected in the many diocesan and regional synods that imposed increasingly harsher penalties for transgressing the law. These penalties included expulsion of the wife, excommunication of the priest and his family, and a prohibition to all women from entry into the priest's house. Despite all these punishments, the union of priests and women continued. The Church no longer called these women wives, but called them concubines or harlots.

In the thirteenth century, contemplative life thrived in Benedictine and Cistercian monasteries, some housing hundreds of members. New mendicant orders like Franciscan and Dominican also fostered celibate lifestyles. These orders grew rapidly and reinforced papal prohibitions against priestly marriages.

Bishops at the Council of Constance (1414–18) and the Council of Basel (1435) voiced opposition to the current discipline. But their words had no effect; enforcement of celibacy laws continued with all rigor. Although the law was never changed, its observance was often privately circumvented.

Bert Peeters documents in succeeding generations an enormous escalation in the number of clergy in the Netherlands.[32] In Utrecht between 1515 and 1518, two to three hundred priests were ordained annually. Parishes supported between 38 and 120 priests. These clerics had to celebrate Masses daily for their income, stipends being attached to each Mass. In the course of this evolution, bishops gave little attention to the selection, education, and spiritual direction of the clergy. Visitation reports between 1550 and 1575 in Europe show that about 25 percent of the clergy had concubines.

In the centuries leading to the Reformation, popes who fathered children held the throne of Peter. Richard P. McBrien[33] records that Pope Clement IV (1265–68) was a widower with two daughters, Pope Innocent VIII (1484–92) was father of three illegitimate children before ordination, Pope Alexander VI (1492–1503) fathered children before and after his election to the papacy, Pope Julius II (1503–13) fathered three daughters as cardinal, and Pope Paul III (1534–49) fathered four illegitimate children before ordination. Ludwig von Pastor further documents that Pope Pius IV (1559–65) begot illegitimate children before receiving sacred orders[34] and Pope Gregory XIII (1572–85) had four sons.[35]

Reformation and Post-Reformation

Abuses and scandals in the Church, even at the highest levels, reached their apex in the sixteenth century. Lust for power, money, and domination ran rampant throughout Europe. As these abuses increased, the voices of reformers clamored more loudly. *Reformatio in capite et in membris* (reformation in the head and its members) was their constant cry. A clash became inevitable.

Reformers demanded greater fidelity to the Scriptures and a way of life more consistent with biblical teachings. Basing their beliefs on a strict reading of the Pastoral Epistles, they advocated married leaders in the Christian community. Luther married in 1521 at age forty-two and always cherished the dignity of marriage and family life. Other reformers — Zwingli and Bucer — also married. Priests in the Northern countries by the droves followed their example. Many in France married also, even though they faced severe punishment, including burning at the stake.

By current standards, behaviors in Spain during the sixteenth century, as reflected in the families of two of the greatest Jesuits, can only be termed bizarre. Ignatius Loyola (1491–1556), founder of the Society of Jesus, had a brother, Pedro Lopez, a Basque parish priest who fathered four children. And Francis Borgia (1510–72), the great-grandson of Pope Alexander VI, grew up in the episcopal palace of his grandfather, Don Alonzo, the archbishop of Saragossa. Francis became the Duke of Gandia and fathered eight children. When his beloved wife, Leonora, died in 1546, he provided for the welfare of his children and then took off for Rome in 1550 to join the Jesuits. He was ordained a priest the following year and for twenty-two years brought fame to the Society of Jesus, serving as its third general.

When the newly elected Pope Paul III in 1534 promised to convene an ecumenical council, he received a stream of recommendations from bishops and sovereigns. Two requests emerged repeatedly: mitigation of the celibacy law and permission to take communion under both species. Emperor Charles V and his successor Philip II argued that the spread of the Reformation could be checked if these two reforms were to be adopted. But such changes were not to be. They were deemed too strong a concession to Protestant reformers.

At the final session of the Council of Trent in 1563, the Fathers declared, "If anyone says that clergy in sacred orders or regulars with solemn vows of chastity can enter into marriage and that such a contract is valid, despite Church law or vow ... and that all those who do not feel they have the gift of chastity, even though they vowed to keep it, can enter into matrimony, let him be anathema" (Canon 9).[36] They further asserted, "If anyone says ... it is not better and more blessed to remain in virginity or in celibacy than to marry, let him be anathema" (Canon 10).[37] They also banned secret marriage (Canon 12); only marriage before a priest and witnesses was recognized by the Church.[38]

The Council made important changes in the education of clergy. In the centuries that followed, bishops prescribed more extensive training for priests. Boys at age twelve were encouraged to enter minor seminaries. After twelve years of study in an all-male, sequestered environment, they were ordained priests and sent into the world. If the priest later tried to marry, the faithful were instructed to regard him as excommunicated and expel him from their communities. Books criticizing celibacy were put on the Index of Forbidden

Books. The entire ecclesiastical system reinforced the ban on clerical marriage.

With the age of enlightenment and the influence of Rousseau, Montesquieu, and Voltaire came further challenges to the traditional discipline. Leaders of the French Revolution argued that no human being could be restrained from marrying. As a result, thousands of French priests married. A few years later, when Napoleon Bonaparte signed a concordat with Rome, Pope Pius VI agreed to allow a return to the lay state for about thirty-five hundred priests who had married or wanted to marry.

The Reigns of Pius XI and Pius XII

After the Council of Trent (1545–63), the Church set up a wall of opposition to all things Protestant, including antagonism to married clergy. Occasionally, however, the Catholic Church has recognized the outstanding work of married priests. In 1929, for example, Pope Pius XI beatified Gomidas Keumurgian, a married Armenian secular priest from Constantinople put to death by schismatics because of his strong advocacy of union of the Armenian Church with Rome. And in *Casti Connubii,* issued on December 31, 1930, the same Pius XI articulated a sacred principle, "No human law can take away from people the original human right to marry."

Other slight changes occurred. Between 1951 and 1953 Pope Pius XII granted a dispensation allowing four Lutheran pastors in Germany to be ordained Roman Catholic priests. Not one had to relinquish marital relations as a condition for ordination. But these were exceptions.

Over a thirty-two year period in the twentieth century, three popes wrote encyclical letters glorifying celibacy: *Ad Catholici Sacerdotii* (On the Catholic Priesthood) by Pius XI on December 20, 1935; *Sacra Virginitas* (On Holy Virginity) by Pius XII on March 25, 1954; and *Sacerdotalis Caelibatus* (On Priestly Celibacy) by Paul VI on June 24, 1967 (discussed below). Each refused to reconsider traditional teaching and reaffirmed current discipline. A storm, however, was brewing.

The Reigns of John XXIII and Paul VI

The accession of Angelo Giuseppe Roncalli to the throne of Peter in 1958 introduced a new climate for change. As Pope John XXIII, the 78-year-old pontiff surprised the world by convening an ecumenical council. Those sessions were conducted in a spirit of collegiality, with the help of distinguished theologians of the day. The Council produced documents that altered church policies in important areas.

Vatican Council II (1962–65). When the bishops of the world were polled before the Vatican Council, they proposed for discussion the restoration of a permanent diaconate, but nothing about celibacy.[39] At the Council, nevertheless, bishops were ready to speak for a married priesthood. The revered Patriarch of the Melkite Catholic Church, Maximos IV Saigh, prepared a text that he never delivered. He was ready to say:

> When you praise the beauty of a celibate priesthood, you must not destroy or disregard the parallel and likewise apostolic tradition of a clergy that has taken upon itself the bond of a holy marriage. . . . Neither Scripture nor Tradition, especially that of the first centuries, do regard celibacy as an indispensable condition for priesthood.[40]

Another text supporting a married priesthood prepared by Bishop Koop of Brazil for delivery at the Council was leaked to the press and published in *Le Monde* on October 12, 1965. He asserted:

> I want to start with a clear announcement that, to save the Catholic Church in Latin America, a married clergy has to be accepted as soon as possible. . . . I therefore propose that the Council considers ordaining qualified laymen who have been married for at least five years. That solution also exists in the Orthodox Churches, which have at their disposal dignified and apostolic priests. Their matrimony, their exemplary life and their socioeconomic status will undoubtedly contribute to the effectiveness of their ministry.[41]

Other bishops were preparing similar interventions.

When he heard of these developments, Pope Paul VI dispatched a letter to the Council with orders to read it before all those assembled. The letter stated, "We know that some Fathers intend to discuss in the Council the law of ecclesiastical celibacy as observed in the Latin Church. Thus, while respecting the assembly's freedom of expression, we would like to offer our personal opinion: this is not the time to debate publicly a subject which requires the greatest prudence and is of such importance."[42] Out of deference to him, Council Fathers cut off all debate. No public discussion occurred.

Patriarch Saigh sent his prepared text, as requested, to the pope with an accompanying note in which he wrote:

> I am convinced that despite the approval which your order found (i.e., not to discuss the issue publicly), this problem is disturbing more than one bishop's conscience. Continuously we receive confidential notes from priests who, by the way, are known for their piety and zeal, who ask that we should raise our voices and break the silence.... If you do not impose upon priests the poverty of monks, which can be practiced much more easily, why do you force them to celibacy?[43]

On December 7, 1965, the Vatican Council issued its "Decree on the Ministry and Life of Priests." In that decree the Council Fathers observed, "It is true that (celibacy) is not demanded of the priesthood by its nature. This is clear from the practice of the primitive Church and the tradition of the Eastern Churches where ... there are also many excellent married priests."[44] In deference to the pope, they went no further.

Sacerdotalis Coelibatus. Seeing that the controversy over this topic continued in private, Paul VI in 1967 issued a new encyclical, *Sacerdotalis Coelibatus,* reaffirming the law of celibacy. In this document, however, he abandoned the arguments that had long been used to justify an all-celibate clergy. No longer were ritual purity and the evil of sexual union offered as justification for this discipline. He wrote instead about the fittingness of celibacy, addressed objections against it, and gave motives for maintaining an all-celibate priesthood.

Moreover, he held out an olive branch to Eastern Christianity when he wrote in paragraph 38:

> If the legislation of the Eastern Church is different in the matter of discipline with regard to clerical celibacy, as was finally established by the Council of Trullo held in the year 692, and which has been clearly recognized by the Second Vatican Council, this is due to the different historical background of that most noble part of the Church, a situation which the Holy Spirit has providentially and supernaturally influenced.[45]

Like John XXIII, Paul VI struggled with this matter. The noted Redemptorist Bernard Häring wrote, "I had the opportunity of speaking with Pope Paul VI on this problem, and I discovered that he was extremely sensitive to it, such that he even sent troubled priests to me for counseling. Even more, he promised to initiate change."[46]

Synod of 1971. The encyclical did not end the matter. In 1971 in response to continued requests from many bishops' conferences, Pope Paul VI summoned to Rome roughly two hundred cardinals, bishops, and general superiors to advise him about the celibacy law. Startling interventions were made. Bishop Valfredo Tepe, for example, presented the majority opinion of the Brazilian hierarchy that married men should be ordained priests. Voices supporting a married priesthood arose from bishops' conferences in Indonesia, Canada, and Chad. Many cardinals expressed themselves in favor: Alfrink in the Netherlands, Suenens in Belgium, Malula in Zaire, Arns and Lorscheider in Brazil, Koenig in Austria, and Vidal in the Philippines.

Cardinal Suenens of Belgium wrote in his memoirs:

> This synod dealt in part with the priesthood. I made several statements, the most important of which was a request that those episcopal conferences that might wish to do so — and this was not the case in my own country — should be allowed to open the priesthood to married men, in circumstances which would have to be defined. What I was seeking was in fact to open up the possibility of a double clergy, the one celibate and

the other married — such as we now have in the Catholic Church of the Eastern Rite and such as existed several centuries ago.[47]

A series of telling arguments were made at the synod. Theo Van Asten, the general superior of the White Fathers, declared:

> How is it that a church that requires from a priest not to enter into matrimony does not demand that they decline dignities and titles, ecclesiastical ones included? And why does it not require from its priests that they abstain from seeking after worldly riches? What can be the significance of somebody who pretends to be a celibate devoted to God, and who does not abstain from wealth, ambition and dignities? Could care for children and love for a woman be more dangerous for a priest than riches and smelling incense?[48]

And in a note addressed to the synod, Bishop Jan van Cauwelaert of Belgium wrote:

> The shortage of priests in the young churches in Africa will not be met by an increase of celibate priests, which in practice can never be materialized. All bishops will confirm the impossibility of sending celibates to straggled villages to reside there isolated and alone. It cannot be solved either by importing expatriate priests, because they are not able to be the real leaders of those communities. All bishops of Africa and many bishops of Asia demand that their catechists be married men. Now these catechists are already in charge of every priestly function, except Eucharist and Confession.[49]

Many an impassioned *cri de cor* was heard from pastorally minded bishops about the need for ordaining married men. A few pleaded in behalf of entire bishops' conferences that had discussed the matter beforehand and reached virtual unanimity in support. Others spoke in their own name. But, despite many interventions of this kind, the 1971 Synod of Bishops turned down a married priesthood. One must note that forty of the bishops at the Synod were appointed directly by the pope and the Roman Curia. If only bishops in pastoral service and delegates of national hierarchies had voted, the ordination of married men would have garnered a majority vote. The final tally was 107 opposed, 87 in favor of changing current discipline.[50]

Schillebeeckx gives a careful analysis of the speeches made during the debate.[51] The reasons cited most frequently in favor of maintaining the law of celibacy were: (1) a fear of escalation — it might open the door to further change, even ordination of women; (2) concern about making changes during a time of crisis — as Cardinal Cooray of Ceylon noted, "The hurricane is not the time to renovate the roof"; (3) concern about a synod changing a recent council declaration — bishops would look foolish, some noted, if they reversed a policy affirmed just five years earlier by the Vatican Council; and (4) awareness of the total availability of celibates — a point stressed by many bishops, without also acknowledging the episcopal power and control entailed in such availability.

In concluding the Synod, Pope Paul VI addressed them: "From your discussions, it emerges that the bishops of the entire Catholic world want to keep integrally this absolute gift by which the priest consecrates himself to God; a not negligible part of this gift — in the Latin Church — is consecrated celibacy." Not one word was said about the strong sentiment for ordaining married men. But despite the tenor of his encyclical in 1967 and the directives of the Roman Synod of 1971, Pope Paul VI continued awarding dispensations, enabling priests to return to the lay state and marry.

The Reign of John Paul II

On assuming the papacy in 1978, John Paul II abandoned the practice of his predecessor. He returned to the sterner discipline of earlier years, making more onerous and time-consuming the procedure for gaining clerical dispensations. When in 1980 Cardinal Justin Darmojuwono of Jakarta told the pope that he would resign if John Paul II refused to allow him to ordain married men, the pontiff promptly accepted his resignation. This highlights John Paul II's intransigence.

Despite such papal response, many bishops privately encouraged married priests. The influential bishop of Orleans in France, Guy

Riobe, maintained a warm friendship with married priests through-out his life. Before his death he said to them, "You should firmly persevere! The day is near that our Church will acknowledge the riches of your lives."[52]

Synods of Married Priests. Beginning in 1983 married priests and their wives have organized international gatherings or synods. On the occasion of the August 1985 Synod, senior churchmen sent let-ters supporting their efforts. Cardinal Evaristo Arns, archbishop of São Paulo in Brazil, wrote, "I understand your impatience and I sym-pathize with you. . . . I shall always do what is possible to me."[53] And Michael Vincent Rowland, bishop of Dundee, South Africa, wrote, "I hope as many bishops hope that the married permanent deacons in the Church are a sign of a move in the Church to have a rethink of priestly celibacy."[54]

Interviews of Bishops. Periodically bishops have been interviewed by journalists and have spoken freely about these matters. Cardi-nal Michele Pellegrino, the archbishop of Turin, in an interview in *Il Regno* on April 15, 1981, said:

> Confronted with this dilemma: either at any cost maintaining the law of celibacy in its present rigor, and in consequence renouncing a full evangelization, or promoting a full evange-lization, which requires Eucharist, and therefore changing the law of celibacy, I believe that we have to choose this way.[55]

Luciano Mendez de Almeida, archbishop of Mariana in Brazil, in an interview in *Rumoz* in June 1987 said:

> The Church cannot escape considering the fact of a massive departure of priests as a sign of the times, which has to be in-terpreted in the light of God's Spirit rather than in the light of canon law. . . . Seen from a merely human point of view, the fact that the Church does not want to accept the services of married priests, in whom she has invested so much education, appears to be nonsense. From a pastoral point of view, and given the chronic shortage of priests, it seems an even greater absurdity to regard all married priests as suspect and not to make use

of their skills and strengths, when they pronounce themselves ready to serve.[56]

Bolder statements have also been made. Jacques Gaillot, bishop of Evreux, at the French Bishops' Conference at Lourdes in October 1988 gave an address that was published in *Le Monde* on November 13–14 of that year. He said:

> Why not grant the dispensation from celibacy to priests who ask for it, along with the desire to stay in communion with the Church? How long shall we deprive ourselves of the service of those married priests who remain prepared for service in the Church? Why do we close our eyes to pastoral situations where the lack of priests is felt like a cry?...The absence of priests has the effect of canceling out in the faithful's minds the knowledge of how significant ordained ministry is in its symbolic and structural value for the Church. Can we continue any longer to administer the shortage, find solutions of delay, instead of doing justice to the needs of the People of God?[57]

International Federation. The gatherings in synods led to the formation of an International Federation of Married Priests. Thirty-four associations of married priests in countries all over the world joined together. In a letter to that federation on the occasion of its gathering in January 1989 Pascasio Rettler, O.F.M., the retired bishop of Bacabal in Brazil, wrote:

> I have not yet lost the hope that one day married men will be ordained, especially to serve small communities. In our diocese we have more than 500 leaders of such communities, many known to me for twenty years. I should not hesitate to ordain them, so that the right of the Eucharist for all baptized Christians might be assured.... And how much do we need those married priests who remain faithful to the Church in their belief and their love — and there are thousands of them.[58]

The 1996 gathering of the International Federation of Married Catholic Priests (IFMCP) in Brasilia witnessed the intervention of

Archbishop Luciano Mendez, who declared, "Married priests are not deserters, but pioneers." At the same meeting, Bishop Ladislao Bernaski said:

> We, bishops, can learn so many things from the witness and experience of married priests.... You can contribute so much to the symbolic and prophetic image of the Church. Perhaps you might not immediately achieve the results of your efforts; but soon people will keep asking: what is the difference whether a priest is married or not?[59]

Pastoral Provisions. In the meantime, contrary to all expectations, Pope John Paul II began restoring a married priesthood in the Western, Roman Catholic Church. That restoration began in 1977 when a few Episcopal priests as a group applied to be admitted to priesthood in the Catholic Church without divorcing their wives or refraining from marital relations. The U.S. National Conference of Catholic Bishops sent their petition to Rome. Cardinal Franjo Seper, Prefect for the Sacred Congregation for the Defense of the Faith, granted that request in June 1980.

With Pope John Paul II's approval, Episcopal and Lutheran pastors who converted to Catholicism were ordained and accepted into the Latin Rite. Priests from the Polish National Catholic Church also converted to Catholicism and had their ordination accepted as valid. They all serve as Roman Catholic married priests. By 1990 over forty had been ordained in the United States; by 2002 over a hundred.

After the special authorization granted to the U.S. Church in 1980, the Holy See gave similar permission to bishops' conferences in Canada (1986) and England and Wales (1995). Married ministers from the Lutheran, Methodist, and Presbyterian communions have also been ordained as Roman Catholic priests in the United States.

In 1996, Pope John Paul II invited a married priest, Khalil Chalfoen, father of three children and professor of dogmatic theology, to the synod of Lebanese bishops in Rome. Addressing the papal entourage on that occasion, Chalfoen asserted, "The Eastern tradition did not know an obligatory celibacy. In the Greek Catholic Church, 92 percent of the priests are married; with the Maronites 33 percent.

They are all members of the Roman Catholic Church."[60] And in canonizing Edith Stein, Pope John Paul II accepted as a miracle attributed to her intercession the cure of the daughter of an Eastern Catholic married priest.

Other Voices. Given the intransigence regarding priestly celibacy, one would expect that the married priest movement would die down at this point, and that the hierarchy would become hardened to their concerns. But evidence does not support that contention. Statements by prominent churchmen show a deeper sensitivity. On ordaining a married former Anglican priest in New York in 1990, Cardinal John Joseph O'Connor said to the press, "It would be uncharitable, unjust and very naive and foolish to say that the sense of hurt on the part of Roman Catholic priests who married and cannot come back is groundless." And in an interview in *The New Yorker* on July 22, 1991, Archbishop Rembert Weakland of Milwaukee said:

> Across-the-board celibacy works to our detriment as a Church. Men who leave the priesthood because of the loneliness are not weak. They are simply good men who have fallen in love with good women.

In Australia in 1996, Bishop Patrick Power of Canberra-Goulburn told a group of married priests and their wives that their resignation from official church ministry signaled a change in direction rather than an end to ministry. He said:

> You are all messengers of hope to people because you have trod the path of pain and suffering as you successfully worked through the crisis of leaving official ministry and began a new life. This journey equipped you to reach out to others as a beacon of hope and a helping hand to them in their time of trial and sorrow.[61]

In Europe, Cardinal Basil Hume of Westminster, referring to the law of priestly celibacy, declared, "There's no reason why that should not change, because it's Church law and not divine law." And, upon retiring in 1998, Bishop Reinhold Stecher of Innsbruck wrote a public letter in which he criticized the treatment of married priests, "Rome has lost the image of mercy and that will have heavy consequences in the next century, despite all the nice words and pompous celebrations at the beginning of the new millennium."

Speaking during a Mass in July 2000 at the annual retreat for about forty married priests, Archbishop Karl-Josef Rauber, the apostolic nuncio to Hungary, acknowledged that these priests had a "very valuable" contribution to make. He recognized that the decision to give up priestly work because of celibacy was painful and that most wanted to remain faithful to Christ and keep in touch with the Church. Nevertheless he expressed uncertainty about how laicized priests might carry on with activities of their former clerical life.

The Third Millennium

Many expected that, with the millennium celebration focusing on reconciliation, the Church would address the treatment of married priests. Cardinal Basil Hume suggested such reconciliation directly to Rome. In the name of the bishops of England and Wales, Hume formally requested amnesty for married priests and for their return. He passed away not long afterward without receiving a response.

The opening years of the third millennium saw a plethora of sympathetic calls for reform. When revelations of clerical sexual abuse in the United States stunned the nation, *The Pilot,* official newspaper of Cardinal Law's Boston Archdiocese, in March 2002 called celibacy an issue that "simply will not disappear." On March 25, 2002, Cardinal Roger M. Mahony of Los Angeles said, "The Eastern Catholic Churches have always had a married priesthood, and it works out fine. . . . So I think it should be discussed."

In July 2001 fifty-two-year-old Bishop Raymond Dumais resigned as Catholic bishop of Gaspé in Quebec and announced his plans to marry. The following year he submitted to Rome his request for laicization. He is now married. In May 2005 Roddy Wright died of liver cancer. Wright was the former Catholic bishop of Argyll and the Isles in Scotland, who eloped in 1966 with Kathleen McPhee. They married in 1998 in the Caribbean, and then emigrated to New Zealand, where he passed away. The editor of the *Scottish Catholic Observer* wrote: "As a priest and a bishop he did a lot of good for a lot of people. There will be many people in the Western Highlands and Islands who remember him for the things he did and the kindness he showed them."[62]

In an April 2002 interview in the *Edinburgh Sunday Herald,* Keith O'Brien, archbishop of St. Andrews and Edinburgh and president of the Scottish Bishops' Conference, declared, "I have no problems with celibacy withering away. There is no theological problem with it ending. The loss of celibacy would give liberty to priests to exercise their God-given gift of love and sex rather than feeling they must be celibate all their lives." And again in May 2005 the now Cardinal Keith O'Brien reiterated the same theme, "Having seen something of the apostolate of married deacons, I can foresee the day when there will be married priests."

In September 2002 Bishop Pat Power of Canberra-Goulburn in Australia said, "Celibacy is something that needs to be looked at. One of the things I have specifically suggested is that those priests who have left the active ministry and marry, that consideration be given to allowing those men to exercise priestly ministry." He reiterated similar sentiments in April 2005, saying that a new pope should allow married men to be priests, including those who have left the priesthood to marry.

The drumbeat continues. Despite all the laws enacted and penalties inflicted, Catholic priests continue to marry, with or without Church approval. Voices of support repeatedly come from every sector: bishops, priests, nuns, laywomen and laymen. Few have so consistently and faithfully supported married priests and their families as the revered Francis Murphy, auxiliary bishop of the Baltimore Archdiocese. His words form a prophetic valedictory. When on his deathbed and dying of cancer in 1999, he penned this note to the leaders of the International Federation of Married Priests:

> I write as a friend and fellow traveler along the journey the Federation has been on these past years.... A great sorrow for me over the years has been the way the process has laid all the responsibility for change on the individual priest, while the church

as an institution has not been willing to review its own procedures or policies. I feel such a profound loss to the church, to the
believing community, from this intransigence on the part of the
institution to address the issue of a married priesthood head-on,
honestly and creatively. As a bishop I remain appreciative and
grateful for the many contributions many of you have made and
are making to the church and world community....

For myself, I am so edified by the love you and your members have for the Church and by your living out new models of
a renewed priesthood....Surely your searching together, your
trying one way, then another, for viable options is the way the
universe and the earth itself has worked out the journey of life.
Your own faithfulness to this path is a sacred trust. My great
hope...is that you...and all the others...take courage and
stay the course even amidst setbacks and difficulties. In the end
a renewed Church for the New Millennium will be born, shaped
in a large measure by your experiences and those of other faithful who carry the wisdom of the Spirit and the yearning of the
community for wholeness and new life.[63]

Chapter 2

Beloved Wives

HOW CAN ONE WRITE about married priests and ignore the women who have been their closest friends, their loving partners, their chosen companions? Too long have they lived in the shadows. These women are the joy of their lives, mothers of their children, symbols of God's richest blessings. They are their beloved wives.

In journeying together, priests and their wives have learned the truth of the apostolic admonitions:

> Love one another as Christ loved the church... Love one another as you love your own bodies. Those who love their partners love themselves. No one ever hates one's own flesh; one nourishes it and takes care of it as Christ cares for the church — for we are members of Christ's body. This is why one person leaves home and clings to another, and the two become one flesh. (Eph. 5:25–31)[1]

When the history of a married priesthood in the Western Church is written, the story of priests' wives will also unfold. Deservedly so. Few have suffered more. The witness of these noble women marks a unique chapter in the annals of martyrdom. Despite the example and clear teachings of Christ, women continue to be subordinated in the Christian assembly. None more than the wives of priests. Their tale needs to be told.

The Example of Christ

In dealing with women, Christ violated the customs of his day. Men at that time were not to speak with women in public, nor travel with them, yet Jesus openly dined with them, comforted them, and came to their aid. Moreover, he welcomed them into his entourage, even those regarded as sinners.[2]

When Mary knelt down at Jesus' feet — the traditional place of male rabbinical students — even Martha, another woman, objected. But Jesus rebuked Martha. Then, like rabbis with their students, Jesus went on to teach the two, pointing out that Mary had chosen the better part (Luke 10:38–42).

Jesus challenged much of the sexist bigotry of his day. He had compassion on the Canaanite woman who knelt before him, begging him to heal her daughter (Matt. 15:21–28). His disciples urged that he send the foreigner away. But no, Jesus cured the girl. He did the same with the woman suffering with a hemorrhage for twelve years (Matt. 9:20–22). He healed her. And when he heard the ruler's daughter being mourned as dead, he entered the home, took the girl by the hand and raised her from her bed (Matt. 9:23–25).

Nor would Jesus ward off a sinful woman who came up to him and washed his feet with costly perfume. His disciples bemoaned the waste, but Jesus praised her and bade her to "go in peace." Then he turned to Simon, the prince of the apostles, and chastised him for failing to understand his behavior (Luke 7:36–50).

Jesus acted with similar kindness to the Samaritan woman at the well. To her entreaties he responded not just with water to drink, but with a detailed explanation of his message. But his disciples just "marveled that he was talking with a woman" (John 4:27).

When scribes and pharisees, trying to trick him, brought before him a woman caught in adultery, Jesus did not give in. Slowly he sketched in the sand and one by one the accusers departed. In the end, no one was left to condemn her. Nor would Jesus (John 8:2–11).

On another occasion, he healed a woman suffering from an infirmity for eighteen years. He boldly responded on the Sabbath, thus angering the rulers of the synagogue (Luke 13:10–17). Neither secular customs nor religious taboos prevented him from responding to women in need.

One must not forget that Christ called both women and men to his varied ministries. Among those most closely allied with him and explicitly named were Mary Magdalen, Joanna, and Susanne (Luke

8:1–3). Magdalen became apostle to the apostles after the resurrection. Joanna, wife of Chusa, Herod's steward, is believed to have given details about Herod to Luke, the evangelist. Susanne was one who "provided for them out of their means" (Luke 8:3). The roles of these three women are significant in the early church.

When Jesus' apostles cravenly abandoned him, women remained near him. When Jesus writhed in agony on the Cross, women stood by him. When Jesus was placed in the tomb, women visited him. And women, yes women, brought the Good News of the resurrection to the frightened apostles. Their faithful love and Christ's sensitive response stand out for all time.

Historical Development

The Early Church

Although slow to learn, the apostles gradually came to understand and follow the example of Jesus. Some changes did occur. Paul identified women as deacons (Phoebe), missionaries (Prisca), prophets (Philip's daughters), apostles (Junia) and leaders of local communities (Lydia).[3] Yet the customs of the day proved a strong obstacle to following Christ's teaching.

Peter the Apostle was married, yet no mention is made of his wife. Many popes and bishops had wives, yet rarely does one hear their names. Down through the ages, wives of bishops and priests remain nameless and forgotten, their heroism known only to God. Copartners in ministry and ministers in their own right, they deserve greater recognition.

For centuries Christian writers heaped the vilest slanders on women. Caricatures arose from a grotesque distortion of the biblical record. Because of Eve's transgression, according to male preachers, God put women in permanent subjection to men. But the biblical narrative paints a different picture. The chief villain in the creation story, the one who seduced Eve and through her Adam, was the devil. Scriptures proclaimed that God would triumph over the beast, but first, God reprimanded the two — Adam would work by the sweat of his brow, and Eve would give birth in pain. Both actions dramatized the hardships of life resulting from sin.

Yet Fathers of the Church continually held women responsible for bringing sin into the world and looked on them as a continuing source of seduction. Tertullian, for example, spoke of woman as "the gate of the devil, the traitor of the tree, the first deserter of divine law; you are she who enticed the one whom the devil was not able to overcome."[4] Origen wrote, "God does not deign to look upon feminine or corporeal things."[5] Ambrosiaster went even further when he wrote, "Women must cover their heads because they are not the image of God. They must do this as a sign of their subjection to authority and because sin came into the world through them."[6]

The Medieval Church

St. Boniface convened a German Council in 742, which decreed that lewd monks and nuns were to be taken to prison and after the third beating imprisoned for a year. Nuns were to have their hair shaved off their heads. The human anguish was incalculable.

Decrees and edicts tried to bar the priest from wife and children and return him to sacred pursuits. Forced separation of women from their clerical husbands became the norm, as penalties grew in intensity, especially against women. Barstow notes the altered language that came about in church law: "the change from *uxor* (wife), *diaconessa* (deaconess), and even *episcopessa* (bishop's wife) to *concubina* (concubine), *meretrix* (prostitute), *scortum* (harlot), *pellex* (mistress) degrades the woman, implicitly denies the possibility of her being fully married . . . and increases the immoral connotation."[7]

The tragic fate of the woman in such alliances has been well documented. Perceived as the femme fatale, the guilty person, and the seducer of a priest, she was frequently abandoned and left to raise children alone in poverty; her husband was urged to return to a "higher calling." Bernard Verkamp observes, "While none showed any concern for the care of the clergyman's wife and children after separation, a number (of decrees) dictated what was to happen to these latter if they did not separate from the cleric. Both the wives and children were made subject to being sold or taken into slavery."[8]

At a synod in Rome in 1050 Pope Leo IX ordered the sale of priest wives as slaves in front of the Lateran Palace. The Synod of Melfi in 1081 gave princes the power to enslave priests' wives. And the Synod of Pavia that same year declared children of priests to be slaves of the Church.

Barstow writes:

> It is not surprising that at this period one hears desperate reactions on the part of wives. When separated from their husbands, some committed suicide while others physically attacked the bishops who tried to separate them. One, maddened by the destruction of her marriage, was said to have poisoned the wife of the lord who had forced her from her husband.[9]

In this climate of perversity is there wonder that theologians and preachers reserved their greatest scorn for wives of priests? Those believed to have lured priests away from their sublime calling became objects of bitter attacks. Normally intemperate outbursts against women rose to scurrilous harangue when dealing with the beloved companions of priests.

St. Peter Damian (1007–72) stands as the prime example of this monumental scorn. He addresses priests' wives in these terms:

> I speak of you, charmers of the clergy, choice food of the devil, castaway from paradise, you, virus of the minds, sword of souls, venom of drinkers and poison of eaters, the very substance of sin, the cause of ruin. I speak of you, female abodes of the ancient enemy, pick-axes, screech-owls, night-birds, she-wolves, blood suckers, crying "Give, give, without ceasing." Come and hear me, you garbage, prostitutes, puckered lips, pigsties for fat pigs, couches for foul spirits, nymphs, sirens, vampires, moon goddesses...you who through the allurements of your fake charm snatch away unfortunate men from ministry at the sacred altars where they are engaged, in order to strangle them in the slimy glue of your own passion.[10]

It gets even worse. Peter Damian is here talking about beloved wives! Good and saintly women! Loving companions on the journey! The self-sacrificing mothers of priests' children! His words reflect neither sanctity nor sanity.

Such degeneracy knew no limits. It continued through succeeding generations. The fifteenth-century work *Hammer of Witches,* produced by two Dominican priests, Jakob Sprenger and Heinrich Kramer, who had been appointed inquisitors by Pope Innocent VIII, declares, "What else is woman but a foe to friendship, an inescapable punishment, a necessary evil, a natural temptation, a desirable calamity, a domestic danger, a delectable detriment, an evil of nature, painted with fair colors." Sprenger and Kramer carried their argument to absurdity, "Women are intellectually like children...she is more carnal than a man...women have weak memories...as she is a liar by nature, so in her speech she stings while she delights me....All witchcraft comes from carnal lust, which is in women insatiable."[11] Little wonder that this work, cited repeatedly at inquisitions, became a tool for sentencing countless women to the stake.

Uta Ranke-Heinemann summarized well the historical development:

> After the age when priests were allowed to marry came the age of clandestine and persecuted priestly marriages. After Trent, concubinage was the only way out, a sad but not infrequently chosen alternative. The history of celibacy was a troubled one, not so much for those who initiated it and pushed it through, as to those whom it personally affected. For many of these people, especially women, it meant disaster.[12]

Can anyone conceive of Christ being associated with such cruel behavior toward women? From everything known of his teachings and example, can one still justify diabolic attacks against the wives of priests?

Modern Church Teaching

Signs of change in the Catholic Church can be found. The 1917 Code of Canon Law tended to treat women pejoratively, relating to them as potential temptresses of clerics.[13] The new 1983 Code, in its corresponding canon (277), is less offensive. As the distinguished canonist Paulist Father John Lynch noted:

> In paragraph two of canon 277, clerics are warned to be careful about those with whom they associate lest their obligation to continence be endangered and the faithful scandalized. The former law (CIC 133) was much more detailed. Clerics were not to live under the same roof with or to frequently visit women so as to give rise to suspicion on the part of others. Clerics were permitted to dwell only with those whose natural kinship (mother, sister, aunt) or whose irreproachable character and maturity obviated any suspicion. Canonists generally understood the advanced age as forty years or older. The revised Code does not single out women as the likely cause of scandal; the association with certain males could be just as harmful.[14]

Moreover, the new Code (Canon 208) stresses the fundamental equality of all the baptized: "In virtue of their rebirth in Christ, there exists among all the Christian faithful a true equality with regard to the dignity and the activity whereby all cooperate in the building up of the Body of Christ in accord with each one's own condition and function."[15]

Pope John XXIII in his encyclical *Pacem in Terris* in 1963 described the emerging role of women as a "sign of our times." And the 1971 Synod on Justice drew attention to the need of the Church to witness to justice, especially to women. Even the *Catechism of the Catholic Church* in 1995 reflected a new direction when it asserted, "In no way is God in man's image. He is neither man nor woman. God is pure spirit in which there is no place for the differences between the sexes. But the respective perfections of man and woman reflect something of the infinite perfection of God: those of a mother and those of a father and husband."[16]

John Paul II has often acknowledged woman's special role. He liked to speak about the feminine genius, his term for the unique contribution that only women can give to the Church and the world.

He expressed that most clearly in his encyclical *Mulieris Dignitatem* in 1988. And in his apostolic letter addressed to the Fourth World Congress on Women as they gathered in Beijing in 1995 he apologized to all women, noting:

> If objective blame, especially in particular historical contexts, has belonged to not just a few members of the Church, for this I am truly sorry.... When it comes to setting women free from every kind of exploitation and domination, the Gospel contains an ever relevant message which goes back to the *attitude of Jesus Christ himself*. Transcending the established norms of his own culture, Jesus treated women with openness, respect, acceptance and tenderness. In this way he honored the dignity that women have always possessed according to God's plan and in his love.[17]

These documents demonstrate progress in recognizing the importance of women and acknowledging injustices against them. But remedial actions remain inadequate. Although women in the Church make up a clear majority, they are not consulted, even in matters that directly affect them. That must change. Respect for the wives of priests must also return. Richard Sipe put matters in perspective when he declared:

> A married priesthood without full rights for women only legitimizes the priest's woman as the parson's wife. Women must take their place with priests as co-ministers, not merely silent, sexless (or sexy) and subservient handmaidens.... The goal is a married priesthood, two people in full partnership, with ordination open to either or both. Nothing less will satisfy the Gospel ideal of life in Christ where there is no distinction in persons, and where the Spirit is not limited by sex in its distinction of roles.[18]

When will the example of Jesus be followed? When will the role of women be respected among his followers? When will women take their place in the councils, the senates, the synods of the Church?

Examples of Courage

Earlier Priests' Wives

The cruel suffering of priests' wives is veiled in historical records. These women remain largely anonymous. The stories of the few that are known deserve to be told worldwide.

TITIA. In the early fifth century, Titia, the daughter of Catholic bishop Aemilius of Benevento, married Julian, the son of a bishop from Apulia. On the occasion of their wedding, the saintly Paulinus wrote a marvelous poem[19] in which he extols Titia as "the holy wife of a bishop's son, the spouse of a boy already consecrated." He admonishes Julian that "a cleric must love a wife who glories in Christ." And more tellingly, "if they consummate physical union, may the chaste offspring to come be a priestly race." Paulinus depicts Titia as a holy and beautiful wife, and wishes the couple many priests as offspring.

Little is known of their life together. In 416 Julian was made bishop of Eclanum. During the Pelagian controversy, he was attacked by the great St. Augustine of Hippo and driven from office. A lifetime of wandering followed. He concluded his life as tutor in a Pelagian family and died in Sicily in 450. Nothing further is heard about Titia.

HELOISE. More poignant is the beautiful story of Heloise and Abelard, heralded throughout the ages. While still an adolescent, Heloise fell for the renowned teacher and priest Abelard. The passionate love aroused was mutual. Nevertheless, the perverse climate surrounding sex in the twelfth century meant that Abelard's career as a brilliant teacher would be jeopardized if they married. She therefore agreed to his plan to marry privately and then, for safety, retire to a monastery. When Heloise's relatives heard of the marriage and escape to a convent, they sent a band of hoodlums who castrated Abelard, ending the marital bliss to which they aspired. Yet her love endured. Her sighs and yearnings leap from the pages of letters penned at her convent many years later:

> Shall my husband never be mentioned without tears, shall his dear name never be spoken but with sighs? ... When I lost you,

dearest, I lost all I loved on this earth, and the manner in which it came about makes my grief inconsolable. . . .

We were content with each other and we passed our brightest days in tranquil happiness. If that was a crime, it is a crime I am yet fond of, and I have no other regret save that against my will I must now be innocent. But what am I saying? My misfortune was to have a cruel family whose selfish creed destroyed our lives; had they been reasonable, I would now be living quietly at the side of my dear husband. How cruel and merciless they were when, with blind fury, they hired thugs to assault you in your sleep! Where was I—where was your Heloise then? What joy should I have had in defending you! I would have guarded you from violence at the expense of my life! . . .

Even now I love you as much as ever. . . . Irresolute as I am, I still love you and yet I know I can hope for nothing. I have renounced life and stripped myself of all that pleased me; but I find I neither have been able to nor can I now renounce you, Abelard![20]

As with Titia, Heloise's husband had the misfortune of drawing the opposition of a great churchman—in this case Bernard of Clairvaux. One can only surmise what importance the earlier love affair between Heloise and Abelard played in the reactions of this Cistercian ascetic. He treated Abelard with scorn.

Heloise spent her final years as abbess, Abelard as abbot. Their monasteries were not far apart, but no evidence is found of their meeting again. Nor has a response from Abelard been discovered. "The story of Abelard and Heloise," Ranke-Heinemann correctly noted, "remains for all time the story of a celebrated couple, first lovers and then married, who fell victim to the laws of celibacy."[21]

KATHERINE VON BORA. When her father remarried, Katherine at age ten was placed in a convent. At sixteen she took vows. Then the whirlwind of the Reformation in the sixteenth century challenged traditional practices in Germany. Many nuns reexamined their way of life. Katherine and eight other sisters at her convent, disquieted in conscience, tried to escape. Even though the civil leader would impose prison on anyone who aided their departure, Martin Luther boldly came to their rescue and helped them find suitors. Among the suitors for Katherine was Luther himself.

After marriage Katherine bore Martin six children, raising them according to Gospel precepts. Besides their own, the couple took in four children of a friend who lost his wife. Nor was this the limit of their hospitality. They hosted for protracted stays tutors of their children, relatives in time of need, refugees from convents or persecution, and distinguished foreign visitors. The Duke joked that Luther was conducting an asylum for renegades.

Wars, pestilence, and strife of many kinds swirled around Martin Luther. He had become world-renowned. Through all their travails, Katherine maintained an atmosphere of comfort and peace at home. She ministered faithfully to her famous husband through all his depressions, illnesses, and eccentricities, and tried to shelter him as best she could. She always remained deferential to him, addressing him as "Herr Doktor."

Although Katherine's words have not survived, she inspired her husband to write, "I would not want to exchange my Kate for France nor for Venice to boot; to begin with (1) because God has given her to me and me to her; (2) because I often find out that there are more shortcomings in other women than in my Kate.... (3) because she keeps faith and honor in our marriage relation."[22]

Current Priests' Wives

In marrying a priest, the religious woman for good or bad enters into the mystique of the priesthood. On the positive side, this means identifying with the calling to Christ's ministry that she shares. Together they respond to that call and encourage each other along the way. On the negative side, she inherits a sacralized priesthood that traditionalists accuse her of thwarting. The latter can be nasty and unforgiving.

Because of the changed discipline under Paul VI and John Paul II, wives of married priests now give open testimony to Christian values in family life. They are no longer bound by anonymity, living in the shadows. Dozens of these beautiful women give glorious witness to the Gospel today. Consider just a few.

LOUISE, a native of Mankato, Minnesota, joined the School Sisters of Notre Dame after high school. As a nun she taught children in elementary and secondary schools and earned a masters degree in speech communication from St. Mary's University in Winona. Then in 1972 she married John, a Catholic priest.

Work in the institutional church was closed to them. Their zeal for the Lord impelled them to found Mission OK Ministries in Minneapolis to teach, preach, and worship the Lord while serving the inner-city poor. Through the last twenty-six years of her life she gave music lessons, ran a preschool program, and taught a home/school junior high program from their house church in North Minneapolis. She showed leadership in different community organizations, like Lovelines, Daystar, Campus Farthest Out, and a Thursday women's prayer group.

Louise fought a twenty-year battle with medullary cancer and, after the disease took over all her organs, she succumbed at last in 1999. Throughout her sufferings, her ever-present smile and Christlike acceptance of her cross inspired many. A gifted artist, teacher, and musician, Louise will be remembered as a strong and dedicated woman who loved the Lord with all her heart, and who was devoted to her husband, John, their daughter, Christie, and the multitudes who came to her for help.

JULIE. Married priest couples try to continue their dedication to Christ by applying their talents to Church ministry. Usually they had met when each labored jointly, often the woman a nun and the man a priest. But not always. A shared spirituality and love for ministry are the chemistry that brings them together. Most often they must abandon their ministry. Julie and Pat, however, journeyed along a different path.

Julie was not a former nun, but a separated mom with two teenage sons, serving as religious education director in her Catholic parish community. When Pat arrived as pastor of that parish, he was already questioning his ability to remain a celibate priest. As his friendship with Julie deepened, he realized the happiness to which God was calling him. He resigned his pastorate and, after a year's courtship, they decided to marry. By then, Pope John Paul II had enforced new procedures, making it impossible to get a dispensation from celibacy before the wedding. They therefore married in a Lutheran church. Pat's petition remained in the local chancery for fifteen years before being processed.

Fortunately, Julie was able to continue working as director of religious education in another Catholic parish. The people there recognized her gifts and admired her Christ-centered ministry. Pastors recognized that she was caught in a "Catch-22." She had received an annulment from Rome and Pat applied for a dispensation, but no action was forthcoming. The archbishop tolerated such situations if they did not become a stumbling block for parishioners. In that progressive parish, pastors and parishioners were aware of Pat's background and respected him and Julie for their commitment to the Church.

After the appointment of Archbishop Thomas Murphy, Julie's job as parish lay minister came in jeopardy. Despite that, her peers chose her as president of the Archdiocesan Religious Education Association. Uncomfortable with this arrangement, Archbishop Murphy offered her a guarantee that she could continue her ministry in the parish if she would step down from the archdiocesan post. She agreed.

Upon Archbishop Murphy's death, the archdiocese again reviewed its policies and asked Pat to reapply for a dispensation so that their marriage could be blessed by the Church. He did. In July 2000 Rome granted a dispensation and they married in the Catholic Church.

Julie and Pat took leadership in organizing married priest couples in the region. That group grew to 140 and worked closely with CORPUS — The Association for an Inclusive Priesthood. Through the last fifteen years, this region has given that organization nationally a treasurer (Pat) and two presidents. In recent years, Pat has also conducted an ecumenical wedding ministry that reaches out to many estranged Catholics and others wanting help in creating a religious wedding celebration. He considers his ministry an important outreach to alienated Catholics that helps build bridges to Church membership.

Julie is highly regarded not only by her parishioners, but also by her peers in ministry. Her staff position in her parish community has enabled her to promote a Vatican II vision of a collegial Church, where laity are truly empowered. In the diocese she now serves in a role similar to that to which her peers elected her years earlier, namely, chairperson of the Association for Lay Ministers for the Archdiocese. Through their ministries in and outside the Catholic Church, Julie and Pat continue to promote Vatican II values. Their marriage bears witness to the successful ministry that emerges through blending the sacraments of matrimony and holy orders in a married priest couple.

LINDA. Linda had two sons, one of whom died at four months, the other at age twenty-two. Devastated by the first death, she divorced, began studies as a medical assistant, and tried to rebuild her life. Along the way she found God and went through a religious awakening that inspired her to begin instructions in the Catholic faith.

Among the instructors preparing her for admission to the Catholic community was Phil, the local parish priest. A warm friendship developed between them and deepened in time. During one class, a song by Joe Wise touched her heart. As she tells it:

> Even though my future did not seem to include falling in love, I had hoped to meet someone. My prayer had always been to find someone who loved God as much as I did. As I listened to the words, "I'm in love with my God, My God's in love with me, and the more I love you, the more I know I'm in love with my God," I opened my eyes and saw Phil as I had never seen him before. It was as though I was looking at him through God's eyes, and I was filled with a depth of love and tenderness that both exhilarated and terrified me.[23]

While receiving counseling and spiritual direction for the next five years, they remained friends. Phil then told his bishop about the relationship and relinquished his clerical state. After their marriage in 1982, Linda was blessed with two more sons.

The plight of a priest's wife can be awkward. Some Catholics cannot accept her, and such rejection is hard to take. Of special concern is the priest's mother. At her first meeting with Linda, Phil's mother expressed strong opposition to Linda's relationship with her son. Her attitude gradually changed after the birth of her two grandsons. In time, she developed a deep love and appreciation for Linda. At the 1991 CORPUS Conference in New York, she joined with all the married priests and their wives in a prayer session outside St. Patrick's Cathedral.

Linda and Phil have endured serious medical complications. When Phil developed severe arterial blockage that the doctor gauged to be inoperable, Linda bought an exercise bicycle and adopted for their family a strict low fat/low cholesterol diet, leading Phil to lose thirty pounds and dropping his cholesterol by 125 points. That was more than twenty years ago. Not long after Phil's ordeal, Linda began losing weight and feeling severe stomach pains. The doctor diagnosed colon cancer, requiring six months of chemotherapy. That was five years ago. Phil and Linda together have survived those ordeals.

Today they minister in the Christian community as much as permitted, supported by many married priest couples in the Akron, Ohio, area. Each year Linda and Phil and their boys stand vigil outside during the ordination ceremony at St. John's Cathedral in Cleveland. Their signs tell the story. At a recent vigil, their son Phil's sign read, "St. Peter was a married priest, and so is my dad"; their son Joshua's, "When I Grow Up I Want to Be a Married Priest"; Linda's, "6 Sacraments Equal Priesthood, 7 Sacraments Equal Married Priesthood"; and Phil's, *"Tu Es Sacerdos in Aeternum"* (You are a priest for eternity).

The Other Women

It is not enough to write about priests' wives. Countless other women must also be mentioned — soul mates, secret lovers, wives in all but name. Their poignant stories remain hidden. Groups like Good Tidings in the United States, Bethany Revisited in Ireland and Sonflowers in England seek to help women who have had relations with priests. Their number is legion; their plight heartrending.

JAN CURRIE was a religious education teacher and youth worker in England. During the course of her labors she fell in love with Father Sean. For ten years they struggled together in what she describes as a relationship that meant everything to us, yet at the same time tore us apart. A relationship in which we both fully appreciated and acknowledged his calling to priesthood, yet felt just as strongly our calling to be married.

In an effort to get away from this situation, she volunteered for two years as a teacher in Zimbabwe, but absence made their hearts grow fonder. Upon returning she became pregnant and Sean broke down under the pressure. His superiors sent him to a treatment center where he lived among pedophile and alcoholic priests. No difference in treatment was accorded them.

The baby Jan carried died in the womb. Five days later Sean calmly walked to the local railway line and lay down across the tracks. An oncoming train mangled his body.

When she heard the story on television, Jan called the diocesan press officer, a priest, who advised her to leave the country for a while. The news broadcast that evening featured an interview of that priest as spokesman for the Church. He commented, "Celibacy is not a problem for those of us who pray." Jan gagged on that, for she knew of Sean's constant prayerfulness. That same clerical press officer is now in jail for, among other sexual offenses, raping a sixteen-year-old girl.

Church officials advised Jan not to attend the funeral. They tried to cover up any mention of her, removing flowers with her name on them from the grave site, tearing out notes referring to her in Sean's books. The coroner's report that mentioned her had that section highlighted and words penciled in on the side: "Do not read out in court."

When news of these events reached him, the wise and saintly Cardinal Basil Hume asked to see Jan. He listened compassionately, consoled her warmly, and assured her that he would never have sent Sean or her away. Today Jan can only reminisce about what might have been. She writes,

Four years after Sean's death the first married ex-Anglican priest was ordained in the Cardiff diocese. He, his wife and two children were warmly welcomed into the Catholic community by the archbishop, priests and people, and rightly so. This move was celebrated as part of his "journey of faith." As I watched the ceremony, I reflected how poignant it was that many of those priests and people present were Sean's friends, colleagues and parishioners.

I thought of all those priests who found themselves called both to the priesthood and to married life with one they truly loved. I thought of those who had then found the courage and integrity to leave the ministry and marry. I thought of those who continued to keep their affairs, and sometimes children, secret: almost it seems, the preferred course of action in clerical circles. And I thought of the man who, had the option existed to be a married priest, would still be alive today. If only.[24]

FRANCES. The legal hurdles and loopholes that govern the marriage of a Catholic priest create problems of their own. Particularly for the women involved.

Frances was a twenty-six-year-old Catholic schoolteacher when she met Efraim Lopez. He was working as a civil servant after leaving the Redemptorist community and requesting from Rome a dispensation from his vow of celibacy. They fell in love and, because word from Rome was slow in coming, the local Catholic pastor decided to perform the marriage ceremony anyway. Six months later the dispensation arrived and the pastor dutifully entered the marriage on the church rolls and issued them a church marriage certificate.

Technically the pastor was not authorized by church authorities to perform the ceremony until the dispensation arrived. Frances nevertheless always felt she was in a Catholic marriage and had the church document to prove it.

Twenty years and two children later, after several failed business ventures, Efraim divorced his wife. He then requested reinstatement as a priest, claiming that the marriage was invalid in the eyes of the Church. The Vatican acceded to his request. He is now pastor of a Catholic Church in Puerto Rico.

In the meantime, Frances was left with a debt of more than $60,000, which forced her into bankruptcy and impoverished her and her children. She is now a public school teacher in Prince William County in Virginia. Efforts to seek redress from the bishop in Puerto Rico have proved fruitless.

Frances stated, "I want the church and my ex-husband to accept the fact that they took him back without any investigation, never contacting myself, my daughter, friends or acquaintances, investigating his creditors or making any kind of provision for me after a twenty-year marriage. The church was so desperate to take him back that they completely ignored my position." As with the handling of clerical pedophilia cases, the lack of episcopal response reinforces the conviction that bishops are overprotective of their clergy, cloaking clerical behaviors in secrecy and showing insensitivity to those who have been wronged by priests.

Summary

This brief review of Church discipline dealing with women, especially those wed to priests, shows a mixed inheritance. From the days of Peter to the present, priests have married and lived with their wives. They continue to do so. In some ages this practice has been respected, in others reviled. Consistent with these reactions, women are either honored or vilified.

Starting in the fourth century, local church regulations began severing the bonds between women and the increasingly sacralized priests. A plethora of regional laws requiring sexual abstention for priests culminated in the Second Lateran Council's absolute ban on clerical marriage in 1139. During the intervening years penalties imposed on all parties grew in severity, but disproportionately so against women.

The terms used to designate the priest's companion simultaneously changed from wife to concubine, harlot, and whore. This coincided often with an exaltation of virgins and a vilification of married women. The resultant estrangement of wives from their priest husbands exceeded the bounds of reason and contradicted the teaching and example of Christ.

The Second Vatican Council, in its closing message addressed to women, declared on December 8, 1965, "the hour is coming, in fact has come, when the vocation of woman is being achieved in its fullness, the hour in which woman acquires in the world an influence, an effect and a power never before achieved."[25] And Pope John XXIII in his encyclical *Pacem in Terris* declared, "because women are becoming ever more conscious of their human dignity, they will not tolerate being treated as mere material instruments, but demand rights befitting a human person both in domestic and in public life."

On the occasion of John Paul II's first visit to the United States as Pope, on October 7, 1979, the courageous Sr. Theresa Kane spoke to him respectfully but firmly, "The Church in its struggle to be faithful to its call for reverence and dignity for all persons must respond by providing the possibility of women as persons being included in all ministries of the Church." With those words she gave voice to the aspirations of women and men throughout the Catholic Church today. Those words continue to be met with silence.

Many women, denied admission to Catholic seminaries, are studying theology at Protestant seminaries. Their desire to gain greater knowledge and apply their talents in teaching, preaching, and other ministry impels them to seek such training. Sr. Joan Chittister noted this development when she addressed the 2001 Call to Action gathering: "If Roman Catholic dioceses continue to refuse to prepare women for participation in the Church, I predict that this movement of Catholic women to Protestant schools of theology will significantly alter the shape of the church — the faith — in the next twenty-five years."[26]

In the light of all that has taken place, one can safely conclude that any breakthrough in the Catholic Church in this day will not come from the circle of male celibates, but from women, married and single, religious and lay. Much as black sisters and brothers after centuries of subjugation finally broke the shackles of slavery, much as Jewish sisters and brothers after countless pogroms and forced wanderings finally laid claim to the Promised Land, so must women in the Catholic community today after centuries of repression finally assert their birthright and gain equality in power and ministry. Anything short of that is unacceptable.

Chapter 3

Organizing Priests

I N ITS "Constitution on the Liturgy," the Second Vatican Council endorsed the work of generations of scholars and pastors. Liturgical scholars like Virgil Michel, Joseph Jungman, and Pius Parsch and pastoral leaders like Martin B. Hellriegel of St. Louis and Cardinal Lercaro of Bologna paved the way. The long heralded liturgical revival had begun.

These first fruits of the Council served as prelude to broader reforms in the Church. Years of scholarship filtered through first-rate theologians emboldened bishops to address matters long considered intractable. Wisely and effectively they tackled ecumenism, revelation, Christian education, religious liberty, and the nature of the Church. Major breakthroughs occurred. A series of decrees and dogmatic constitutions confirmed for the faithful an outpouring of the Holy Spirit.

Council directives urged greater collaboration among bishops, priests, religious, and laity. The Decree on the Bishops' Pastoral Office in the Church, for example, declared that "diocesan priests should be united among themselves and should be genuinely zealous for the spiritual welfare of the whole diocese."[1] The apostolic letter on implementing that decree added, "There is to be in each diocese a council of priests, a group or senate of priests, representing the presbyterium, which by its advice will give effective assistance to the bishop in ruling the diocese."[2] Bringing together all the Church's resources was the next logical step in renewal.

The Rise of Priest Organizations

With its long democratic tradition and its practical know-how, the Catholic Church in the United States proved fertile ground for these ideas. Collaborative structures arose almost overnight. The pragmatic American bishops, more inclined to diligent action than scholarly disputation, resolved to follow through methodically on the entire agenda of reform. In quick order they set up priest senates, sisters councils, and diocesan pastoral councils.

The National Federation of Priests Councils (NFPC)

All over the country the organizing of priests began. "Forty-five senates were in operation by the end of 1966 and 135 by the first of the year."[3] Less than two years after the Second Vatican Council, most dioceses in the United States had set up a senate or association of priests. Formation of local senates and associations was understandable in light of the mandate of the Second Vatican Council and the American penchant for democratic structures. Logically the next step was to unite all these bodies into a national organization. This was a bolder move fraught with danger, but necessary if effective action and leadership were to be supplied by the priests of America. A national assembly was needed.

In February 1968, clergy representing senates across the country met in an exploratory meeting at the Sheraton-O'Hare Motor Hotel in Des Plaines, Illinois, to review the progress of priest organizations and discuss the feasibility of forming a permanent national body. Participants concurred almost unanimously, 283 to 1. The following May, in the same hotel, a constitutional assembly convened. This was the first official gathering of the newly formed National Federation of Priests Councils (NFPC). Delegates chose as president Patrick O'Malley of Chicago. A Burt Lancaster look-alike, he spoke firmly and instilled confidence about the future.

A year later, the Second National Conference of the NFPC convened at the Jung Hotel in New Orleans under heightened tension. The papal encyclical *Humanae Vitae* had recently been issued, followed by a tidal wave of discontent over its teaching on birth control. At the conference, delegates listened to the plight of priests in Washington, D.C., who appealed for help in their struggles with Cardinal Patrick O'Boyle. Similar requests, resulting from the *Humanae Vitae*

debacle, soon came from other bodies of priests across the country —
in Buffalo, Los Angeles, and San Antonio.

In those first meetings, the organizational skill and professionalism of the Chicago priests was impressive. They seemed to come
from a different mold. While diocesan senate meetings plodded along
with unclear agendas and more than occasional ramblings, Federation meetings were highly organized, guided by agendas addressing
the needs of the day, and led by articulate spokesmen skilled in par-
liamentary procedure. NFPC deliberations always were conducted in
a congenial atmosphere that left one proud of one's priesthood and
deepened one's commitment to the Church.

Pat O'Malley's successful term as president ended with the election of a native of the Rockford, Illinois, Diocese, one of the original
NFPC organizers, Frank Bonnike. A former naval business officer
with immense energies and personal charm, Bonnike fostered growth
and development of the NFPC. He launched the National Association of Church Personnel Administrators (NACPA), the National
Organization for the Continuing Education of the Roman Catholic Clergy (NOCERCC) and the Catholic Church Personnel Group
Benefit Trust. Today these organizations meet the needs of priests
nationwide.

Bonnike also led the NFPC into new and uncharted waters. During
his tenure, he gained passage of an extraordinary document titled
"The Moment of Truth." This bold statement was hotly debated by
delegates at the convention in 1971, but passed by an overwhelming
193–18–3 vote. For progressives, it marked the high point in the
history of the NFPC; for traditionalists, its nadir. In chancery offices
and rectories across the country, the document evoked great passion,
enthralling proponents and galvanizing opponents of reform.

"The Moment of Truth" took as its theme the words of Ecclesi-
astes 3:1–8: "There is an appointed time for everything . . . a time to
tear down and a time to build . . . a time to keep and a time to cast
away . . . a time to be silent and a time to speak. . . . " Its concluding refrain echoed loudly: "That moment is now!" In the document, NFPC
delegates boldly advocated shared responsibility between bishop and

priests and new forms of ministry. Noteworthy were its words on celibacy: "We are convinced that the present law of mandatory celibacy in the western church must be changed.... We ask that the choice between celibacy and marriage for priests now active in the ministry be allowed and that the change begin immediately.... In a spirit of brotherhood, we ask that priests who have already married be invited to resume the active ministry." Theologian Anthony Padovano was a principal author. Every bishop in the United States received a copy of that historic proclamation.

Priests nationwide had great expectations for the Roman Synod about to start in the fall of 1971. They expected that the hierarchies of many nations would speak out on celibacy and reform. As noted earlier, some bishops did address the issue, but with little effect. Despite strong interventions, the final balloting at the synod dashed all hope of reform, as bishops reaffirmed the discipline of celibacy. Disillusionment set in for many priests. In September 1973, Bonnike resigned as president of NFPC. He later married.

National Association for Pastoral Renewal (NAPR)

Even before the national federation, another important initiative was under way. Less than a year after the close of the Vatican Council, some priests from St. Louis proposed a survey of priest attitudes on clerical celibacy. Robert Hoyt of the *National Catholic Reporter* (NCR) offered seed money, priests the rest, and Joseph Fichter, S.J., a recognized social scientist, undertook the study. The survey showed that an astounding 62 percent of the clergy nationwide favored freedom of choice for priests to marry. In December 1966, the group mailed the full report to all bishops and simultaneously released it for publication in the NCR.

Before publishing the report, the priest organizers set up an advisory board of volunteers — Robert Francoeur, George Frein, Frank Matthews, Alfred McBride, John O'Brien, and Joseph Fichter. In January 1967 they announced the formation of the National Association for Pastoral Renewal (NAPR). A membership drive followed.

With few resources, this small group made its presence felt. They conducted surveys, organized local chapters, lobbied bishops at their annual meetings, ran national symposia in St. Louis and the University of Notre Dame, and gained the support of many theologians and priests. Their board of directors included Daniel Maguire of Catholic University and Monsignor Henry G. J. Beck, the distinguished seminary professor at Darlington Seminary in New Jersey. Their national advisory board consisted of such luminaries as John O'Brien and John L. McKenzie, S.J., of Notre Dame, Eugene Burke, C.S.P., and Alfred McBride, O. Praem., of Catholic University, Joseph Fichter, S.J., of Harvard, the Trappist monk Thomas Merton, O.C.S.O., and others.

Merton's letter to the Board reflected his views on clerical reform. From cloistered walls he wrote:

> I am happy to accept the invitation to become an advisor of the NAPR to help study and solve the critical problem of a married secular clergy. This problem must be faced though many would prefer to ignore it.... There is no hope of it "going away." It will become more and more urgent from day to day and I think every one realizes that it involves the future of the Church in the modern world. That is why some find it so frightening: they are still not ready to admit that drastic change in many fields is required if the church is to continue her mission successfully.[4]

In reading the literature of NAPR today, one cannot ignore its pervasive optimism regarding Church reform. NAPR members, like early disciples awaiting the coming of the Lord, were convinced that repeal of the celibacy law would soon occur. Encouraging signs had emerged. Survey after survey showed many priests marrying, and more and more laity receptive to that development. In a letter to Carl Hemmer, one of the organizers, Cardinal Joseph Ritter of St. Louis wrote, "Our Holy Father [Pope Paul VI] is fully aware of the problem and I think, like his predecessor, wishes to do something about it."[5]

National Study of the Priesthood

Responding to repeated requests, the U.S. Catholic bishops undertook an unprecedented study of Catholic priests. Cardinal John

Dearden entrusted the project to Bishop Joseph Bernardin, General Secretary of the National Conference of Catholic Bishops (NCCB). The study would entail a full analysis of the social, psychological, historical, and theological dimensions of priesthood in the United States. Great expectations were aroused. In bringing together outstanding professionals from each discipline and allowing them to conduct their investigations independently, the bishops tried to come to grips with the full scope of problems facing the priesthood.

The project, titled *The Catholic Priest in the United States,* pooled teams of scholars under superb leadership. The distinguished historian John Tracy Ellis headed the historical investigations, published in 1971; Eugene C. Kennedy and Victor Heckler the psychological in 1972; and Andrew Greeley the sociological, also in 1972. Carl J. Armbruster, S.J., led the theological investigations. The bishops, however, never permitted that study to be published because they disagreed with certain aspects of the research. The entire study is the most perceptive and scholarly analysis of priests ever undertaken.

In his foreword to the sociological investigations, Cardinal John Krol wrote:

> The study is an irrefutable evidence of the deep concern of bishops for their priest workers. The National Conference of Catholic Bishops used the instrumentality of a massive sociological and psychological survey to enable the priests to speak frankly and directly about themselves and their problems to their bishops and religious superiors.[6]

Despite such positive feedback, bishops quietly put aside the entire study. Thirty years later, Bishop Thomas Gumbleton reflected the view of many priests when he stated:

> It is important to grasp what that study revealed. It was saying that we had in our midst some priests who were severely handicapped from a psychological point of view; they were maldeveloped persons capable of inflicting great harm on people they were supposed to be ministering to. And there was

this very large number of priests who would be considered underdeveloped. In my judgment a major failure was the refusal on the part of the bishops to follow up on these studies.[7]

These studies of the priesthood remain today largely unread and forgotten.

Society of Priests for a Free Ministry (SPFM)

The NAPR Symposium in St. Louis in September 1968 opened a fissure in the married priests movement, which reverberated through the years. Delegates at that gathering debated whether to respond to the recently issued encyclical *Humanae Vitae.* A slight majority rejected any challenge to papal authority. They regarded optional celibacy as their main concern, and were reluctant to take on other matters. Many priests, however, considered freedom in the Church a more fundamental problem. They caucused separately and laid grounds for a new organization, the Society of Priests for a Free Ministry (SPFM), which before long eclipsed NAPR.

These two approaches show the enduring division between organized groups of married priests. Some want to maintain relations with Church leaders, stay connected with their local Catholic parishes, and work within current norms of the Catholic Church. That was the basic tenor of NAPR and CORPUS (discussed below), at least from the start. But others aspire to a free ministry, in which they respond openly to the growing sacramental needs of disenfranchised Catholics and other Christians. SPFM, FCM, and CITI embody this central idea. William Powers articulated that philosophy well in his book *Free Priests.*[8]

During the 1980s and 1990s, as Church leaders hardened their opposition, discouraged further dialogue, and ignored requests for dispensations, married priests aligned themselves increasingly with the latter initiatives. Dialogue and docility they deemed fruitless. Response to the needs of God's People they considered their only option, their priestly duty.

Federation of Christian Ministries (FCM)

The Society of Priests for a Free Ministry, like NAPR, was short-lived. The growing conservatism in the Church, the seeming reversal of support from NFPC, and the frustrations of holding the group together took their toll on presidents Bianchi and McGoldrick. They were unable to draw a larger membership and sustain momentum.

In 1973, the election of William Manseau from Lowell, Massachusetts, as president of SPFM changed its direction. Soon SPFM became the Fellowship of Christian Ministries (FCM), a term that better described its new direction. Bill advocated a less confrontational stance with Church leaders and encouraged newer forms of ministry. He set up a certification system for ministers, greater participation of women, and a more ecumenical ministry open to other Christian communities. This gave the organization new life.

The name Federation supplanted Fellowship in 1981; FCM today stands for the Federation of Christian Ministries. This change reflects a move toward greater diversity in ministry and pluralism in operations. It subordinates priestly ordination to the baptismal call to ministry.

In three decades of operation, FCM has had its ups and downs, with some conventions sparsely attended, and with occasional lapses in direction. But time and again the organization has renewed itself. Members formed small faith communities in which women and men minister as equals and profess the vision of Jesus Christ at the heart of the Gospel. They have done much good.

In recent years the Federation has shown renewed vigor. Its certification program enabled many, not just married priests, to exercise Christian ministry legally if challenged by the courts. Such certification results in a flourishing marriage ministry and permits many women to assume leadership roles.

FCM maintains it is "a prophetic community empowered by the Spirit of Jesus in which women and men serve humanity with compassion, act as equals and partners in ministry, celebrate inclusivity in language, ministries and structures, preach the Gospel, engage in interfaith dialogue, welcome the alienated members of church and society, design rituals, witness marriages, conduct funerals, and provide pastoral and spiritual care." It maintains a Web site at *www.FederationofChristianMinistries.org.* FCM also publishes every two months a newsletter, *Diaspora,* which tries "to keep members current with the organization and its activities, to provide ideas to further ministry and to further community building among local FCM groups and the national organization."

CORPUS

Frank Bonnike's resignation as NFPC president in 1973 did not signal his abandonment of priestly ministry. He became, as a Catholic, chaplain of crisis ministry at Lutheran General Hospital in Park Ridge, Illinois. Soon he began organizing married priests and their wives in small gatherings in the Chicago suburbs. From these meetings emerged CORPUS, originally conceived as the Corps of Reserve Priests United for Service, an acronym suggested by Frank's wife, Janet.

A bishop was overheard saying to fellow bishops, "Listen, I know those guys (married priests) and, believe me, they are not interested in coming back to the priesthood. They are only interested in sex and money." Hearing this, the small neighborhood group, which by then consisted of the McGraths, Hunds, Nemmerses, Wilburs, and Bonnikes, decided to test that assertion. They put together a statement affirming the married priest's willingness to serve as a reserve unit in the Church, much as reserves assisting the military during wartime.

The Chicago area couples distributed copies of the document to about seventeen hundred married priests whose names they secured from chancery offices and private sources. Of those reached, over six hundred promptly endorsed it. Frank McGrath concluded, "at least one third of the resigned/married priests remain committed to their priesthood and are ready and willing to serve the Church." That statement distributed in 1975 launched CORPUS. And the bishop who spoke about married priests five years earlier apologized for his remarks.

For the first ten years, CORPUS was not much more than a post office box in Chicago, managed by a few married priests called facilitators. But, like the NAPR, it loomed strongly on the national scene and had a more lasting effect. Their periodic newsletter continued to arouse interest, and more and more married priests, when they heard, signed the statement. The Chicago couples saw CORPUS not as an organization, but as people who affirmed their readiness to serve. Activists, however, wanted more vigorous action. They began urging a professional approach to public relations, a formal dialogue with the bishops, and greater service to CORPUS signers.

In 1980 the facilitators brought together 35 coordinators from across the country to discuss the structure of CORPUS. At that meeting participants recommended hiring a full time executive director to work on fund raising and organizing. Four more years elapsed before the facilitators accepted the idea. To lead the new effort, they chose a married priest from Minneapolis, Terry Dosh. A former Benedictine monk, Terry, and his wife, Millie, a former Poor Clare nun, lived consistent with their monastic roots. Not interested in worldly wealth, Millie and Terry raised their sons, Martin Luther King Chavez Dosh and Paul Gandhi Joseph Dosh, in the same spirit. On a meager budget, they did much for the reform movement.

As executive director, Terry energetically expanded the CORPUS membership and raised its stature. Crisscrossing the country, visiting every organized band of married priests, he orchestrated radio and newspaper interviews at each site. Always certain about the future of a married priesthood, he beamed optimism and confidence. And CORPUS benefited.

Under Dosh's leadership the CORPUS mailing list grew to almost eleven thousand, including every Catholic bishop and many newspapers. He published *CORPUS Reports* six times a year and increased the coordinators to over two hundred. He put the national movement in high gear. In six years, Dosh generated over twelve hundred media stories, including appearances on national TV programs (*The MacNeil/Lehrer News Hour, 60 Minutes*), over a hundred radio and TV interviews, and a front page story with photo in the *New York Times*. Today he continues to spearhead the reform movement

as editor of the newsletter *Bread Rising,* and as member of the board
of the Association for the Rights of Catholics in the Church (ARCC),
on which he has served as president.

In 1988, Dosh proposed to the facilitators the formation of a national board for CORPUS. From his journeys, he had become well
acquainted with married priests in all parts of the United States.
He recommended a diverse board representing every region. The
facilitators discussed possible candidates and reached agreement on
whom to invite on the first board. For president, they chose Anthony
Padovano.

Anthony came well prepared for national leadership. A Rome-
educated theologian with an S.T.D. from the Gregorian University
and a Ph.D. in literature from Fordham University, he had been professor of systematic theology at Immaculate Conception Seminary
in Darlington, New Jersey. When *Humanae Vitae* was published, he
was serving as adviser to the U.S. Catholic bishops on their Sub-
committee on the Systematic Theology of the Priesthood. He helped
to prepare the U.S. Bishops' pastoral letters "The Church in Our
Day" (1967) and "Human Life in Our Day" (1968). After marrying
Theresa Lackamp, he became a professor of literature and religious
studies at Ramapo College of New Jersey, an institution he helped
to found. They have raised four children and Anthony has authored
twenty-seven books.

The first gathering of the CORPUS Board occurred in November 1988. The excitement of those first meetings was palpable.
Board members felt they could change the world. They plunged into
projects like the publishing of a national directory, the development
of a prayer service for departed married priests, and a collaborative
reaching out to other reform groups. Mike Breslin from Brooklyn
continually prodded the board to bolder stands. Pat Callahan from
Seattle pleaded for fiscal restraint and accountability. Tom Abel of Baton Rouge as secretary kept record of the deliberations with warmth
and humor. But the intellectual leadership of the movement rested
with Padovano.

After assuming the presidency of CORPUS, Anthony Padovano became the most articulate spokesman for married priests in America.

His writings covered the full range of issues faced by them. Whenever the press focused on current topics that had to do with priesthood — pedophilia, homosexuality, financial abuse — Padovano was ready with a wise and thoughtful response. He could always be relied on to give a penetrating commentary. He also became active in international affairs, serving as CORPUS ambassador and vice-president of the International Federation of Married Priests.

No one has uplifted the hearts and sharpened the vision of married priests more than Padovano. In his bold keynote address at the first National Conference on a Married Priesthood at American University in Washington in 1988, he declared:

> Where was our sanctity lost? Did we lose sanctity in the arms of our wives? We found grace there and were blessed by our wives. Did we lose sanctity in the children we conceived and held in our arms, willing to die for them if need be? We found God in our children, in their hearts, and they blessed us. Did we lose sanctity because we asked God to be with us as we took our word of celibacy and made it a vow of marriage? We were given two sacraments at that moment and summoned to be doubly committed, to marriage and to priesthood until death. Mysteriously, both sacraments became one lived reality in us so that all the commitments of marriage and priesthood became one life. In our wives and children, Christ was formed for us as he became bone of our bone, flesh of our flesh. What God put together in us, let no mortal power put asunder.[9]

The task of running a nationwide organization at the cutting edge of reform was not easy. Faced with the hardening of positions in Rome and the appointment of rigidly traditionalist bishops at home, Padovano kept hope alive. The married priest movement worldwide will always be indebted to him.

In 2002 the CORPUS Board changed its clarifying subtitle from "Association for a *Married* Priesthood" to "Association for an *Inclusive* Priesthood." In undertaking this move, the Board articulated more accurately the direction in which it has long headed. CORPUS combines the goals of a married priesthood and a female priesthood.

Both are now major focuses. CORPUS offers annual conferences, an attractive Web site (*www.corpus.org*), effective member services (508-822-6710) and an excellent journal published by David Gawlik every two months, *CORPUS Reports*.

Celibacy Is the Issue (CITI)

With the decline in celibate priests, more and more laity have called on married priests for help. This development gave rise to yet another new organization. Louise Haggett of Massachusetts deserves credit for this next major step in the evolution of the married priest movement.

In the early 1990s, Louise could not find a priest to minister to her mother at a senior assisted living home. Noting the growing shortage of clergy to offer such services, and realizing the availability of thousands of married priests, in 1992 she began an effort later called Rent-a-Priest. This irreverent, lighthearted approach arose from a reverent, serious-minded Catholic. With her savvy marketing skill and public relations talent, she set about trying to identify the twenty thousand married priests in the United States and nudging them back into ministry.

The organization she set up, Celibacy Is The Issue (CITI), tries to restore the dignity of married priests by acknowledging them and encouraging the ministry to which Jesus called them. CITI seeks after the full use of Roman Catholic priests in responding to the spiritual needs of the faithful. Like CORPUS, it tries to dialogue with the Catholic community; like FCM, it urges married priests to minister to the People of God.

The revised mission statement of CITI says: "Living our faith in Jesus Christ, we affirm, invite and educate married Roman Catholic priests and other People of God to utilize their gifts in providing for the spiritual and pastoral needs of the faithful." To foster such work, CITI keeps a sacramental registry of all baptisms and weddings performed. It has identified married priests in all fifty states willing to respond when requested. It publishes the list as *God's Yellow Pages*. In 2002 these priests were responsible for 2,500 marriages, 300 funerals, 250 baptisms, and 650 anointings of the sick.

Based in Framingham, Massachusetts, CITI Ministries Inc. maintains a Web site (*www.rentapriest.com*), managed by the resourceful John Shuster. This advanced computerized network matches people with priests. In recent years, CITI has spread to other countries and has become the fastest growing movement of married priests today.

Collaborative Efforts

Many reform groups arose in the aftermath of the Second Vatican Council. With the shift in Church leadership towards more traditional and conservative ways, reformers realized that they had to join forces for greater strength. They needed to rise above their separate agendas and work to achieve collaborative goals. Much effort has been expended in recent years.

National Coalitions

One of the energizing catalysts providing impetus to reform groups nationally has been Call to Action, a movement begun by the U.S. bishops. In 1971 an international synod of bishops in Rome declared, "The Church recognizes that anyone who ventures to speak about justice must first be just in their eyes; hence, we must undertake an examination of the modes of action, of the possessions, and of the lifestyle of the Church itself." The U.S. bishops took those words seriously. When they returned home, they launched a dialogue involving over eight hundred thousand Catholics nationwide. These discussions lasted several years and culminated in the historic Call to Action Conference in Detroit in 1976.

Through three memorable days of debate, 160 bishops, 1,340 voting delegates, and 1,500 observers discussed and voted on topics that arose from the nationwide consultation. Results were startling. At the final meeting, delegates affirmed that the Church must stand up to the chronic racism, sexism, militarism, and poverty in society. They called for the Church to reevaluate its positions on birth control, an all-male clergy, priestly celibacy, and homosexuality. They also asked for involvement of the entire Church in making important decisions. Each diocese was urged to act on these recommendations.

After the conference, bishops distanced themselves from the event. Because this consultation with lay, clerical, and religious leaders in the Catholic community resulted in advice they did not want to hear, they disowned the event. The genie, however, had escaped from the bottle. The voice bishops gave to lay leaders would not be silenced.

In 1978, the autocratic actions of Cardinal John Cody of Chicago triggered a Call to Action gathering involving over four hundred priests, nuns, schoolteachers, and other laity. This group continued to convene annually in Chicago, growing to eighteen hundred in 1981. It produced a document titled "Call for Reform in the Catholic Church," published by the *New York Times* on February 28, 1990. In a few years twenty-five thousand people added their names and the national Call to Action movement was in full swing. Its annual conferences attract thousands of progressive Catholics.

At the November 1991 Call to Action meeting in Chicago, a dozen reform groups gathered separately to plan strategy, agreeing that they could reach their goals more advantageously if they joined forces. They formed Catholic Organizations for Renewal (COR), which claims to be not so much an organization as "a coalition of Catholic groups, inspired by Vatican II, to further reform and renewal in the Catholic Church, and to bring about a world of justice and peace, reflecting the sacredness of all creation." About thirty national and regional organizations in the United States and Canada come together under their banner. Call to Action provides staff support and coordination.

In the following decade, COR undertook important initiatives: signature ads in major newspapers, a Gallup Poll of Catholic opinion, support for the We Are Church referendum, a White House meeting with presidential staff, a meeting with the bishops' staff at NCCB, and a combination of public forums, news conferences, and press briefings in conjunction with the visit of Pope John Paul II to Denver.

International Coalitions

In 1983, married priest groups united internationally. Synods with representatives from many countries convened in Chiusi (1983) and Ariccia (1985) in Italy. In response to an initiative at the Synod in

Ariccia, participants formed the International Federation of Married Catholic Priests (IFMCP), an ongoing coalition of national organizations aimed at fostering dialogue and promoting joint action. The group met for the first time in May 1986, and in November of that year Anthony Padovano became its vice-chairman. The IFMCP held international congresses at Ariccia, Italy, in 1987; Doorn, Netherlands, in 1990; Madrid, Spain, in 1993; Brasilia, Brazil, in 1996; and Atlanta, U.S.A., in 1999; and a General Assembly in Madrid in 2002.

Besides the American married priest groups, thirty-four other organizations aligned themselves with IFMCP. These include well-established groups like Epiphany in Australia, Advent in England, Leaven in Ireland, four associations in Italy, three in France, and two in Spain. The major work of organizing this Federation began in Europe. Today The IFMCP embraces South and Central American countries like Argentina, Bolivia, Brazil, Chile, Colombia, Ecuador, Guatemala, Mexico, and Paraguay; also the reemerging Central European countries like the Czech and Slovak Republics, Hungary, and Poland.

Efforts at greater solidarity among married priest groups have resulted in the development of regional federations, organized to meet common cultural needs. The first of these was the Latin American Federation of Catholic Married Priests, coordinating efforts among Latin American married priests. Similarly, on January 8, 2003, the North Atlantic Federation of Married Catholic Priests came into existence, uniting the efforts of priests in Austria, Belgium, England, Germany, Hungary, Ireland, the Netherlands, and the United States. A third development, a Mediterranean Federation, is now being planned.

These federations enable married priest groups to address matters specific to their region. As Padovano explains:

Certain issues have reached a more intense level of expression in the North Atlantic community: the sexual abuse of minors; the ordination and leadership of women; effects of affluence; collegial structures for the church; the legitimacy of dissent; spiritual values in our secular lives.[10]

At their Sixth International Congress in Wiesbaden, Germany on September 15, 2005, the International Federation of Married Catholic Priests decided to reorganize itself as a confederation of federations: (1) Latin-American Federation, (2) Filipino Federation, (3) European Federation, and (4) North-Atlantic Federation. Each group represents significant numbers of married priests and their wives.

The Next Steps

What are the next steps on this journey? Just as no one could have anticipated the New Pentecost at the Second Vatican Council or its aftermath, so also no one can predict the workings of the Holy Spirit in the years ahead. One married priest organization has folded (NAPR), another has altered its structure (SPFM to FCM), and others were started (CORPUS and CITI). The last three grow and interact amicably. Although agendas differ, these organizations support each other's programs. Married priests and their wives are found in the leadership of all three groups.

The pattern of evolution is clear. In response to directives from the Second Vatican Council, local groups were formed, then a national coalition. For celibate priests this meant formation of senates and associations of priests followed by the National Federation of Priests' Councils (NFPC); for married priests, it meant local groups meeting together and joining under the leadership of FCM, CORPUS, or CITI, sometimes all three. These organizations have expanded their memberships to include friends who support their goals.

To gain greater strength, these groups formed coalitions with similar national bodies in different parts of the world. The chief vehicle for married priests was the International Federation of Married Priests, organized in 1986. Over thirty organizations worldwide are united under their umbrella. The married priest movement also joined hands with other Church reform groups nationally (COR) and internationally (We Are Church).

Much has taken place since the exciting days of the Second Vatican Council. The impulse given to church reform has borne extraordinary and unanticipated fruit. The spontaneous emergence of organizations of priests, religious, and laity throughout the world and the formation of coalitions can be ascribed only to the Holy Spirit. That work, however, has just begun.

Barriers between reform groups and traditional groups, between clergy and laity, must yet be broken down. In light of Post–Vatican II's tumultuous history, it would be presumptuous to predict the future. One certainty remains. The Holy Spirit is in charge. She will not abandon the Church.

Part Two

Post-Clerical Journeys

Chapter 4

The *Humanae Vitae* Debacle

THE YEAR 1968 marked a turning point in the United States and in the Catholic Church. The murders of Martin Luther King Jr. and Robert F. Kennedy spawned unrest in America, especially through the peace movement and the civil rights movement, reaching its climax at the Democratic National Convention in Chicago. The Catholic Church, in contrast, reached a more rapid and dramatic escalation of tension through one event — publication of the papal encyclical on birth control, *Humanae Vitae*.

Rarely does a single document, a letter no less, cause public clamor. Except for Church bureaucrats affected by them, most papal encyclicals go unnoticed. Not so with *Humanae Vitae*. In the years before its publication, concerns about birth control steadily rose. Refined methods of contraception and a growing consensus about the need for responsible family planning led people to expect a reversal in Church teaching. Experts chosen by Pope Paul VI to advise him recommended just that. But despite all these developments, the pope chose to reiterate traditional teaching. He dropped a bomb.

The encyclical challenged emerging structures. Methods of broader consultation — episcopal conferences, pastoral councils, priest senates, parish councils, sisters' associations — had recently been put in place. The Vatican Council encouraged this, urging deeper involvement of the People of God in activities of the Church. Yet these same bodies were caught by surprise. To ignore these consultative bodies and the counsel of experts on matters that affected adversely the lives of the most ardent faithful appeared to be dramatically shortsighted. For the remaining ten years of his papacy, Pope Paul VI would not undertake another encyclical.

Priests in parish ministry were left in a quandary. Some welcomed the encyclical, affirming obedience to the pope as the only response. Others were vexed by it and openly said so. The majority followed a middle course of respecting Church authorities, while looking for ways to respond with sensitivity to the plight of their people. They sought a pastoral solution.

Reactions to the encyclical across the Catholic world were swift and fierce. Some theologians tried to interpret the encyclical benignly; others opposed it openly. Rome, through its apostolic delegates, urged each bishop to proclaim fidelity to the voice of Peter. Most did so, choosing their words skillfully. But few bishops had ever faced such immediate and concerted challenge to official Church teaching. Their leadership was tested. Because of their apostolic authority, many bishops felt they had to assert themselves and support papal teachings. Prudence and charity did not always prevail.

On the right were clergy who saw their prime responsibility as defending Rome and demanding adherence to its teaching. They spoke of requiring signed oaths of loyalty. On the left were theologians and clergymen convinced that an error had been made and that a more enlightened response to the faithful was needed. They voiced strong opposition. A few on each side proved intractable.

Several bishops tried to dispel the passions of the moment. They downplayed the matter in public and calmed down extremists in private. Cardinal Lawrence Shehan of Baltimore, for example, responding with understanding and solicitude to troubled clergy, averted clashes like those that soon followed in Buffalo, San Antonio, and Los Angeles. The newly formed National Federation of Priests' Councils weighed in with support for censured priests. In every instance, Federation leaders urged that bishops and priests submit such conflicts to binding arbitration. Bishops were reluctant to do so.

The Archdiocese of Washington

Of all the confrontations that followed, none achieved greater notoriety or nationwide exposure than that between bishop and theologians and between bishop and clergy in the Archdiocese of Washington,

D.C. Home of the apostolic delegate to the United States, site of the nation's premier pontifical university, center of the nation's political and ecclesiastical life, the scene was ready-made for prime time.

The protagonists were unlikely adversaries: the bishop — Cardinal Patrick O'Boyle, a respected church leader outspoken in defense of the poor and disenfranchised, ahead of his times in the racial integration of schools and churches; the theologians at Catholic University — emerging as intellectual leaders of the American Church and advocates of the progressive reforms of the Second Vatican Council; the Association of Washington Priests (AWP) — led by some of the best educated and most respected priests in the archdiocese, emboldened by the support of major theologians, adopting what they considered the right pastoral response.

Events unfolded with stunning swiftness. On July 29, 1968, Pope Paul VI issued his encyclical on birth control, *Humanae Vitae.* By nightfall, eighty-seven Catholic theologians in America burned up the telephone wires constructing a response to which they agreed to add their names. Leadership in this initiative came from the theological faculty of Washington's pontifical Catholic University. The statement they released to the press asserted:

> It is common teaching in the Church that Catholics may dissent from authoritative, non-infallible teachings of the magisterium (teaching authority) when sufficient reasons for doing so exist. Therefore, as Roman Catholic theologians, conscious of our duty and our limitations, we conclude that spouses may responsibly decide according to their conscience that artificial contraception in some circumstances is permissible and indeed necessary to preserve and foster the values and sacredness of marriage.[1]

Members of the Association of Washington Priests quickly came together and announced that they would not support the Church's traditional teaching against birth control. Paralleling the statement by theologians, they published a "Statement of Conscience." It said:

This dissenting position is perfectly compatible, we feel, to loyalty to Christ and the Church. The integral pastoral ministry must take into account not papal statements alone, but also the practical day-to-day lives of those who are striving to live in the grace of Christ. As preachers of the Word and ministers of the sacraments of penance, we feel that the theologians' judgment...requires a pastoral response on our part. This response means that we will respect the intelligently and responsibly formed conscience of people who follow this theological judgment.[2]

Cardinal O'Boyle also responded immediately. Upon receiving a copy of the encyclical, he sent a message to Pope Paul VI expressing gratitude and appreciation. His congratulatory telegram and that of Cardinal James Francis McIntyre of Los Angeles were posted prominently the next day in the Vatican newspaper, *L'Osservatore Romano*. O'Boyle also issued a public statement, "As the bishop of Washington, I call upon all priests in their capacity as confessors, teachers and preachers of God's word to follow without equivocation, ambiguity or simulation the teaching of the Church on this matter as enunciated clearly by Paul VI."[3] The battle lines had formed.

Temperate statements of other bishops and bishops' conferences supported the dissenting priests. The bishops of Scandinavia stated: "If someone...cannot be convinced by the argument of the encyclical, it has always been conceded that he is allowed to have a different view from that presented in a noninfallible statement of the Church."[4] And the bishops of Austria published a joint pastoral letter advising Austrian Catholics that they could in good conscience act contrary to the encyclical and "receive Holy Communion without having confessed."[5] In a similar vein the Canadian bishops asserted in their pastoral letter:

We must make every effort to appreciate the difficulty experienced by contemporary man in understanding and appropriating some points in the encyclical.... Since they are not denying any point of divine and Catholic faith nor rejecting the teaching

authority of the Church, these Catholics should not be considered or consider themselves shut off from the body of the
faithful.[6]

The pastoral letters of the bishops of Belgium and Scandinavia followed the same line. Other bishops' conferences (Belgium, CELAM,[7]
France, Indonesia, the Netherlands, South Africa, Switzerland) introduced different mitigating circumstances. But as the former auxiliary
bishop of St. Paul, Minnesota, James Shannon, noted: "No matter
how cautiously the draftsmen of such letters phrased their arguments,
they were rejecting the central thesis of the long-awaited encyclical."[8]

Cardinal O'Boyle saw things differently. Rome had spoken. The
matter was finished. All the faithful, especially the clergy, had a duty
to accept this teaching. Successor to the apostles, he saw his role as en-
forcing loyalty to papal decrees, which he accepted as the teachings
of Christ. He tolerated no dissent. The Association of Washington
Priests, in contrast, looked on the encyclical as an erroneous teaching, rejected in theory by theologians and opposed in practice by the
faithful. They too refused to back off. There was no middle ground.

Ensuing events sharpened the conflict. On August 4, the Association of Washington Priests sent to Cardinal O'Boyle a "Statement of
Conscience," signed by fifty-two priests of the archdiocese. By August 15, each of the fifty-two had received a ten-page letter from the
cardinal clarifying his position and requesting a personal, not collec-
tive, response. Nine priests responded. On August 23 and 24, O'Boyle
met with most of the signers, giving them a "canonical admonition,"
an official warning in accord with Church law. On August 27, five
members of the Executive Committee of the Priests' Association held
discussions with Cardinal O'Boyle for two and a half hours. The
priests delivered to him a letter restating their position.

On August 31, the cardinal met with thirty-five signers of the
statement and on September 2 with fifteen more. They were given
until September 14 to retract their statement. The Association leadership got in touch with Cardinal John Dearden, president of the
National Conference of Catholic Bishops, and requested mediation.
Dearden replied the same day that all requests for mediation should

be addressed to Cardinal Lawrence Shehan of Baltimore, head of a committee designated by the bishops to handle such matters. On September 9, the Association wrote to Shehan. His reply, on September 12, shared with Cardinal O'Boyle, showed his willingness to help, if each side agreed to turn the matter over to arbitration. O'Boyle would not.

Bishop Alexander Zaleski of Lansing, Michigan, chairman of the U.S. Bishops Commission on Doctrine, offered the following guidelines to bishops dealing with dissent over *Humanae Vitae:*

- It is possible that a person in good faith may be unable to give internal assent to an encyclical.

- As a loyal member of the Church such a person must beware of voicing dissent in the wrong way.

- Dissent can be expressed but it must be done in a manner becoming to a docile believer and a loyal member of the Church.

- Such dissent must show that it is an expression from a believing person — a person of faith.

- Such dissent can only be expressed in a manner that does not disturb the conscience of other believing people.

- Dissent must be accompanied by an open mind and a willingness to alter one's view in the light of new evidence.

- Such dissent must be brought to the right authorities in the proper manner and quietly.[9]

In Baltimore seventy-two priests signed a public document expressing reservations about the encyclical. Cardinal Shehan met privately with them and they reached a common understanding. The matter was ended. In St. Paul, ninety-one priests signed a similar statement, indicating that they could not accept the pastoral implications of the encyclical. Again, the archbishop addressed the matter privately. In Washington, however, Cardinal O'Boyle handled dissent differently. The saga played out daily in the national press.

On September 14, forty-four priests released to the press another statement reaffirming their position. On October 1, O'Boyle announced his response. He evicted five priests from their rectories. He relieved fifteen of the right to hear confessions, preach, and teach; seven more of the right to hear confessions and teach; and nine others of the right to hear confessions. Two voluntarily relinquished their right to hear confessions. One at his own request was granted a year's leave of absence.

Prayers for guidance and support rose up in churches of the archdiocese. On Sunday morning, September 23, Cardinal O'Boyle demanded that priests in every parish read from the pulpits a letter prepared by him. In unusually strong words, the letter addressed those who would set their own desires above God's will as expressed by the pope. They were admonished with words reminiscent of the book of Deuteronomy, "The wrath and the jealousy of the Lord will blaze against such a man; every curse written in this book will fall on him, and the Lord will blot out his name from under heaven." When O'Boyle entered the pulpit of St. Matthew's Cathedral and began reading the letter that Sunday, many stood up and walked out; when he finished, those remaining applauded. The headline of the *Washington Post,* the city newspaper, on September 23 read: "400 Walk Out on Cardinal at Masses"; the headline of *The Catholic Standard,* the archdiocesan newspaper, read: "Cardinal Applauded After Reading Letter."

Similar reactions followed in churches all over the archdiocese. Among those walking out at one parish was an unlikely protester — Shane MacCarthy, one of the cardinal's trusted friends and his own media advisor. MacCarthy had been Grand Knight of the Knights of Columbus, president of his parish Holy Name Society, announcer at the Archdiocesan Mass for Shut-ins and aide to the cardinal in other public activities. But his son was a dissenting priest. Shane and his wife walked out of Mass that Sunday in protest and stood outside until the letter was read, then returned for the rest of church services. Many others did also. His behavior led to dismissal as lector in his home parish and withdrawal of the invitation to speak at the upcoming Communion Breakfast of the Knights of Columbus.

The anguish of censured priests was expressed by George Spellman in a letter to the *National Catholic Reporter* three decades later:

I, with 44 colleagues, all priests working hard in the Archdiocese, was suspended on the same day with different remedial punishments. Fired! What a way to end a career.... Scared to death and far from home, what will happen next? Not only me but my friends and colleagues and how about those who were not with us on these issues? We all had to reexamine our relationships to the Church and to each other. Some were sympathetic, others very angry with us. More work, less workers! It was disappointing to learn that in the Presbyterate and the Mystical Body only one Bishop, Charlie Buswell, offered us sanctuary until there was some resolution. Can you imagine just one? I eventually concluded that this is not the institution I wanted to devote the rest of my life to. In some strange manner I was being liberated from the organization and didn't realize it.[10]

A third of a century has gone by and most of the chief players are no longer on the scene. Viewing the entire landscape today, one views an unhealed wound. Publication of *Humanae Vitae* sparked the departure of many priests, including a few bishops, from clerical ranks. Countless faithful turned to other Christian communities. Rome, after 1978, began imposing ever more conservative episcopal leadership throughout the Church — bishops committed to affirming papal prerogatives and maintaining traditional teaching.

Since the debacle, each side has hardened its stand. The hierarchy is adamant about upholding papal teaching on birth control. According to recent surveys, however, the overwhelming majority of practicing Catholics reject that teaching. Although the official Church position remains clear, widespread rejection endures. Faithful churchgoers do not want to publicize their dissent, but are intent privately on following their consciences.

Much can be gained from reexamining this bit of history and from reviewing the principal actors. Their integrity is unquestioned. In the intervening four decades, they remained dedicated followers of

Christ. This loyalty to Christ comes as no surprise to those who knew them.

The Cardinal Archbishop

Cardinal O'Boyle is central to the controversy. As a newly ordained priest in Manhattan in 1921, he was assigned to St. Columba's, just south of Hell's Kitchen, where he saw firsthand the poverty of the inner city. That image stayed with him for life. His success working with the poor in those early years brought him to the attention of Cardinal Hayes, who then assigned him to New York's Catholic Charities offices. As supervisor, O'Boyle oversaw childcare agencies and other charitable organizations. His hard work and compassion led to more important and more responsible assignments.

In 1943, he became director of War Relief Services of the National Catholic Welfare Conference (NCWC) and arranged for the distribution of 66,500 tons of food and supplies to forty-eight countries in Europe and Asia. Then, after the war, he was appointed the first residential bishop in the nation's capital. Never before had a priest in the United States been made an archbishop without first serving as bishop.

As new archbishop, he gained a deserved reputation as fearless leader. One of his first acts was to order the desegregation of all schools and churches in the Archdiocese of Washington. Six years before the Supreme Court desegregated the nation's public schools, O'Boyle courageously did the same in Catholic institutions. The *Washington Post* called his action "one of the most influential acts of moral leadership in the city's history."

O'Boyle attended all sessions of the Second Vatican Council in Rome from 1962 through 1965. True to his deepest convictions, he addressed the Fathers of the Council on October 28, 1964, urging that a condemnation of racism and racial segregation be adopted:

> [The Council document] should include a forthright and un-
> equivocal condemnation of racism in all its forms.... It should
> also emphasize the obligation which rests upon all the members

of the Church to do everything within their power to eliminate the cancerous evil of racial injustice and to advance, through all available means, the cause of interracial brotherhood under the fatherhood of God.[11]

This intervention during discussions on Schema 13 became enshrined in the historic *Gaudium et Spes* (On the Church in the Modern World) document.

His work at the Council was interrupted by an important event — the 1963 March on Washington for civil rights. When Martin Luther King Jr. rendered his memorable "I Have a Dream" speech, O'Boyle stood on the dais, having just given the invocation. In succeeding days he continued to speak out for new civil rights legislation. Moreover, as chairman of the American bishops' Social Action Department, he stood in the forefront of bishops advocating interracial justice. Later, in 1972, he would support Cesar Chavez and the lettuce boycott to protest working conditions of farm laborers. This son of working class parents never forgot his roots.

As expected, not long after the Council ended, he was in 1967 created a cardinal. The ceremony of installation confers on the man distinctive red garments and reminds him to be ready to shed his blood, if need be, in defense of the faith. O'Boyle took that symbolism seriously. One year and one month later, *Humanae Vitae* gave him the opportunity to stand firm in defense of Rome's official teachings.

A liberal on civil rights and social issues in America, O'Boyle nevertheless became unyieldingly conservative on matters asserted by Rome. He staunchly opposed sterilization, birth control, and legalized abortion, comparing them to Hitler's slaughter of the Jews. On these matters, like the Vatican, he stood implacable.

In 1971, on reaching the mandatory retirement age of seventy-five, O'Boyle sent to Rome his resignation. Two years later it was accepted. He continued to live at the cathedral until his death on August 10, 1987. Those who knew him well verified the great toll his priests' opposition took on his health. Their disobedience pained him. To the end, he was certain he did the right thing. Today, his successors in the hierarchy support him.

With censured priests, one similarly finds no regrets for their actions. They too remain convinced about the course they had taken. Traditionalists in the Catholic Church today support the cardinal; progressives stand by the censured priests. No compromise has been found.

Three Who Returned

Priests involved in this controversy underwent intense pain and anguish. Each one tried to respond as his intelligence guided him and his conscience prodded him. Much prayer and soul-searching were entailed. No villains are found here. All continue to this day their commitment to Christ. They followed different paths in life, but stood firm with Christ to the end. Consider first three dissenters who died as celibate priests.

HORACE B. MCKENNA, S.J. Known as the saint of the poor, Horace McKenna lent his support to this struggle. His involvement troubled Cardinal O'Boyle, who had always held him in high regard. But those who knew McKenna recognized how typical this was of him. When convinced of a course of action in pastoral ministry, McKenna followed it relentlessly. Above all, he championed the oppressed.

In the first years of his priesthood as a Jesuit, Horace worked among blacks in Southern Maryland and looked after their welfare. Later he did the same in the slums of Philadelphia and Washington, D.C. He identified with his people, and they loved him for it. His labors at times brought him into conflict with religious superiors. When they forbade him from participating in the famous March on Washington in 1963, he obeyed. But when *Humanae Vitae* was published and countless faithful were troubled, he could not give full support. With other priests, Horace signed the letter of dissent. O'Boyle promptly withdrew his priestly faculties.

Horace always held his ground, especially on matters that affected the poor and disenfranchised in Church or state, but he would not speak publicly against church leaders, even when he considered them wrong. He bore his punishment in silence. He never gave up his work with the poor. The cardinal later lifted the suspension.

McKenna started several programs for the needy in Washington. He helped found S.O.M.E. (So Others Might Eat), a soup kitchen, clinic, housing, and job program; Sursum Corda, a community-owned housing project; Martha's Table, a soup kitchen and center for homeless women; and the McKenna Center, a social service provider at St. Aloysius Roman Catholic Church. He worked in our nation's capital until his death in 1982, recognized throughout the city as a friend of the poor, a living saint. He showed how to be a Christian in the turbulent twentieth century.

JOSEPH BYRON. Joe Byron was among the most admired priests in the archdiocese. Like many in those days, he became enthralled by what he saw as the work of the Holy Spirit in the events of the Second Vatican Council. He was chaplain at American University, where he eagerly put in place liturgical reforms. He preached a renewal consistent with documents of the Council. He would say later, "It was great to be a priest at that time." Nevertheless, when rumors of innovation and experimentation reached the chancery office, the archbishop transferred him from the university and appointed him pastor of St. James in Mt. Rainier, Maryland.

Byron always had the deep respect of his fellow priests. They chose him as their representative and leader of the newly formed Association of Washington Priests. That meant dealing with the cardinal in behalf of dissenting priests. Like them he also received the full censures. He was the only pastor among the nineteen priests who appealed to the Vatican for intervention. But O'Boyle would not be moved.

Byron's travails endured for three years until he signed a statement of agreement with the general principles of *Humanae Vitae*. In taking this step, he noted that signing his name "didn't change anybody's mind," but "nobody talked about it any more." This act broke the impasse and readmitted him to full priestly service.

In 1983 O'Boyle appointed him pastor of Our Lady of Mercy in Potomac, Maryland, where he spent his last nine years. Once again his fellow clergy elected him as their leader and spokesman. He became head of the Archdiocesan Priests' Council. This reflected the esteem in which his peers continued to hold him. He was a priest's priest.

In his final days Byron suffered from Alzheimer's disease, which increasingly ravaged his body. He celebrated Mass falteringly and prepared his sermons painstakingly. The deacon assigned to help him would often have to preach in his stead. Eventually, a co-pastor was appointed to work with him. Then in August 1992, the Lord summoned him to his long awaited reward.

ROBERT HOVDA. From his youth, Robert Hovda was a maverick and nonconformist. He grew up in a Methodist household and during high school years participated in Methodist youth groups. Later as a conscientious objector, he joined the Episcopalian Peace Fellowship. Acquaintance with the Catholic Worker inspired him to enter the Catholic Church and begin studies for the priesthood. At last he found his home. After ordination he served for ten years in the Diocese of Fargo, North Dakota.

The Second Vatican Council, especially its proclamation on the liturgy, stirred him. Having studied at the feet of the great liturgical reformers at St. John's Abbey in Collegeville, Minnesota, he became inflamed with zeal for reform. In 1965, the Liturgical Conference in Washington hired him as editor, a post he held for thirteen years. He became a stalwart of the liturgical movement in America, preaching and writing ceaselessly about liturgical reform. His column "Amen Corner" appeared regularly in *Worship* Magazine. He also helped to develop a document for the Bishops Committee on the Liturgy titled "Environment and Art in Catholic Worship."

The publication of *Humanae Vitae* impelled him to join with priests in Washington. As with his opposition to warfare during the Second World War, so also now he stood firm. Although censured by Cardinal O'Boyle, he continued his labors at the Liturgical Conference, which was not diocesan controlled. The censure did not diminish his work for liturgical reform.

In 1980 he moved to New York. By then his physical condition deteriorated as his voice progressively weakened. In 1992 he died of heart failure.

Five Who Married

The majority of censured priests who dissented from papal teaching on birth control later married. Forced to find work in unrelated fields, most succeeded in their adopted professions. They created new lives for themselves and their families. Fidelity to Christ and his teachings continued to motivate them. The following five will serve as examples.

JOHN E. CORRIGAN. One could not find a more gifted priest to guide the Association of Priests in perilous times than John Corrigan. On that all agree. Recognized for his spirituality and theological understanding, he articulated as no other the concerns of the Washington priests. His charisma won over many. Never selfish or out to steal the limelight, he was able to give voice calmly, charitably, and respectfully to the deep convictions of priests in the face of strong episcopal pressure. In the end, he received the brunt of ecclesiastical penalties.

With his fellow priests, Corrigan was forced to find new work. For the next thirty years he applied his energies to economic development, achieving national recognition for his work. In 1972 he was named regional director of the Economic Development Administration (EDA) in the U.S. Department of Commerce, a job he held for twenty-six years. From his office in Philadelphia, he managed programs in thirteen northeastern states, Puerto Rico, and the Virgin Islands. His innovative ability led to adoption of several concepts considered basic economic development tools today: an employee stock ownership plan in New York, the first federally funded incubator in Brooklyn, the first EDA revolving loan fund in Newport, the first micro-lending program in Camden, and the first defense conversion project in Brooklyn.

These deeds merited major honors for him. He gained the Lifetime Achievement Award for excellence in economic development from the National Council for Urban Economic Development, the South Bronx Visionary Award for twenty-five years of dedication to "building a better Bronx," and the first Star of the Southeast Award given by the Austin Regional Office of the Economic Development Administration.

In 2000, the Federal Economic Development Administration presented its first annual distinguished award to the agency employee who contributed significantly to economic development. Because of Corrigan's achievements, the award was named after him. He set a high standard in his profession. That commitment to excellence marked him all his life.

In the midst of these labors, Corrigan raised two children. His wife, Marcia, his faithful companion and an experienced lawyer, succumbed too early to cancer, leaving him to raise his children alone. Retired with them in Florida, he continues to work as a consultant for the federal government.

GEORGE SPELLMAN. If Jack Corrigan was the intellectual and spiritual leader of priests in the Association, George Spellman was its advocate and prime organizer. Gifted with management skill combined with warm friendliness and political savvy, Spellman could hold together a body of men through thick and thin. Whether in the "scotch and scripture" gatherings of clerics in earlier days or through the days of recollection for married priests in later years, he has remained the major organizer of priests in the Greater Washington region.

Spellman's clerical years were spent in the era of civil rights, the Vietnam War, and Vatican II reform. The inner-city parish to which he was assigned in 1962 went from 80 percent white to 75 percent black in one year. Late night meetings on civil rights, the war against poverty, and liturgical reforms were followed by 6:30 a.m. Masses in a non–air conditioned church. Those were challenging times. With youthful exuberance, he applied his energies and showed leadership among his brother priests.

After his censure, George married Susan and raised two sons. His management and organizational skills began to grow. For over twenty-five years, he held important jobs with nonprofit and government agencies: ten years as executive vice-president of Joint Action in Community Services (JACS), where he designed pre-service and in-service training programs for over six thousand volunteers in ten regions of the country; two years as country director of the Peace

Corps in Nigeria; and three years as executive director of Big Brothers/Big Sisters in Greater Williamsburg. Returning at last to religious service, he accepted an ecumenical chaplaincy at the oldest mental hospital in the United States.

Spellman has been recognized professionally for his achievements. He became a board member of Meals on Wheels, agency representative of the United Way, and president of the Greater Williamsburg Association of Volunteer Administrators (GWAVA). Long active in adult education programs, he has given courses for Elderhostel and the Christopher Wren Association. He has also been honored for his work by the American Society for Training and Development (ASTD).

Especially noteworthy has been George's work with priests in transition. To help them, he formed the Warren Barker Foundation. This called for counseling for long hours, investigating the right jobs, and at times even financially supporting former clerics. During the past thirty years he has organized countless gatherings of married priests and their wives. He is the prime activist in the region.

FRANK RUPPERT. His contemporaries at the North American College in Rome remember Frank as Curly in a memorable production of *Oklahoma*. Gifted with handsome looks, a marvelous baritone voice, and a warm, pleasing personality, Frank Ruppert has always taken joy in music, from his early days as assistant pastor at St. Matthew's Cathedral to his later days giving the Schubertiades, musical reflections on Schubert, at the Chevy Chase Retirement Home. In between there was *Humanae Vitae*.

Many priests who left in the wake of that encyclical found jobs with the government or with nonprofit organizations. Frank followed a different route. In the period of conflict that followed, he began graduate study at American University and earned a doctorate in educational counseling. There he met Betty Todd, who was completing her doctorate in educational psychology and who became his life's partner. Together they raised two daughters.

After serving as administrative director of the Leary School for children with learning disabilities, Frank switched careers and founded a real estate company. Since 1970 he has worked to promote low-income housing in inner-city Washington. During those years he privately studied the relevance of the early nineteenth-century music of Franz Schubert to today's mystical themes. This study motivates him to offer reflective and inspirational hours for the elderly at retirement homes.

Typically, Frank philosophizes over recent events in the Church. He recognizes that for some, the ongoing tension between man or woman and Church authorities has meant isolation; for others, a deepening, maturing, and liberating experience. As he sees it, "the living sacraments of wife, children, society, and nature have graced life with more intense meaning and magical, indescribable beauty." He contends that many married priests have beautifully wedded spirituality and lay life. He keeps a philosophical and spiritual bent, while firmly committing himself to the Christian message.

RALPH DWAN. Another Rome-educated priest in the Association of Washington Priests was Ralph Dwan. After graduating from the University of Michigan Law School, he decided to study for the priesthood. The archbishop recognized his talents and sent him to finish his theological studies in Rome, the West Point–like training grounds for future church leaders. Returning from Rome, Dwan became assistant chancellor and was urged to begin part-time study in canon law at Catholic University. His heart, however, lay in the inner city, not in chancery offices.

Ralph surrendered his chancery career to work with the poor in Anacostia and other parts of Washington. He ran the Southeast Center, which did much good for local residents. Archbishop O'Boyle respected his work and visited him at the center to foster his efforts. Ralph developed a summer program for children near St. Joseph's on Capital Hill, then succeeded Gino Baroni in running the Parish Center at St. Augustine's. He would later serve at St. Teresa's.

The papal encyclical changed Ralph's life. It was a moment of truth. After the censures imposed on him, he remained in the inner city, returning to the legal work for which he had originally studied. Over the next thirty years, he continued to offer legal services to the poor and the needy in Washington.

Ralph found a lifetime companion and soul mate in Mary, a former Holy Cross Sister. Mary served for many years on the board of

North Capital Neighborhood Development, providing assistance in housing for people in the inner city. Together they helped to set up the Spring Creek Foundation, which has given much-needed financial aid to the urban poor. They have also been strong supporters of Catholic causes, like Ralph's alma mater, Gonzaga Boys High School, and *Commonweal,* the lay Catholic magazine. Theirs is a lifetime of commitment to Catholic and urban programs.

SHANE MacCARTHY. Shane was a talented priest just three years out of the seminary working in a parish among urban youth when the entire controversy erupted. He and his brothers had followed the example of their parents in dedicated service to the Church, but the plight of the faithful after the encyclical on birth control troubled him. He decided to stand in solidarity with other priests and theologians in voicing opposition to the papal ruling. For that he paid dearly.

Because of his stand, Shane was censured and forced to leave the diocese. He married and took a job with the United States government. He went on to serve as director of the Peace Corps in Ghana for two years, then worked with the United States Agency for International Development (USAID) for over twenty years. While in Africa, Shane assisted the local Anglican bishop by traveling long distances and leading church services in remote jungle villages. This gave him the opportunity to preach the Good News once again to people who yearned for that message.

His wife, Karen, sacrificed with him amid the poverty of Africa. She taught first in Ghana and then in public schools in Northern Virginia. In the midst of all these activities, they raised a son and a daughter.

The Teaching on Reception

With the passage of more than a third of a century, one would expect that this controversy in the Church would be resolved. Far from it. Although official church teaching remains unchanged from the day Pope Paul VI issued his encyclical, widespread observance of its teaching is yet to be achieved.

Pope John Paul II was adamant in reaffirming papal teaching on contraception as doctrine. Bishops appointed under him were screened on the topics of birth control, celibacy, and women's ordination. The conservative wing of the lay church has been equally strong in affirming these teachings and reporting on dissenters. No compromise is accepted.

Rank-and-file Catholics, even regular churchgoers, behave differently. William D'Antonio and his colleagues at Catholic University analyzed the attitudes of the most committed Catholics and found much independence on ethical matters. According to their study, fifty-nine percent thought one could be a good Catholic without obeying the birth control teaching.[12] Their findings coincided with the Gallup Poll of Catholics in 1971, which gave the figure at 58 percent; and a 1977 study in which 73 percent said that Catholics should be allowed to practice artificial means of birth control.[13] In another Gallup Survey in 1992, 68 percent of American Catholics strongly agreed that "the Church should permit couples to make their own decisions about forms of birth control."

James Coriden, dean emeritus of the Washington Theological Union, argues, "for a law or rule to be an effective guide for the believing community it must be accepted by that community."[14] This teaching on reception is a longstanding principle in the Church. The theologian Yves Congar, O.P., argued that non-reception does not show that a teaching is false; it simply means that the teaching "does not call forth any living power and therefore does not contribute to edification."[15]

Many examples can be given of laws proclaimed but never accepted. The Third Lateran Council in 1179 ordered a "truce of God" (a temporary suspension of all hostilities) to be observed during some seasons of the Church year and commanded bishops to punish violators with excommunication. The 1917 Code of Canon Law demanded that provincial councils be held every twenty years and diocesan synods every ten years. And Pope John XXIII in February 1962 issued an apostolic constitution, *Veterum Sapientia*, insisting that teaching in all seminaries be conducted in Latin. Not one of these laws was received by those for whom they were intended.

The theologian Bernard Häring put the matter in perspective when he wrote,

> In this debate also, as on the question of ordaining women and the supposedly intrinsic evil of contraception, we see looming once again the double problem of reception or non-reception. On all these issues, which he has treated with such urgency, Pope John Paul II never "received" the statements of the Council, the findings of current theological research, or the clear indications from the people of God about their sense of the faith. The unavoidable reverse side of this is the non-reception by the people of God of firm papal teachings. Obsolescent models of thought cannot prevail against new findings and viewpoints. "The future has already begun." [16]

It is abundantly clear that overwhelming majorities of Catholics worldwide have not accepted Church pronouncements on contraception. Such behavior has turned the ancient saying on its head: *Roma locuta est, sed causa* non *finita est* (Rome has spoken, but the matter is not yet settled). The future has already begun.

Chapter 5

Working for the Church

D URING THE 1950s and 1960s many Catholic young men entered seminaries and young women convents, surrendering to God their lives. Theirs was a covenant with the divine. Later decisions to marry in no way diminished that bond. In most instances, the joys of family life in a loving relationship deepened their commitment to God and God's People.

In marrying, many faced a dilemma. They would like to respond to God's Call to ministry as married people in the Roman Catholic community. That proved an illusion. Priests soon realized, if they did not before, that they could not with the approval of church leadership continue in priestly ministry and sacramental marriage. Church rules for centuries allowed no exception, no honorable alternative to the ban on marriage after ordination. Recently dispensations have been granted (under Paul VI), then denied (under John Paul II). But ministry is forbidden.

Priests' wives faced the same barriers; in many instances further work in the Catholic community was closed to them. Some turned to other Christian churches — Episcopal, Presbyterian, Methodist, Lutheran — where they could offer pastoral service.

A few married priest couples have been successful in ministries within the Catholic Church — teaching in parochial schools and Catholic colleges, working in diocesan agencies that offer social services to the needy, assisting as chaplains in hospitals, nursing homes, and retirement communities. To bring this about, however, a sympathetic bishop or administrator was needed.

Those who continue working for the Church are fortunate in many ways. They can apply their talents as before and work among people with similar dedication, but in doing so they embrace a lower living standard. Tuition for their children is frequently reduced, but the problems of raising a family on limited income calls for much sacrifice.

The stories of men and women who work under these conditions show an enduring dedication to Christ and the Church. The journeys of the following extraordinary Catholics attest to that.

Religious Educators

Addictions counselor, philosophy teacher, religious education director, nighttime janitor, substitute teacher, adult education instructor — these are a few of the jobs Bob held over a thirty-year period. Never making a full professional salary befitting his education and experience, he and his wife, Ann, maintain a loving home for their family despite many hardships.

Their love story shattered the mold. Bob was Jesuit pastor of an inner-city parish; Ann, a religion teacher. An unlikely romance developed. When they realized what was happening, Bob sent a letter to his superiors, requesting a dispensation to marry. This occurred during the Pope Paul VI era, when such petitions were accepted and reviewed. Nevertheless, they waited more than two years before Rome gave permission. Only after their church celebration did they begin their life together.

Determined to use their talents as religious educators, they sought jobs in Catholic institutions. Whenever interviewed for a job, Bob and Ann were hired; their geniality, Christian joy, and religious competence always showed through. In Illinois, New Mexico, and Alabama, they worked together as parish directors of religious education. A diocesan post in Wisconsin and a teaching job at a college in Pennsylvania also marked stays on their journey.

In every way Ann complemented Bob. Her graduate degree in religious education prepared her for a lifetime of teaching at home and in Church. Besides being a full-time mother, she substituted as a religion teacher.

The oddity of a married priest and his wife leading religious education at a Catholic institution was discomforting for some Catholics.

Awkward scenes arose, especially for Ann. Not long after they arrived in one parish, she was shopping at the local grocery store when she overheard a few women talking. One said, "She must be some glamorous dame to lure a priest away from his ministry!" Ann, eight months pregnant, gently introduced herself. At another parish a woman accosted her, saying: "I can't believe that you would allow those sacred hands to touch you!" Ann bit her tongue.

Overall, Bob and Ann enjoyed good relations with Church officials. At one parish they were getting along well with the people, warm and generous souls, and with the pastor, a kind and thoughtful man, who suddenly was transferred. The new pastor could not adjust to this environment, so Bob and Ann had to leave. At another parish the pastor ordered Bob, as religious education director, to dismiss an instructor. When Bob did so, the pastor supported the instructor, never volunteering that he had instigated the move. Too much a gentleman to put the pastor on the spot, Bob endured the humiliation. Again they moved on.

The plight of children in such an environment highlights some poignant episodes. Their oldest daughter, for example, took pride in her father being a priest, and could not understand why she should not tell her teacher about it. Ann sternly cautioned against sharing that information.

Bob was in his late forties when they married, but God granted him good health and an adequate livelihood. Four children followed. Each received a Catholic grammar school, Catholic high school, and Catholic college education. Today in his late seventies, after teaching in colleges, high schools, and adult educational programs, Bob provides counseling at a hospital; Ann teaches full-time in a local Catholic high school and part-time at a college.

Advocates for Catholic Causes

Anyone who studied at the North American College in Rome at the start of the 1960s will know Bill. A native New Yorker, trained canon lawyer, and gifted storyteller, he could keep an audience in laughter with humorous anecdotes one after another. His academic credentials include a bachelor's degree *cum laude* from Cathedral College in New York, a licentiate in theology *magna cum laude,* and a doctorate in Canon Law *summa cum laude* from the Gregorian University in Rome, where he was ordained a priest. To this day, he maintains close friendship with his seminary classmates, some of whom head major dioceses in the United States.

After ordination, Bill worked at the Chancery Office in New York under Cardinal Terence Cooke as the associate director of Christian and Family Development. His success led to appointment to the U.S. Catholic Conference (USCC) in Washington as head of the national religious education office and chairman of the last National Congress on Religious Education, held in Miami in October 1971. With an attendance of eight thousand, that congress was the largest meeting of its kind. The same year he coordinated the English-speaking delegation to the first International Catechetical Congress, organized by the Vatican. That Congress fostered the progressive, Vatican II–inspired catechetical movement throughout the world.

Bill's marriage to Judy reinforced their commitment to the Roman Catholic faith. Their three sons, like them, attended Catholic grammar schools, Catholic high schools, and Catholic colleges. Bill's support for those institutions entailed coaching soccer teams, forming political action networks, and chairing financially successful development drives. Judy coordinated an ecumenical, multi-parish, social service agency, the Annandale Christian Community for Action (ACCA).

Bill has shown leadership on several fronts. In his local parish, he manages the annual Catholic lecture series and serves as Eucharistic minister. Regionally he coordinates the Catholic Education for Parish Service Program in Virginia, an instructional series that prepares countless faithful to assume liturgical and catechetical roles in parishes. Nationally he founded the Early Childhood Legislative Coalition, whose goal is to restructure federal programs according to parent choice principles. To further those efforts in private institutions, he began and administered an accreditation system for early childhood programs. Again he set high professional standards.

Bill has gained prominence nationally as executive vice-president of Americans for Choice in Education, the largest coalition of national and regional organizations supporting parental choice in education. In that role, he became a focal point and organizer for school choice. By setting up nationwide networks, guiding legislative activities, and coordinating diverse agencies and organizations, he has performed herculean labors on behalf of Catholic education.

Hospital Chaplains

Most parishes and dioceses will not accept a married priest into even peripheral church service. But exceptions are found. Occasionally a bishop will intervene positively; at times priests will warmly welcome and employ a married priest and his wife.

Del's story followed that pattern. An ordained priest with a licentiate in canon law from Rome, he resigned as vice-chancellor and assistant pastor to marry. His priest friends recognized his talents and hired him as counselor at Catholic Family Services. After two children were born, Del gave up this work to become "Mr. Mom." His wife, Ruth, became chief breadwinner through her job as parochial school teacher in the parish where Del had served as assistant pastor. They survived on a meager income as Del filled in with volunteer jobs for the diocese.

When the children entered school, Del returned to the work force, again with the diocese, first part-time as auditor, assessor, and judge at the Diocesan Marriage Tribunal, then full-time as chaplain at a Catholic Hospital. Here he found his niche. For the past eighteen years, he has been visiting with patients and their families, contributing to the liturgical life of the medical community, and assisting in policy development on a range of ethical matters. His theological and human services training have helped patients and staff.

If any ministry matches the skill and aptitude of a married priest, surely chaplaincy at hospitals and nursing homes does. As Del has written, "With the ever-increasing shortage of celibate priests in today's Catholic world, greater utilization of thousands of available married priests is a viable, visible response to the ever-increasing pastoral needs of Christ's faithful."

Many married priests across the country have tried to follow his example. Occasionally they have succeeded. More often they have met rejection by either the bishop or local hospital officials. Bob, a former Divine Word missionary, worked similarly at a Catholic hospital in the East. Luckily, the local auxiliary bishop vouched for him. Another public hospital hired George to give nondenominational ministry to patients. Del, Bob, and George exemplify effective ministry by married priests to the sick and the dying.

Prison Ministers

A work of mercy rarely adverted to in the Christian community is visiting the imprisoned. Yet Christ identified his followers with such ministry. In the memorable parable about discipleship, he said to the sheep, "I was in prison and you came to me" (Matt. 25:36), and to the goats he said, "I was...sick and in prison and you did not visit me" (Matt. 25:43). Few have responded more ardently to those admonitions of Christ than Pauline and Charles.

Pauline was a School Sister of St. Joseph of Carondolet; Charles, a priest of the Diocese of Mobile, Alabama. During the antiwar and civil rights protests in the early 1970s, they had their first taste of imprisonment. This made an indelible impression. The experience alerted them to severe injustices and changed the course of their lives.

After a jail sentence in San Antonio for protesting the treatment of prisoners, they began a bus service for families of the imprisoned, and publicized prison conditions, calling attention to the overcrowding and lack of privacy during visiting hours. Auxiliary Bishop Patrick Flores supported these efforts. The success of their activities led them to champion broader, related issues — abolition of the death penalty, strengthening of prisoner/family relationships, and promotion of job training and rehabilitation for prisoners.

In 1975, they formed Citizens United for Rehabilitation of Errants (CURE), an organization aimed at reducing crime and reforming the criminal justice system. Their office is six blocks from the U.S. Capitol, in space offered by St. Aloysius Parish. Pauline and Charles insist, "The whole criminal justice system is racist and classist." They argue further:

> We have two million people in prisons, half under thirty years of age, most for nonviolent drug offenses, and there's no money to provide drug treatment because it's all going into buildings. This doesn't make sense. It's like building hospitals to end diseases. Building prisons doesn't end crime; prisons promote crime.

Today they get more help from the Roman Catholic Church than from any other organization. They value the moral leadership being shown increasingly by Church officials. Pope John Paul II, for example, reminded the faithful that the need to execute people has become rare and almost nonexistent. The president of the National Conference of Catholic Bishops, Joseph Fiorenza, called on Attorney General Janet Reno to suspend federal executions. And Bishop Walter Sullivan of Richmond, in a state with one of the highest capital punishment records, requested that after each execution the churches in his diocese toll their bells in mourning.

Pauline and Charles have come a long way from the days of her teaching in parochial schools and his pastoring in diocesan churches. *America* magazine described them:

> Charlie and Pauline continue living simply and cheerfully in a small apartment without a phone ... in a drug-infested neighborhood. Bikes are their mode of transportation, and thrift shops supply their clothing. As people guided by their faith, they have never stopped leading religious lives of service to the outcast and vulnerable.[1]

Home Missionaries

Arnie and Kathy gathered up all they owned recently and moved to rental property in rural Kentucky to promote efforts of the Passionist Volunteers. They made this transition after raising five children, including three adopted from abroad. After setting their offspring on their own, they gave themselves once again to ministry to the needy.

Kathy and Arnie's commitments are lifelong. As a Vincentian priest, Arnie lived in the spirit of St. Vincent de Paul. After marrying, he continued in that spirit, directing for many years an agency assisting the blind in the Greater Washington, D.C., area. Then he became a member of the national board of Save Our Aging Religious (SOAR), an effort to give pensions and retirement support to elderly religious sisters.

Now living in the heart of Appalachia in Southern West Virginia, Arnie is a professor of social work at Mountain State University in Beckley. Catholics in the region are not comfortable with the fundamentalist churches there, yet the Catholic Church in the region has been plagued by scandals and a shortage of clergy. This is a fertile field for the ministry of Arnie and Kathy.

Kathy's dedication to these causes is no less intense. With a degree in liturgical music, she has been active her whole life in liturgy and music. Playing the guitar and singing at church services, she provides the spirit and joy in home and community. Together they have assisted many people as true Vincentians.

Foreign Missionaries

Maureen, a former nun, and Maury, a former Trinitarian priest, have continued on a similar course of Christian ministry. Their journey took them from positions of prominence in religious life to housing initiatives in the inner city, management training for senior executives, mission work in the jungles of Africa, and back home again to offer programs for returning foreign missionaries.

As a Trinitarian priest, Maury worked in a rural Mississippi parish whose members lived well below the poverty line. Later he became a housing specialist in Appalachian Kentucky and in Southern Virginia. He studied real estate and urban development at American University, then was appointed the first executive director of Catholics for Housing (CFH) in Northern Virginia. Simultaneously he was named executive director of the Robert Pierre Johnson Housing Development Corporation (RPJ), which sponsors the development of low- and moderate-income housing in the Washington area.

Maureen, as a nun, held administrative positions in Catholic higher education, then ran management training programs for senior executives. She also volunteered in and supported Maury's housing activities. They were an accomplished team.

For the past seven years, Maureen and Maury have worked for an organization that assists missionaries returning to the United States. Its board and members consist mostly of Catholic priests and nuns. The organization conducts workshops and offers audiotapes and booklets to missionaries before and after their service, so that they understand the violence and the trauma that often accompany their labors. The violence takes many forms: war, oppression, physical and sexual abuse, poverty caused by corrupt governments, and all the isms like sexism and racism that mask violence.

Maureen and Maury are suited for this ministry. During their work as lay missionaries in Africa, Maureen was savagely attacked. Maury's solicitude throughout that ordeal, and Maureen's continued dedication, enabled them to survive. Today they share with many audiences their experience of violence, reflecting a mature, professional approach, Christ-centered and healing.

Trade Association Executive

Fred's early priestly assignments took him to the Archdiocesan Seminary in Boston as professor of Latin and Greek, dean of men, academic dean, and music director. He holds a master's degree in classical languages from Boston College and has taken advanced study in classical philology at Harvard's Graduate School of Arts and Sciences. To seminarians, he was scholar and friend.

After leaving clerical ministry to marry, Fred was hired by the National Catholic Educational Association (NCEA) in Washington as director of research and technologies and as executive assistant to the president. In those roles he directed nationwide support services for

Catholic education, which entailed running many workshops, seminars, and conferences. He became a specialist in applying modern technologies to Catholic schools.

Fred's scholarly work includes contributing editorship of the three-volume edition of *Encyclopedia Dictionary of Religion* put out by Corpus Instrumentorum. He has been a guest lecturer at the Sloan School of Management at the Massachusetts Institute of Technology, a member of the Advisory Board of the Challenger Space Center at NASA in Washington, and a member of the National Ad Hoc Committee on Educational Technologies. He now serves as an independent consultant. In that role he has held contracts on Web and Internet strategies with the William H. Sadlier Publishing Company, and on satellite video conferencing and marketing multimedia products for the University of Notre Dame. He is also a consultant for performing arts production for the Duffern Pell Catholic School District in Ontario. This entails coordination among the Toronto Symphony Orchestra, the Stratford Festival, the National Ballet of Canada, and the Royal Conservatory of Music in Mississauga.

Fred's talents could have been applied with greater financial reward in many diverse fields. But his heart was always with the Catholic Church. He preferred to work for Catholic education where his efforts made a difference.

The Future

The commitment of the people described here to the Catholic Church has often led to heroic sacrifice. Most live modestly. Using their talents in ministry in the Roman Catholic community, they have continued a lifetime of service. Many more would follow their example, but are not allowed. Rejected, they apply their talents to secular pursuits, where some gain great success. One can only imagine what could have been accomplished if those talents had been applied as priests in the Catholic community.

Raymond Brown commented perceptively:

Until we face the fact that the Word of God and living it out is the real source of sanctity in the Church, constituting true rank and privilege and honor, and until we appreciate this in our hearts, we will not understand what the NT teaches us about priesthood. That is the challenge that the Church will have to face in these next years as believing men and women, who have heard their dignity praised in Vatican II, ask how they can exercise that dignity in the service of Christ.[2]

Brown lays down a challenge to all the faithful. The work of the Church is abundant, but the laborers are few. This scarcity of workers comes neither from God's failure to call, nor from the faithful's lack of generosity. Many women and men, married and single, hear God's call and yearn to give themselves to ministry. The bottleneck remains — clerical, celibate, male control of all positions of power and authority in the Church.

Married priests and their wives, like faithful lay men and women throughout the Church today, recognize the challenge posed by the Second Vatican Council. They continue to respond to the call in whatever way they can, following the inspirations of the Holy Spirit. A new day is dawning.

Chapter 6

Diversity among Married Priests

WHO ARE these priests who marry? Judases who betrayed Christ, as Pope Paul VI once intimated? Laborers who removed their shoulders from the plow, as Pope John Paul II alleged? Men who spurned their solemn vows and sacred calling, as others charge? Such images serve no good purpose. Reality is much more complex.

So who are these men? They are surely a diverse group, representing the full spectrum of political thought and religious conviction. Politically, married priests range from Phil Berrigan on the left to John McLaughlin on the right. Religiously, they run the gamut from conservative, traditional Catholics to liberal, post-denominational Christians. And yes, some married priests have abandoned their faith. Some also, after a life of wandering, return to the womb of Holy Mother Church. Such was the story of Ed Sponga, the former provincial of the Maryland Jesuit community who, after suffering the pain of a failed marriage and dispersed family, chose to be buried in the Jesuit graveyard at Woodstock.

Stereotypes of the married priest persist. Surely one must not view them with rose-colored glasses. At an early national conference of married priests, one couple participated in a panel and described their experiences in joint ministry. The man, Marty Drew, stood out because he insisted on wearing a Roman collar; his wife, Regina, was introduced as an ordained Methodist minister. They had worked out a good collaborative ministry and were eager to share their success. How startling it was to find out a short time later that in a fit of rage Marty killed his wife and himself! Observers noted a fierce diabolic hatred in his eyes as he performed the dastardly deed. This, unfortunately, was a priest who married. One can also recall the serial pedophile, James R. Porter. After a history of pedophilia as a Roman Catholic clergyman, he married, and his actions as married man were no less notorious than as celibate priest. Today he sits in jail.

These cases are exceptions to the norm. To consider Marty Drew and James Porter typical married priests is as outlandish as to regard Boston's John Geoghan and Paul Shanley as typical celibate clergymen. They are not. Married and celibate priests show the range of human behaviors, good and bad.

Saints can be found among married priests, ranging from St. Peter the Apostle in the first century to the Armenian Catholic priest beatified in the twentieth. Martyred married priests in Russia during the Communist reign showed heroic virtue. One could also cite models of everyday sanctity among the remarkable men and women who once held clerical or religious status, and are now scattered in the diaspora.

Some married priests have endured a breakdown of their marriage — not as many as detractors would like to believe, but they do occur. Some have seen bonds broken with siblings, parents, and children. Every rupture in a family brings pain and sorrow, but this is the human condition, and married priests are not safeguarded from such tragedies.

The following pages identify some married priests and wives in the Maryland, District of Columbia, and Virginia region. Their stories cannot be called representative; each is unique. But taken together they show the diversity of married priest couples today.

Tim and Sally

One of the staunchest defenders of John Paul II and an inveterate letter writer to all who would defy the pope's teachings is Tim. A former Franciscan priest from the Midwest and a retired Army chaplain with service in Vietnam, he married Sally and raised two sons.

Through the years Tim has moved politically and religiously far to the right. Not only does he volunteer to work in Republican political campaigns, Tim also has become an articulate spokesman for traditional pro-life, anti-tax, and pro-defense causes. He can be unyielding in his advocacy. This conservatism carries over to his Catholic faith, which he adamantly defends.

In recent years, Tim and Sally made pilgrimages to Marian shrines and visited other sanctuaries sacred to Catholics. This passionate devotion has led Tim at every turn to defend current Catholic leaders. His letter writing to newspapers and magazines follows upon every perceived misunderstanding of Rome's teachings. Whether *Dominus Jesus, Humanae Vitae,* or the *Catechism of the Catholic Church,* he can be relied on to defend papal pronouncements every time.

Yet Tim joins with, prays with, and supports the prayerful efforts of married priests, whose regional and national gatherings he has attended. Despite a broad divergence in political philosophy with many in the group, he continues the walk with them. He remains committed to his Church and his priesthood.

Joe and Kathy

At the other end of the political spectrum was Joe, a seminary classmate of Avery Dulles. A Jesuit theologian, Joe headed the theology department at Wheeling College and wrote a well-received book titled *Theology of Marriage.* Later he felt embarrassed by his naiveté in writing that text. He would have liked to update it, but never did.

After Joe married, the Christian Brothers hired him to teach at a college in the Midwest, but lay members of the board rebelled against employing a married priest. He had to leave. Joe yearned to spread the fruit of his vast learning and experience but realized that teaching theology was no longer open to him, even in secular institutions. He undertook other jobs, working as headmaster of a private school, then as administrator of a home for troubled children. Later years he spent at the U.S. Department of Education in Washington.

Joe enjoyed a happy marriage with Kathy, a former Sister of Mercy who once vowed never to marry a priest. She met Joe and everything changed. In many ways they complemented each other. The joy and happiness in their lives were obvious to all who knew them.

From his seminary days, Joe delighted in entertaining friends. He composed songs and wrote plays, singing and performing with gusto before his Jesuit confreres and later his married friends. With Kathy and their friends Carl and Pat, he started the Sunday Bunch, a group of people with similar backgrounds who met in each other's homes, celebrating the Eucharist, sharing the Word of God, and developing a camaraderie that endured. Those gatherings were always happy, Christ-centered events.

A carcinoma curtailed his retirement and ended his journey too soon. With Joe gone, Kathy returned to her family in Chicago. The Sunday Bunch, however, continues to meet and pray.

Carl and Pat

As a Jesuit instructor in economics at Fordham, Carl could not have foreseen his future role as a senior official at the U.S. governmental agency overseeing the effects of world overpopulation. Always articulate and knowledgeable, he would represent the U.S. government at international meetings where discussion focused on ethical concerns related to birth control, contraception, and the AIDS epidemic. Vatican officials attending those gatherings had no idea of the background of this American.

Carl's marriage with Pat, a trained pharmacist, brought him to Washington and set him on a course that would lead him to all corners of the globe. In the meantime they raised a son who graduated from the Air Force Academy and piloted Special Operations transports in the Afghan War, and a daughter who became a schoolteacher and married mother of two girls.

Active in civic affairs, Carl served six years as an elected Councilman in Fairfax City. In 1967 he and Pat helped to form the National Association for Pastoral Renewal (NAPR), the first of the post–Vatican II reform groups advocating for optional celibacy. They were original members of the Sunday Bunch and have coordinated that group for the past ten years. They also organized and hosted the National CORPUS Convention in Virginia in 1994.

Helping Christians celebrate their weddings with dignity, Carl has been officiating at weddings for over thirty years. In that time, he and

Pat have participated in almost every local meeting of married priests. They are pioneers and veterans of the priest reform movement.

Ed and Joan

Many married priest couples served in the military, but few equal Joan and Ed's achievements. Joan spent twenty-six years as a Marine, retiring as Lieutenant Colonel; Ed, twenty-three years as a Navy chaplain, retiring as Commander. Before that, Joan had been a Missionary Sister of the Most Blessed Trinity; Ed a Conventual Franciscan priest.

In earlier years, Ed pastored an inner-city parish in Louisville, Kentucky, not far from Muhammad Ali's family home. A participant in the civil rights movement, he strongly supported efforts of his black parishioners. He marched with Martin Luther King Jr. before that became popular, then undertook a long term as military chaplain.

Upon retiring and marrying, Ed and Joan tried to minister wherever they could. Ed is often called upon by military officials and local mortuary firms to officiate at funerals. He gives comfort to families in bereavement and does this often without pay. Joan assists Ed in much of his work. She also worked for ten years as shelter director for the Salvation Army.

More recently, Joan was ordained a priest in the Free Catholic Church by Bishop Thomas Charles Cleary, who has apostolic succession through the Old Catholic Church. Like Ed, she is called upon to officiate at weddings and lead services for a small parish. They serve as co-pastors of the St. Mary of Magdalene Free Catholic Community in Virginia.

Jim and Peg

Priest couples across the land know Jim and Peg. In June 1988 they planned and coordinated the first national gathering of married priests and wives in Washington, D.C. A stirringly successful convention, it marked a turning point for CORPUS, then identified as the Corps of Reserve Priests United for Service. The event brought greater solidarity and public exposure to the married priests' movement.

Though many know Jim and Peg, few are aware of their past. Jim was a pastor and naval reserve chaplain in the Peoria Diocese in Illinois. His success with reserves led to appointment as national Chief of Chaplains at the Veterans Administration. There he worked closely with Bishop John O'Connor, then chief of naval chaplains and later cardinal archbishop of New York.

In the Washington area, Jim met Peggy, a music teacher at Stone Ridge Academy. She was a widow with married children and Jim, a retiring military chaplain. Their marriage proved a blessing for each. With the freedom and security they enjoyed, they devoted themselves to priests and their families in transition, especially in the Maryland-D.C.-Virginia area. They helped many.

A few years ago Peg and Jim moved to San Diego, so Peg could be closer to her children and Jim could help at and benefit from the nearby naval community. He continues to minister as chaplain in local hospitals and hospices. A member of the advisory board of the hospice center, he is recognized as "Father Jim" by the patients, who have grown to love and appreciate his ever smiling and courteous service. He also enjoys a good relationship with local chaplains who welcome his help in ministry.

Gus and Carmel

With the decline in priests and sisters, many Catholic institutions had to be abandoned. The Jesuit seminary buildings in Hyde park, New York, New York were turned into a culinary institute, St. Francis Seminary in Pennsylvania became a federal penitentiary, and the spacious Immaculate Conception Seminary grounds in New Jersey gave way to a real estate development of luxury homes. Many other lesser-known institutions were transformed. In an unusual twist, Trinitarians relinquished their seminary in Virginia to a public agency and the former rector became its director. Gus now heads the Central Virginia Community Services Board, in the same office building where he once worked for the Church.

The leap from church management to community services management is a small one. Similar skills are needed. Religious life often provides such administrative experience. It prepared Gus and Carmel for ministry in a different environment.

Gus is a former Trinitarian priest from Boston; his wife, Carmel, a former Religious of the Sacred Heart from Roscommon in Ireland. Each came from large Catholic families — Carmel one of nine, Gus one of ten. They have one daughter. Living in the Bible Belt among fundamentalist Christians, they keep their Catholic identity, and are active in their parish community. Gus chaired the building committee for many years, supervising the physical development of the entire parish complex; and Carmel applies her educational talent and religious expertise.

Gus's role at a state agency makes him aware of job opportunities, which he dutifully sends to WEORC, a virtual job clearinghouse for priests and nuns in transition. In this way he has helped many to gain employment. Annually Gus and Carmel made the long trek to Maryland and Northern Virginia for the Days of Recollection for married priest couples. They maintain their commitment to Christ, to priesthood, and to the Catholic Church.

George and Florinda

When Fidel Castro took control of Cuba, he aroused high expectations. He had served as an altar boy, studied under the Jesuits, married in the Church, and fought the revolution with a rosary around his neck. But upon assuming power in September 1961, he promptly rounded up over a hundred Catholic priests and deposited them on the freighter *Coradonga* bound for Spain. Among them was a young Salesian priest from Camaguey Province named George.

A few years later George was teaching at the Salesian seminary in New Jersey while pursuing graduate study in classical languages at Fordham University. After he fell in love with Florinda, he was dispensed by Rome, married, and moved to the Washington area.

For three decades, George has taught Latin and Spanish in Montgomery County Public Schools in Maryland. He also served on the national board of the Cuban Committee for Democracy (CCD), which tries to build new lines of communication with Cuba. He has lobbied Congress and Cuban exiles to change the prevailing hard line, embargo-prone attitudes. With his wife and daughter, he has always remained a loyal participant in activities at his local Catholic parish.

In 1989, George returned to Cuba for the first of several trips to see family and friends. In 1997, parishioners invited him back to Our Lady of Charity, the Church from which he had been whisked away in 1961. As he prepared to speak from the sanctuary to his old friends, he was filled with emotion. They gave him a five-minute standing ovation.

When Fidel Castro welcomed Pope John Paul II to Cuba in 1998, a historic celebration followed. George traveled to Havana Airport to participate in that festive event. Proudly he stood in the Plaza de la Revolución on January 25 as the pope celebrated Mass and addressed the throngs. George prayed earnestly for a change in the political climate of his homeland.

Will and Jo

The older the priest when he marries, the fewer his job opportunities. That is all the more true if he lacks advanced degrees and is not certified in a secular field. Will faced that challenge. A gifted preacher without pulpit, an admired counselor, without certification, a dedicated priest without collar, he had to deal with a stagnant job market.

A native of Ireland, Will had traveled as a young man to England to spread the Word of God. For decades he worked in parishes outside London, becoming a popular pastor, revered family counselor and respected school administrator. Then he met Jo, a nurse from America, with whom he fell in love. His life changed dramatically.

After he resigned from his pastorate, Will and Jo married and moved to the United States to be near Jo's family in Virginia. Their marriage was blessed with a son, Kieran. In search of spiritual nourishment, they have visited Catholic parishes in their neighborhood and have tried to apply their talents in the community. But the transition was burdensome.

Will has held a variety of jobs: as trainer, substitute teacher, and jack-of-all-trades. He also responds to the religious needs of the young who call upon him for marriage. With his vast pastoral experience and warm disposition, he is able to counsel and minister to them. Jo is a licensed nurse and has had a steady job. They work hard and maintain a happy and blessed household.

Marie and Ed

The commitment to Christ by nuns and priests often impels them after marriage to continue to give themselves in ministry to the poor, the sick, the needy. Devotion to the Roman Catholic Church, furthermore, leads many to prefer ministry within the Catholic community. Marie and Ed nobly demonstrate that preference.

Marie is a former nun and school principal trained in teaching educationally challenged children. After marriage, she continued working in special education programs in public schools and stayed active in Catholic community affairs. She performs volunteer work at two area hospitals, is a member of the board of the hospital auxiliary, participates in parish religion programs for adults and children, and serves as a Eucharistic minister at her parish and at a local nonsectarian hospital. Ten years ago, as member of her parish council, she organized a soup kitchen to feed the poor in their neighborhood. With her husband, Ed, and a few others, she continues to operate that kitchen weekly. She also works with the ladies' guild of the local Knights of Columbus.

Before leaving canonical ministry, Ed was a hospital chaplain and assistant pastor. After being dispensed by Rome, Ed and Marie were married in the Catholic Church by Ed's brother, a missionary in Latin America. Ed took a job with the federal government and began attending evening classes at a local university, from which he gained a second master's degree. Later he became a counselor in inner-city public schools.

Ed serves as lector, cantor, Eucharistic minister, member of the parish finance committee, and president of his parish council. In the broader church community, he has been a member of the Knights of Columbus Council, serving as editor of their newsletter for six years, church activities director for eight years, and chairman of the Council's Right to Life Committee for two terms. He has also held elective offices in the Council, including Grand Knight.

Unsuccessful in their efforts to have children, Ed and Marie became foster parents. In retirement, besides caring for their grandchildren, they continue their extensive round of religious and community activities. As former clergy and religious, they have gone as far as they can in permissible ministry under the current discipline of the Catholic Church.

The Future

Though these narratives are centered on married priest couples in the Maryland-D.C.-Virginia area, such stories can be found in every region of the country. These people are called to fullness of life. They are summoned to heal the brokenhearted, to pour salve on open wounds, to straighten crooked paths. As former clergy and religious, they like so many others journey through uncharted waters along diverse routes.

◆ Some remain loyal to traditional Church teachings and attend Mass regularly, even daily. A few even listen faithfully to Mother Angelica's TV programs, and admire the pope, supporting him in everything.

◆ Some continue to attend services in local parishes, taking leadership roles in prayer groups, social action outreach, and religious education programs. More frequently, though, they remain passive observers in their Church community, taking a back seat unless invited forward.

◆ Some join floating parishes, meeting in school halls or church auditoriums where they attend services conducted by a hired priest. They are more likely to gravitate to reform groups in the Church and are open to a wider range of Catholic practice.

◆ Some gather in each other's homes, taking turns at celebrating the Eucharist, sharing reflections on the Scriptures and applying those teachings to their daily lives. Through life's crises they support each other, learn from one another, and focus on Christ's message.

• Some, frustrated at the slowness of reform in the Catholic Church, have transferred to Lutheran, Episcopal, Old Catholic, or other churches. Wives often find there a greater acceptance of their gifts, leading at times to ordination. Zeal for Christian ministry motivates them.

• Some have given up the struggle and no longer walk with their former companions. They have chosen to remove themselves from organized religion, usually because of painful events they cannot forget.

All these are part of the diaspora, the dispersion of former clerics and religious in our day. The model for each remains Jesus — the Jesus who ate with publicans and sinners, the Jesus who protected the woman caught in adultery, the Jesus who calls the faithful to follow him wherever he leads them.

Chapter 7

Prominent Former Clerics

MANY PRIESTS who leave the clerical state steal away silently into the night and move far away, never to be heard from again. After years in priestly ministry, they assume a new persona in a different environment. Some transit gracefully, but others struggle all their lives, dealing with unemployment, unfulfilling jobs, chronic illness, broken marriage, wayward children, or a host of other adversities. Journeys vary.

Not all leave in secrecy. Some priests had already achieved great prominence in specialized fields. Their escape can be neither private nor quiet. What makes it easier for them is that they had achieved success in a profession that permitted a ready transfer to the secular world, usually at a much higher salary and with even greater visibility. At times their academic training as theologian, psychologist, or writer assured a smooth transition. Others apply themselves to acquiring additional skill, and climb rapidly on the ladder of success, achieving even greater prominence than before.

The following stories depict married priests who excelled professionally. In most instances they built upon skills acquired before departure from clerical ministry. Some were well known before, others achieved greater visibility after, marriage. Their stories are untypical.

James Patrick Shannon

An admired progressive leader in the post–Vatican II era in America, James Shannon graduated from Yale University with a doctorate in history, and became the youngest Catholic college president in the country. He was named auxiliary bishop of St. Paul, Minnesota, in

1965 at the age of forty-four, whereupon he promptly attended the final session of the Second Vatican Council in Rome. That experience transformed him. Returning home, he fulfilled his assigned task of explaining and promoting Council reforms in the archdiocese.

That same year all U.S. bishops came together at the Catholic University of America and reorganized themselves in the National Conference of Catholic Bishops (NCCB). Shannon, only an auxiliary bishop, became the youngest member of a new forty-member board. His familiarity with the press and his skill as a speaker resulted in appointment as vice-chairman of the Conference's press department. Most bishops were paranoid about dealing with the press. Shannon was comfortable in that role.

Shannon's leadership made him the darling of progressives but earned the contempt of traditional churchmen. When he persisted in opposing the Vietnam War, he antagonized Cardinals Spellman and McIntyre. The latter called the apostolic delegate in Washington and demanded that he be silenced. All came to a boil when Shannon appeared as interlocutor on a TV special "The New American Catholic," in which he spoke frankly about progressive developments in the Church. McIntyre fumed with rage. He sent a letter to Archbishop Dearden, president of the National Conference of Catholic Bishops, denouncing Shannon and urging Dearden to declare positions articulated by Shannon heretical. At 83, the curmudgeonly McIntyre attacked all that smacked of modernism.

Problems only escalated for Shannon. Besides protesting the Vietnam War, he also stood with Martin Luther King Jr. and other clergy at Selma, the only Catholic bishop there. With the passage of *Humanae Vitae,* a more serious crisis arose. Shannon's growing discomfort with that encyclical, McIntyre's recruitment of the new apostolic delegate against him, and the sense of abandonment by his immediate superiors, Archbishops Binz and Byrne, left him with few options.

In accepting appointment as vice-president of St. John's College in Santa Fe, Shannon severed his ties with the archdiocese and the institutional Catholic Church. Not long afterwards, he married Ruth

Wilkinson, a widowed legal secretary. He gained a law degree from the University of New Mexico and began the practice of law.

Shannon's life took another turn when he accepted directorship of the Minneapolis Foundation, a move that brought him back to his former place of ministry. Success in foundation management led to the executive directorship of the larger General Mills Foundation and service on the boards of five national watchdog agencies. He emerged a recognized expert in corporate philanthropy and foundation management.

Shannon and his wife maintained a commitment to service, a dedication to Christ, and a respect for the Catholic Church, despite his excommunication. A story is told of his attending a Catholic Mass, sitting in the rear of the assembly and refraining from approaching the altar for Communion. An elderly nun, after receiving the Sacred Bread in her hands, walked to the back of the church where Shannon was kneeling and shared the Communion wafer with him, saying: "I know that Christ would not want you to be separated from him." The gesture moved him deeply.

Shannon's autobiographical account, *Reluctant Dissenter,* tells his fascinating story. The well-respected Monsignor George Higgins of Catholic University of America describes the book in his cover endorsement: "He has told his story here engagingly, with great dignity and sincere love for the Church and, to his credit, without the slightest trace of anger, bitterness or malice." Shannon remains a revered figure to progressive Catholics.

In past centuries the marriage of a Catholic bishop resulted in automatic excommunication, and that was Shannon's fate when he married. The new code of Canon Law under Pope John Paul II, however, abolished that penalty. By special permission of the pope, furthermore, Shannon spent his last years in full communion with the Catholic Church. He worshipped regularly, first at St. Joan of Arc Church in Minneapolis, then for fifteen years at Holy Name of Jesus Church in nearby Medina in his native Minnesota.

On August 28, 2003, he died of a stroke. His body draped in a blanket from the college (St. Thomas) he served as president, placed in a pine box made by the monks of St. John's Abbey in Collegeville, surrounded by many priest friends and former vice-president Walter Mondale, James P. Shannon at age eighty-two went to his eternal reward. His beloved wife, Ruth Wilkinson, attended the service, as did three Catholic bishops. Bishop Richard Pates, representing the Minneapolis Archdiocese where he had labored, made it clear in a prepared statement that Shannon had been reconciled with the Catholic Church. Bishop John F. Kinney of St. Cloud and Bishop Paul V. Dudley of Sioux Falls also participated in the services.

Horace Deets

In 1988, Horace Deets became chief executive of the American Association of Retired Persons (AARP), the second largest organization in the United States (based on membership). The largest is the Roman Catholic Church. Over a thirteen-year period, Deets had climbed the career ladder at AARP, from consultant to personnel director, chief of staff, acting director of legislation, and acting director of public relations. He would serve another twelve years as executive director.

In earlier years Deets had been a parish priest, high school teacher, and religious education director in his native Diocese of Charleston, South Carolina. Even then his hard work and dedication were recognized. That augured well his future accomplishments for the elderly. Leading an organization known for its vast lobbying and membership services may be far removed from clerical, sacramental actions. Yet it entails the same commitment to service.

Horace has always been reluctant to talk about his clerical past and has tried to downplay it in interviews and in his official biography. But as with AARP, so also in his earlier labors as a priest he worked unstintingly. Under Deets's leadership, AARP has grown to a membership of 34 million. Besides guiding its at times thorny relationship with Congress, he introduced many new programs and expanded the list of services offered to senior citizens. He became an untiring advocate and articulate spokesman for the elderly in America.

Horace has enjoyed the support of his wife, Connie, who once served as secretary to the priest director of the Office of Priestly Life and Ministry at the National Conference of Catholic Bishops. They have two children and several grandchildren.

A. W. Richard Sipe

The continual scandals resulting from pedophilia and other sexual abuses by clergy are unpleasant to read about. They cannot be glossed over. For years Church leaders, by simply sending the accused pedophile on retreat and transferring him to another community, and by placing a guilt trip on victims and refusing to deal with their families, have added to the gravity of the crimes. Such behavior has harmed innocent lives, tarnished the image of the priesthood, and compromised the credibility of the Church. To overcome this disaster will take time and effort.

Anyone who writes about such clerical conduct will be accused of sensationalism, prurient interest, or anti-Catholic bigotry. A. W. Richard Sipe has heard it all. Yet few come as qualified as he to address these sensitive matters. A former Benedictine monk who keeps close ties with that monastic community, he has spent over forty years counseling hundreds of priests dealing with normal and abnormal psychosexual behaviors.

Sipe studied at St. John's Seminary and University in Collegeville, Collegio Sant Anselmo in Rome, the Menninger Foundation in Topeka, and the Seton Psychiatric Institute in Baltimore. He taught at three Roman Catholic major seminaries, served as instructor in psychiatry at Johns Hopkins School of Medicine, and headed the Department of Family Services at Seton Psychiatric Institute. His wife, Marianne Benkert, is a practicing psychiatrist. Their son, Walter, was born in 1973.

Sipe's talents have put him in the limelight in courtrooms and in the media as an expert. His writings include dozens of published articles and three books: *A Secret World: Sexuality and the Search for Celibacy* (1990); *Sex, Priests, and Power: Anatomy of a Crisis* (1995); and *Celibacy: a Way of Loving, Living, and Serving* (1996). He has appeared on major TV networks in the United States, England, and the Netherlands.

In all his efforts, Sipe comes across as a voice of moderation. He aims not to shock or exaggerate but to testify to the truth in matters that affect the credibility of the Catholic Church. He remains faithful to that Church and to the message of Christ in these troubling times.

Eugene C. Kennedy

As a Maryknoll priest, Eugene Cullen Kennedy was well known and admired in Catholic circles. His early writings, chiefly in psychology and religion, earned the Catholic Press Association Book Award in 1968 and the Thomas More medal for contributions to Catholic literature in 1972 and 1978.

Kennedy taught at the Catholic University of America in Washington and Maryknoll College in Glen Ellyn, Illinois, then spent most of his professional career as professor of psychology at Loyola University in Chicago from 1969 to 1995. In 1977 he married Sara Connor Charles, a physician who collaborated with him on his books. Kennedy has published over forty works.

After marrying he broadened his writing into different literary genres. In 1978 he published a biography, *Himself: The Life and Times of Richard J. Daley,* for which he received the Carl Sandburg Award. His book *Father's Day* earned the Midland Authors Fiction Award in 1981. That same year he was also given a second Carl Sandburg Award. He has composed a TV play about Pope John XXIII produced by CBS and writes a syndicated column for the *New York Times.*

Through the years, Kennedy developed a growing admiration for Cardinal Joseph Bernardin. This resulted in inspirational books about his friend: *This Man Bernardin* in 1996, *Bernardin: Life to the Full* and *My Brother Joseph: The Spirit of a Cardinal and the Story of a Friendship* in 1997. A gifted prose stylist, he continues to write and gain the respect of readers throughout the world.

Kennedy has also shed light on the growing conflict in the Catholic community. *Tomorrow's Catholics, Yesterday's Church: The Two Cultures of American Catholicism,* published in 1990, interprets that scene today. His latest, in 2001, *The Unhealed Wound: The Church and Human Sexuality,* is a penetrating study of the dilemma Catholics face in dealing with human sexuality. With the growing scandal of clerical pedophilia in 2002, he has become a perceptive commentator in the press and on the airwaves.

Francis MacNutt

As a Dominican priest, Frank MacNutt was the leading figure in the Roman Catholic Charismatic Renewal Movement. He drew a crowd of fifty thousand to a healing service in Giants Stadium in New Jersey; thirty thousand to a rally in Latin America; twenty thousand to a rally in India; and enormous throngs to Catholic Pentecostal rallies at Notre Dame University. A graduate of Harvard with a doctorate of philosophy from Aquinas Institute, he ranked among the top preachers in the country. He served as president of the Catholic Homiletic Society and founding editor of its journal *Preaching*. Then he married Judith Sewell in 1980.

Reactions were swift and unforgiving. The Dominican Order dismissed him. The Association of Christian Therapists, which he founded, rejected his membership. The National Service Committee, directed by his long-time friend, published a statement referring to his marriage as "a serious sin" and "a personal tragedy." Frank was ostracized from Catholic circles.

Today Frank and his wife, Judith, run the Christian Healing Ministries in Jacksonville, Florida. They hold weekly healing services at an Episcopal Church. Frank spends about a third of his time on the road, conducting prayer services in different churches. Judith cares for their two children, and joins him in ministry.

Frank's most important book, *Healing*, has sold one million copies. It remains a best-seller for Protestants and lay Catholics. In recent years, he has lectured at many universities and medical colleges on the evidence of healing in response to prayer.

James Carroll

A former Paulist priest, James Carroll attained a distinguished career as a writer. He is chairman of PEN/New England and the author of a weekly op-ed column in the *Boston Globe*. He has written many books of fiction, including *Madonna Red* (1976), *Mortal Friends* (1978), *Fault Lines* (1980), *Family Trade* (1982), *Prince of Peace* (1984), *Supply of Heroes* (1986), *Firebird* (1989), and *Memorial Bridge* (1991). The *New York Times* named his *The City Below* a Notable Book of 1994.

Carroll's best-received work is an autobiographical journey, which earned him the prestigious National Book Award for Nonfiction in 1996. *An American Requiem: God, My Father, and the War That Came Between Us* describes his relationship with his father, a powerful Air Force general working at the Pentagon when James was developing strong convictions against the Vietnam War. The book paints a nostalgic picture of growing up in Washington, D.C., during the 1940s and 1950s, and reflects sensitively the growing peace movement of the 1960s. The portrayal of his inner anguish as a dovish priest dealing with a hawkish father is riveting.

Like Kennedy, Carroll also sheds light on the current Catholic scene. *Constantine's Sword* (2001) outlines through two millennia the sorry history of Christian-Jewish relations. He undertook extensive research for this book during a fellowship year at the Center for the Study of Values in Public Life at Harvard's Divinity School. The book inspired symposia at Harvard and Brandeis Universities, and interfaith dialogues in the United States and Canada. He is also a regular participant in Jewish-Christian-Muslim dialogue at the Shalom Harman Institute in Jerusalem.

During his clerical career Carroll for five years filled the role of Catholic Chaplain at Boston University. He is married to novelist Alexandra Marshall, and they have two children, Elizabeth and Patrick.

Bernard J. Cooke

Few priests after marriage are able to continue their theological work in Catholic circles. That Bernard Cooke successfully does this reflects recognized competence and scholarship. He is respected at theological conferences and university programs, where he continues to inspire listeners across the land. He remains insightful in his commentaries, and always respectful of the Catholic tradition.

As a Jesuit priest, Cooke had been professor and chairman of the theology department at Marquette University from 1958 to 1970. After leaving the Jesuit community in 1970, he married Pauline Turner and raised their daughter, Kelly. He became professor of religious studies first at the University of Windsor, then the University of Calgary, followed by professorships in theology at Holy Cross College (1980–92), Incarnate Word College (1992–98) and the University of San Diego (1999–).

Cooke received the John Courtney Murray Award of the Catholic Theological Society in 1979, and was named Wilson Center fellow and resident fellow at Yale Divinity School. His writings cover the entire field of sacramental theology. Among them are: *Sacraments and Sacramentality* (1983), *Reconciled Sinner* (1986), *The Distancing of God* (1990), *God's Beloved* (1992), and *The Future of Eucharist* (1997).

Philip Berrigan

After serving in artillery and infantry divisions of the U.S. Army during World War II and graduating from Holy Cross College, Philip entered Sacred Heart Seminary of the St. Joseph's Society (S.S.J.) and was ordained a priest in 1955. Soon after that he developed the radical commitment to peace that drove him the rest of his life. He became the first priest to participate in a civil rights Freedom Ride in 1962.

As cofounder of Catholic Peace Fellowship, he planned protests aimed at ending the U.S. government's aggressive and dangerous military policies. To call attention to these policies, he undertook provocative public actions, resulting in his arrest over forty times and imprisonment for many terms. With brother Dan he organized the Catonsville Nine in 1968, followed by the Harrisburg Seven and the Plowshares Eight, repeatedly plotting bold moves to stir the conscience of the nation.

In an unprecedented occurrence, the two Catholic priest brothers — the Jesuit Dan Berrigan and former Josephite Phil Berrigan — were posted on the FBI's most wanted list in 1969. Their crimes consisted of opposing the Vietnam War through acts of civil disobedience. In opposing violence, they attacked instruments of war; in pursuing peace, they sacrificed their lives. After being pardoned in 1972, they continued their protest actions.

The biblical idea of turning weapons into plowshares forms the basis of the plowshares movement, which Philip helped to organize. It aims to do just that. On one occasion with accomplices, Phil slipped into the General Electric plant at King of Prussia, Pennsylvania, and damaged the missile cones. Then in 1988, he pounded on cruise missile launchers aboard a destroyer in Virginia, and, in 1993, he did the same to an F-15E fighter in North Carolina. For each of these actions, he was apprehended and put in prison.

Philip completed a thirty-month sentence for his role in "Plowshares vs. Depleted Uranium," where he and a team of associates disarmed two A-10 Warthog aircraft at the Maryland National Guard base in Middle River, Maryland, in 1999. He pointed out that the U.S. government had launched depleted uranium from those aircraft in military actions against Iraq and Yugoslavia. After the terrorism of September 11, 2001, the U.S. government put Phil in solitary confinement and denied his family every contact. He was later released.

His wife, the former nun Elizabeth McAlister, matched his commitment to these causes. With her Phil founded Jonah House, a nonviolent resistance community in Baltimore. Amid the turmoil of their lives, they raised three children: Frida, Jerry, and Kate. Elizabeth was given a two-year prison sentence and served many shorter jail terms; Phil spent over eleven years behind bars. On December 6, 2002, Phil died of cancer at his Baltimore home, surrounded by family and friends. Elizabeth carries on the struggle.

John McLaughlin

Few have achieved prominence and visibility in media like the sardonic John McLaughlin. Journalist, broadcast executive, television producer, and political commentator, he has climbed to the top of his profession, garnering many awards along the way.

A native of Rhode Island, McLaughlin entered the Society of Jesus (Jesuits) and received graduate degrees in philosophy and English from Boston College and a doctorate from Columbia University. Ordained a priest in 1960, he taught at Jesuit institutions and served as associate editor of *America* magazine. In 1969 his writings gained the Excellence in Journalism Award from the Catholic Press Association.

The political and religious turmoil of the 1960s impelled him to run as a Republican candidate for the U.S. Senate from Rhode Island in 1970, but he lost. President Nixon then appointed him deputy assistant and speechwriter on his staff from 1971 to 1974. In that role McLaughlin strongly supported the American bombing of Vietnam and Cambodia, earning the enduring animosity of peace activists.

In 1975 he left the Jesuit community and married Ann Lauenstein Dore, a corporate executive who later became Secretary of Labor in the senior Bush administration. As Washington editor of the *National Review* from 1981 to 1989, McLaughlin received the News Media Award of the Veterans of Foreign Wars (VFW). He persuaded Jack Welch, the head of General Electric, to finance a new TV show, *The McLaughlin Group,* which premiered in 1982. It soon garnered an impressive following and was named by *Washington Magazine* as Best Political Talk Show for the years 1987–93.

McLaughlin's popularity resulted in cameo roles in films, where he played himself: *Dave* (1993), *Getting Away with Murder* (1996), *Mission Impossible* (1996), *Independence Day* (1996), and *Bulworth* (1998). He also made TV appearances on *Cheers, Murphy Brown,* and *Dateline.*

His talents have been displayed in almost every medium. He combines conservative political convictions with a bombastic style, which many find amusing. In 1992 he divorced his wife, Ann, and in 1997 married Cristin Vidal.

Daniel C. Maguire

A recognized leader in Christian ethics, Daniel C. Maguire has held the presidency of the Society of Christian Ethics and the Religious Consultation on Population, Reproductive Health, and Ethics. A graduate of St. Charles Borromeo Seminary in Philadelphia and the Pontifical Gregorian University in Rome, Maguire taught ethics at Villanova University, St. Mary's Seminary, and Catholic University. Since 1981, he is professor of moral theology and ethics at Marquette University in Milwaukee. He is also founder and president of The Religious Consultation.

Maguire was ordained in 1956 and served as a priest of the Philadelphia Archdiocese until his marriage to Marjorie Riley in 1971. They raised two sons, Daniel and Thomas.

Maguire's classic work *The Moral Choice,* published in 1978, earned for him the Best Book of the Year Award from the College Theological Society and the Best Scholarly Book of the Year Award from the Wisconsin Author Association. *Ms. Magazine* named him one of the "40 male heroes of the past decade, men who took chances and made a difference." The University of Notre Dame named him one of the ten best teachers in 1983–84.

Other significant publications include: *A New American Justice: Ending the White Male Monopolies* (1980), *The New Subversives: Anti-Americanism of the Religious Right* (1982), *The Moral Revolution* (1986), *The Moral Core of Judaism and Christianity* (1993), *Sacred Energies* (2000), *What Men Owe Women* (2000) and *Sacred Choices* (2001).

William X. Kienzle

Over a twenty-year period William X. Kienzle worked as assistant pastor in five parishes in the Detroit Archdiocese. For the final twelve years of that ministry he was editor-in-chief of *Michigan Catholic,* the Archdiocesan weekly newspaper. His journalistic achievements were recognized by the Knights of Columbus, which honored him with its journalism award for general excellence in 1963, and the Catholic Press Association, which awarded him honorable mention for editorial writing in 1974.

After marrying Javan Herman Andrews, an editor and researcher, in 1974, he devoted his efforts to writing mysteries. In 1979 he published his first and most popular novel, *The Rosary Murders.* The story was made into a film starring Donald Sutherland. Kienzle went on to become a best-selling mystery novelist, and published more than twenty novels. He created the fictional character Father Robert Koesler, an amateur sleuth, whose adventures are followed through a series of books.

The public has well received Kienzle's series of detective stories. He died in December 2001. His wife, Javan, a former journalist with the *Detroit Free Press,* tells his moving story in the recently published *Judged by Love: A Biography of William X. Kienzle.*[1]

John Dominic Crossan

John Dominic Crossan rose from boyhood at Tipperary, Kildare, and Donegal in Ireland to the pinnacle of biblical scholarship in America. He would become one of the world's foremost Jesus scholars, co-director of the Jesus Seminar and chair of the Historical Jesus Section of the Society of Biblical Literature in America. His monumental work would also spark scholarly debate and gain front-page coverage in *Time, Newsweek,* and *U.S. News and World Report.*

While in Ireland Crossan joined the American province of the Servite Order, a monastic community dating back to the thirteenth century. He completed his theological studies at the Servite major seminary near Chicago, followed by graduate study at Maynooth College in Ireland, the Pontifical Biblical Institute in Rome, and the Ecole Biblique in Jerusalem. He secured degrees from each. After completing those studies he taught biblical courses at Servite College and St. Norbert's Abbey in Wisconsin.

Several Catholic institutions invited him to full-time teaching. But when he revealed his intention to leave the monastic priesthood and marry, Notre Dame and Loyola promptly withdrew their invitations. De Paul University alone had the courage to hire him on the basis of his scholarship and teaching competence. Out of gratitude he remained there for twenty-six years, ultimately receiving the Via Sapientiae Award, De Paul's highest honor.

During the course of his career, Crossan received numerous academic distinctions, including the American Academy of Religion

Award for Excellence in Religious Studies in 1999. He authored eighteen books, including *The Historical Jesus* (1991), *Jesus: A Revolutionary Biography* (1994), *Who Killed Jesus?* (1995) and *The Birth of Christianity* (1998). His most recent work is *Excavating Jesus: Beneath the Stones, Behind the Texts* (2001), co-authored with archaeologist Jonathan Reed.

In 1969 he married Margaret Dagenais, professor of fine arts at De Paul University, with whom he enjoyed summer adventures at their home in the Balearic Islands of Spain. She died of a heart attack in 1983. He retired as professor emeritus at De Paul in 1995 and now lives near Orlando, Florida, with his second wife, Sarah Sexton, a retired social worker.

Despite his controversial work, Crossan insists that he never separates the historical Jesus from the Christ of faith. He explains, "Jesus Christ is the combination of a fact (Jesus) and an interpretation (Christ). They should never be separated nor confused, and each must be found anew in every generation, for their structural dialectic is the heart of Christianity."[2]

Luke Timothy Johnson

Efforts to research the historical Jesus have aroused controversy among biblical scholars. This has redounded among the faithful. While Crossan as co-chair of the Jesus Seminar showed leadership on the left, Luke Timothy Johnson attained prominence through scholarly opposition from the right.

Normally reluctant to enter into polemical controversies, Johnson nevertheless was led to challenge basic foundations of the Jesus Seminar Movement and historical research as reported in the popular press. Arguing that many experiences are profoundly real and yet nonhistorical, he sought to demonstrate that the real Jesus is the one experienced in the present through faith, rather than in the past through historical reconstructions.

Johnson is a 1967 graduate of Notre Dame Seminary and holds a master's degree in divinity from St. Meinrad's School of Theology and a doctorate from Yale University. He served as a Benedictine monk and priest before delving into biblical scholarship. He taught at Yale Divinity School (1976–82) and Indiana University (1982–92), and is currently the Robert W. Woodruff Professor of New Testament and Christian Origins at the Candler School of Theology at Emory University.

Johnson's skills as a teacher have long been recognized. At Indiana University he received the President's Award for Distinguished Teaching, became a member of the Faculty Colloquium on Excellence in Teaching, and won the Brown Derby and Student Choice Award for teaching. At Emory University he twice received the On Eagle's Wings Excellence in Teaching Award.

In recent years Johnson has become a foremost critic of the Jesus Seminar. Author of hundreds of articles and reviews, he has published 21 books. Most notable are *The Real Jesus: The Misguided Quest for the Historical Jesus* (1996), *The Letters of James: A New Translation with Introduction and Commentary* (Anchor Bible, 1995), and *Living Jesus: Learning the Heart of the Gospel* (1998). He has written for *America, Commonweal,* and *Christian Century.*

After leaving his Benedictine community, Johnson married Joy Radazzo, with whom he now shares seven children, eleven grandchildren, and three great-grandchildren.

Summary

Most married priests were foot soldiers in the clerical system, and continue today in similar supportive roles in other organizations. Not so with these men. Their accomplishments mark them as outstanding achievers in their fields. Some accomplished much as clerics; others achieved even more as laymen. One can only surmise what might have been accomplished for the Church if these men had continued to use their talents as canonical priests. But that would be pure conjecture. The Living God has guided them along different paths, where they have influenced countless others. Such achievement might not have been possible within the clerical system.

The great drama of life calls for diverse roles. Some become major players on that stage; others appear in cameo roles. The Master Producer who manages the entire production guides the destiny of all. Critics will comment positively or negatively according to their tastes and biases, but in the end God alone will be the Final Judge.

Chapter 8

The Swinging Door

IN RECENT YEARS hundreds of Roman Catholic priests have joined other Christian churches — Episcopal, Lutheran, Methodist, Presbyterian — where they serve as pastors and even bishops. At the same time dozens of married clergy from those same Protestant communities have become Catholics and resumed ministry as Roman Catholic priests. The door is swinging both ways.

Such movements have a long history. After the break between Eastern Orthodoxy and Western Catholicism in the eleventh century, many clerical transfers occurred. Greek Catholics, Ukrainian Catholics, and Armenian Catholics bear witness to the move toward Rome. In the seventeenth century, however, three million Greek Catholics together with their Metropolitan Joseph Siemashko returned to the Orthodox Church. Since the Reformation in the sixteenth century, the same can be observed between Roman Catholic and Protestant Churches. Cardinal Newman and the Oxford Movement reflect conversion from the Anglican community to Rome. But moves in the other direction have also occurred, notably among Hispanic Christians.

More recently many Roman Catholic priests, discouraged by the slow pace of reform after the Second Vatican Council, married and joined other Christian communities. In turn many Protestant clergy, objecting to liberal practices like ordaining women and solemnizing gay unions, turned to the Roman Catholic Church and were ordained as Catholic priests. The door swinging has sped up in each direction.

From Episcopal to Roman Catholic

In the past, an Episcopal clergyman wanting to become a Catholic priest had to separate from his wife by mutual agreement, and she had to enter a convent. This posed a formidable roadblock. In 1835, for example, the Episcopal Rector of Trinity Church in Natchez, Mississippi, Pierce Connolly, and his wife, Cornelia, converted to the Roman Catholic Faith. Shortly after that, he petitioned the Vatican to be ordained a Catholic priest and agreed to separate from his wife. After Rome issued its decree in 1845, Pierce was ordained and Cornelia entered the Convent of the Sacred Heart. Later he recanted and turned for redress to the Anglican ecclesiastical courts. Cornelia, however, chose to remain a nun.

In 1966 Episcopal priest Louis Sigman was the first ordained by an American Catholic bishop, John Franz of Peoria. Sigman's ordaining prelate had been consecrated by a Polish National Catholic Church bishop who had been consecrated by the Catholic archbishop of Utrecht. Therefore Franz ordained Sigman conditionally. Two years later another Episcopal priest, the celibate John Jay Hughes, was ordained conditionally by Bishop Joseph Hoffner in Munster, Germany.[1]

In 1977, a number of Episcopal clergymen in America applied as a group to be admitted to the Roman Catholic Church, asking that they be allowed to continue their ministry without separating from their wives. This request followed the contentious 1976 General Convention of the Episcopal Church in Minneapolis, which endorsed women's ordination.

Not until June 1980 did the Vatican permit the American hierarchy to admit married Episcopal clergy into the Catholic priesthood. Rome then issued the Pastoral Provisions, a set of procedures and guidelines to be followed, and appointed Bernard Law, then bishop of Springfield-Cape Girardeau in Missouri, as Ecclesiastical Delegate to oversee this effort. In June 1982 the Reverend Luther Parker became the first married priest ordained under those provisions. The official Web site — *pastoralprovision.org* — noted, "Since 1983 over seventy men have been ordained for priestly ministry in Catholic dioceses of the United States; seven personal parishes have been established and the Book of Divine Worship has been authorized."

One married Episcopalian bishop, Peter Watterson, now works as a Catholic priest in Florida. Another, Clarence Pope, the Episcopal bishop of Fort Worth, Texas, resigned from the Episcopal House of Bishops and joined the Roman Catholic Church. As the date for him to be re-ordained as a Catholic priest neared, he began to have second thoughts. He withdrew his application and returned to the Episcopal fold, saying, "I was finding myself more and more compromised in my theology and simply had to come back home where I belong."

PETER DALLY. The book *Married to a Catholic Priest* describes the experiences of Mary Vincent Dally, wife of an Episcopal priest now serving as a Roman Catholic priest. Reading about their long wait for admission and their many sacrifices, one cannot but admire their steadfastness.

Peter, her husband, served as Episcopal priest for thirty years, the last 16 as Vicar of Holy Spirit Episcopal Church on Vashon Island, near Seattle. A lifelong high churchman, he considered himself part of the historic Catholic Church, and hoped the Anglican branch of the ancient Church would acknowledge its unique identity within Catholicism and reunite with Rome. But after the 1976 General Convention that approved women's ordination, he felt deserted. He therefore formally joined the Roman Catholic community.

Mary records their rejections, resentments, and perplexing plight. She describes a religious journey to remain faithful to God's call despite misunderstandings. After five years of struggle, Peter was ordained a priest and assigned to a Catholic parish in Tulsa, Oklahoma. Mary writes about their adjustment to life in a Catholic parish:

> We found that our relationship to the laity, and the whole question of priests who had left the priesthood to marry, required our most heartfelt sensitivity and warmth. Indeed, this became a heart breaking symbol of the 60s for Peter and for me as well. . . . This small diocese, where only four percent of the population is Catholic, had lost nearly half of its priests in the years following Vatican II. The pain of that loss was still very much a part of their lives. We were looked upon as undeserving outsiders, and there seemed to be no thought that we, too, might be sensitive to the loss of so many of their brothers and sisters in Christ.[2]

Their four children were grown when Mary and Peter settled into their new life in the Diocese of Tulsa. They were one of the first couples to take this journey under the Pastoral Provisions.

CHRISTOPHER PHILLIPS, along with twenty Episcopal clergymen, petitioned the Vatican in the early 1980s to become a Roman Catholic priest. After completing theological studies, he was ordained a Catholic priest on August 15, 1983, by Archbishop Patrick F. Flores of San Antonio. He is married with five children, two of whom were born after ordination.

Flores appointed Phillips pastor of Our Lady of Atonement Church, the first parish authorized under the "common identity" authority of the Vatican-approved Pastoral Provisions, which enable communities to transfer to the Catholic Church and keep their Anglican liturgical customs. Called personal, common identity, or Anglican-use parishes, they respect their Anglican liturgical heritage and acknowledge allegiance to Rome. The vibrant Atonement parish has grown from eighteen original members to over twelve hundred today. The community runs an elementary school and plans to build a new high school.

JAMES MOORE, a married Episcopal priest, entered the Catholic Church in 1984. Since 1981, he and many others in his community had been seeking admission to the Catholic Church. On April 7, 1984, Bishop Fiorenza incorporated the community as a Catholic parish, the second Anglican-use parish set up under the Pastoral Provisions. He then re-ordained Moore and appointed him pastor of that community, now under the title of Our Lady of Walsingham.

ALLAN R. G. HAWKINS, a married priest with two children, served as pastor of the Episcopal parish of St. Mary the Virgin. Like Moore, he also guided many parishioners to withdraw from the Episcopal Church and attain full communion with Rome. On June 12, 1994, Bishop Joseph P. Delaney of Fort Worth received 120 of their members into the Catholic Church. A few days later he re-ordained Father Hawkins, and allowed him to continue shepherding the community as a Roman Catholic priest.

RICHARD STERLING BRADFORD, a married priest and Episcopal Church rector, led twenty-nine members of his Episcopal parish of

All Saints in Boston into the Catholic Church on September 28, 1997. Cardinal Law of Boston re-ordained him and appointed him Catholic chaplain of the community, now known as the Congregation of St. Athanasius.

On October 3–5, 2001, Our Lady of Atonement Catholic Church in San Antonio hosted an Anglican Use Conference for eight parishes, mostly in Texas, that help make up the Anglican-Use Catholic community in the United States. The Conference featured Solemn Evensong, Benediction of the Blessed Sacrament, and an address by Patrick J. Zurek, auxiliary bishop of San Antonio. The number of such parishes continues to grow.

In 2002, Fred Luhmann identified seventy-four priests ordained under the Pastoral Provisions between 1983 and 2000.[3] A review shows that twenty-one (or 28 percent) live in Texas; another twenty-one (or 28 percent) in other southern states. The seventy-four priests serve in forty-eight dioceses around the country. Rome has authorized similar provisions for the Catholic Church in Canada, England, and Wales. Former Episcopal priests are also known to have been ordained in Australia, South Africa, and the Caribbean.[4]

Unheralded was the ordination on January 24, 2003, of Alan Stephen Hopes as auxiliary bishop to Cardinal Cormac Murphy-O'Connor of Westminster. Hopes was an unmarried Anglican priest who converted to Catholicism in 1992.

From Methodist to Roman Catholic

Clerical transfers to the Roman Catholic priesthood are not limited to the Episcopal Church. Methodist, Lutheran, and Presbyterian pastors, have traveled the same route.

JOHN GILES, a married pastor in the United Methodist Church, developed a close friendship with Catholic priests who influenced his decision. On May 23, 1985, he and his family entered into full communion with the Catholic Church. Two and a half years later, John was ordained for the Lake Charles, Louisiana, Diocese, where he serves as associate pastor of Our Lady Queen of Heaven parish. After directing the diocesan Office of Marriage and Family Ministries, his wife, Carol, now heads Friends of Families, an ecumenical agency providing help to the homeless.

SCOTT MEDLOCK followed a similar path. For nine years, he worked as a Methodist minister. After attending Notre Dame University, he married a Catholic and raised his three children in the Catholic faith. Occasionally joining his wife at Catholic services, he was led to request admission to the Catholic Church and ordination to the priesthood. Archbishop Francis T. Hurley of Anchorage, Alaska, agreed to sponsor him and ordained him a Catholic priest.

From Lutheran to Roman Catholic

Martin Luther never intended to separate from the Catholic Church. He tried to reform it. With the doctrine of justification no longer a barrier in our day, and with the Eucharist distributed to laity under both species, some stumbling blocks to full communion are being overcome.

The union of Luther's followers in a reformed Catholicism would not strike him as strange.

In 1951, Pope Pius XII deviated from normal practice when he allowed Rudolf Goethe, a seventy-one-year-old German Lutheran pastor, to be ordained a Catholic priest. The next year two young Lutheran ministers, Eugen Scheytt and Otto Melchers, were ordained, and the following year one more, Martin Giebner. Although all were married, none had to relinquish marital relations, nor were wives urged to enter a convent. These exceptions were limited to Germany. Since Pastoral Provisions were put in place, however, many more Lutheran pastors have been ordained as Catholic priests in America and elsewhere.

After their three children had grown, Lutheran minister **LARRY HEIMSOTH** and his wife, Betty, requested admission to the Catholic Church. On July 10, 1999, he was ordained for the Diocese of Austin, Texas, and assigned as associate pastor of St. Luke's Catholic Church in Temple, Texas.

LAWRENCE BLAKE, a married Lutheran minister with three children, was ordained a Catholic priest by Archbishop Harry Flynn on December 12, 1999. He serves in the Archdiocese of St. Paul and Minneapolis as business administrator at St. Hubert's Church in Chanhassen.

Former Lutheran pastor **DAVID MEDOW** studied at Georgetown University and married Jane, a lifelong Catholic. On June 2, 2001, he was received into the Roman Catholic Church. Bishop Joseph Imesch ordained him a Catholic priest at the Cathedral of St. Raymond in Joliet, Illinois, and assigned him to St. Mary Immaculate Church in Plainfield, Illinois. His wife, Jane, teaches in the parish school. They have two children, Nikolai and Hannah.

From Presbyterian to Roman Catholic

An eleven-year journey ended for **LARRY STEROID,** former Presbyterian minister and father of three children, when he was received into the Catholic Church. The journey began when he attended a retreat at the Trappist Monastery in Oregon. Since 1996 he has served as Catholic priest in the Archdiocese of Portland.

From Roman Catholic to Episcopal

Movement in the other direction has also been steady. Many examples can be cited of Roman Catholic priests transferring to other Christian churches. These include two current Episcopal bishops — Jerry Lamb, formerly a priest in the Archdiocese of Denver, now Episcopal bishop of Northern California, and Mark Dyer, formerly a Benedictine priest and later Episcopal bishop of Bethlehem, Pennsylvania.

JOHN HORTUM. After being ordained to the Roman Catholic priesthood, John worked for nine years in his home diocese of Arlington, Virginia, before requesting a leave of absence. In a fatherly talk before his departure, Bishop Keating made clear that if either of John's parents died while he was on leave, the bishop would forbid John to officiate at their funeral. Although this was spoken to deter him from leaving, John had already made up his mind. Because securing a dispensation from Rome to marry would take years, John and

Leslie married before an Episcopal priest who urged John to minister in that Church. A few more years elapsed, but John eventually joined the Episcopalian community.

In accepting him for service, the Episcopal bishop noted an anomaly. Episcopal priests transferring to the Catholic Church are routinely re-ordained because of doubts about apostolic succession. No need to re-ordain John, the bishop observed, because apostolic succession of John's ordaining prelate was never challenged. After completing his studies in Rome, John was ordained by Pope Paul VI.

Today John serves as pastor of a flourishing Episcopal community with parochial preschool in Alexandria, Virginia. He succeeded a female pastor who had also been raised a Roman Catholic. In the meantime, John had the privilege of officiating at the funeral service of his parents. They remained Catholic all their lives, but chose to be buried in services officiated by their son, John, in his Episcopal parish.

BISHOP MARK DYER. A priest celebrating the funeral liturgy of his parents is common. Knowing the appeal of that practice, Bishop Keating had threatened John. But different bishops handle matters differently. A New England Catholic bishop was willing to allow Mark to officiate at his mother's Catholic funeral. Besides being a former Benedictine priest who married, Mark was an ordained Episcopal bishop. Through the years he kept close relations with members of his monastic community. All monks from the monastery attended his mother's funeral and concelebrated the liturgy, with the abbot presiding and Mark preaching.

Today Mark teaches systematic theology and spirituality at the Episcopal Seminary in Northern Virginia. This permits him to bring together the fruit of his remarkable life. A former monk and trained theologian, he studied at universities in Louvain and Ottawa. His views on ecumenism prompted his leaving a teaching job at the Benedictine seminary. The Episcopal community welcomed him and hired him as a spiritual director guiding the religious formation of its priests. He was later ordained bishop for the Episcopal Diocese of Bethlehem, Pennsylvania.

Mark married Mary Elizabeth, the first wife of a bishop to be ordained a priest. Together they raised three adopted children, including a child requiring lifelong care twenty-four hours a day. Mary Elizabeth died recently, leaving Mark with the home chores and a full-time teaching load at the seminary.

Today he chairs the international ecumenical dialogue between Episcopal and Orthodox churches. In twelve years, Mark has helped to produce important documents fostering better ecumenical relations. Through all these efforts, he keeps a commitment to Benedictine spirituality and unity of the churches.

JOHN NEGROTTO. Put into intolerable pastoral assignments with no recourse, many young priests see no other option but to leave the clerical system. Such was the plight of John. His first appointment took him to a large suburban parish, where bingo was run five nights a week to repay the huge debt resulting from the recently constructed school, convent, church, and rectory. His fellow clergy at the rectory, he discovered, were an alcoholic pastor and a pedophile priest. John looked in vain for understanding from church officials. A third assistant was appointed who, grasping what was taking place, tried to alert the bishop. To no avail. He and John were labeled malcontents and soon left the diocese. John is now happily married.

Today John is completing his twenty-fifth year as pastor of an Episcopalian parish in northern New Jersey. Well respected in his community, he serves as chaplain to the fire and police departments and aide to the bishop on diocesan committees. As experienced counselor, he advises loyal parishioners, Catholics in transition, and occasional agnostics.

JERRY GALLAGHER. Rome-educated and destined for advancement in the Diocese of Brooklyn, he gave that up to marry. Alongside his wife and four children he now shepherds an Episcopal community in the hills of New York State. That parish recently celebrated its 150th anniversary, with Jerry as pastor the past fifteen years. The twinkle in his eyes and the ever-present smile on his face bespeak the joy in his heart.

The precise number of priests leaving ministry and transferring to other denominations is difficult to calculate. Various estimates have been given. An Episcopal churchman who studied these movements for many years estimated that in his lifetime about six hundred Roman Catholic priests have affiliated with the Episcopal Church.

From Roman Catholic to Lutheran

With his emphasis on the Word of God and his reverence for marriage and family life, Martin Luther has become a model for Catholic priests who marry. This is reflected in the lives of the following men.

FRED DONOHOE. The call to ministry was an overriding passion for Fred, impelling him, after marriage to Joan, to continue ministry in the Lutheran community. Ecumenical relations as a Catholic priest in the Altoona Diocese had acquainted him with clergymen in other churches. This led to appointment as assistant pastor of Messiah Lutheran Church in South Williamsport, Pennsylvania, for seven years. He was then called to found a new Lutheran parish in Northern Virginia. St. Peter's Lutheran Church in Stafford stands as a monument to Fred's vision and hard work. Close to a thousand parishioners are housed in a spacious church building with modern classrooms for religious instruction.

In marrying Joan, a widow with four children, Fred gained instant family. A fifth child soon followed. As they gave themselves to family and ministry, they recognized marriage as a blessing from God. They blended marriage, ministry, and family life.

Fred always preached well. As a Catholic priest, he spent four hours a week working on his sermons; as a Lutheran pastor, ten hours. As a Catholic priest he was accustomed to daily Mass as the focus of his prayer; as a Lutheran pastor he gave greater prominence to the weekly Eucharist and intensified his daily prayer life.

After twenty-two years, Fred retired, leaving behind a thriving Christian community. He has returned to the Divine Office, praying it twice daily as in earlier years. Today, with grandchildren to dote on and with hospital and community social work to turn to, Fred and Joan enjoy a blessed retirement.

RAY SHECK. Studying theology at the Catholic University of America in Washington in the late 1960s, seminarians were caught up in the enormous ferment in the Catholic Church. Major changes after the Second Vatican Council, explosive opposition to the encyclical *Humanae Vitae,* and the ecumenical climate of burgeoning reform groups all had their effect on the lives of active priests and nuns. The journey of Joan and Ray must be seen against that background.

Joan was a School Sister of Notre Dame; Ray, a diocesan priest. Their awakened love and the kind pastoral response of Cardinal Lawrence Shehan resulted in a lifelong deep respect for their Catholic roots. Marriage, nevertheless, separated them from the Christian ministry to which they felt called. This led to their accepting ministry in the Lutheran Church.

God blessed them with two biological and two adopted children. One daughter graduated from her mother's alma mater, Notre Dame College in Baltimore, and works among the poor in the Hispanic community. She recently decided to return to the Catholic faith with her parents' full support.

Uppermost in the mind of Ray and Joan is servant leadership. They see their role as mentoring others in the faith and making disciples in accord with Christ's final mandate. With that in mind, Joan visits the sick, counsels the young, and teaches Bible classes. Ray, on the other hand, spent more than twenty-five years as pastor of Redeemer Lutheran Church in Damascus, Maryland, a community of over six hundred people. His devotion to sacramental ministry impels him to offer well-planned weekly Eucharistic celebrations. He also insists upon regular Bible study for all parishioners. He has guided many in bible-centered, servant leadership not only in his parish, but also in other churches.

Review of the Phenomenon

Clergy who have transferred from Catholic to Protestant Churches and from Protestant to Catholic Churches manifest sincere commitment to their new family of faith. Reports show that they are well received in both communities and are making unique contributions to the American Church. They are plowing new ground.

These stories of interdenominational transfers show many similarities. Each person looks for peace in fidelity to Christ. Former Roman Catholic clergy found Church structures oppressive, celibacy laws unjust, and some papal decrees wrong. In transferring to Protestantism, they often cite the desire to grow, the acceptance of diversity, and the joys of marriage and family life. Former Protestant clergy found their church vacillating and deviating too far from Christian norms, especially in accepting women's ordination and homosexual unions. In transferring to Catholicism, they are more likely to note unity in teaching, faithfulness to tradition, clarity in moral and religious matters. Each clergyman finds comfort in his current place. They all maintain they have come home.

A Jesuit sociologist and perceptive observer of this scene, Joseph Fichter, notes in his book on the Pastoral Provisions:

> The tendency among the Episcopalian laity is to complain that their Church officials are changing too rapidly, while the Catholic laity tend to complain that Rome and the Bishops change too slowly. In the Episcopal Church, it looks as though many of the laity are trying to "hold the line," while in the Catholic Church the hierarchy is remaining steadfast. The forces of change in both American Church bodies — though from different sources — are resulting in a deeper cross-creedal understanding between Episcopalians and Roman Catholics. If there is a constant element common to both churches, it is that the conflict centers around the same major issues: women clergy, liturgy, authority, secularism, and sexual morality. No one in either Church can escape these modern problems by transferring into the other.[5]

What is written about Episcopal–Roman Catholic relations could also be applied to other Christian bodies. The dream of Christian unity continues to haunt all Christ's followers. If achieved, that unity would go far to overcome the climate of suspicion and mistrust; it would transcend the controversy over marriage and celibacy; and it would move Christians closer to the mind of Christ, who prayed, "That they may all be one; even as you, Father, in me, and I in you" (John 17:21).

In 1965 Orthodox Patriarch Athenagoras and Pope Paul VI embraced and removed the excommunications shamefully inflicted on each other centuries before. In a joint statement they declared:

> This reciprocal act of justice and forgiveness...cannot suffice to put an end to the differences, ancient or more recent, which remain...and which...will be overcome thanks to the purification of hearts, regret for historical errors, and an effective determination to arrive at a common understanding and expression of the apostolic faith and its demands.[6]

Would that similar gestures could be shown to Lutheran, Episcopalian, Presbyterian, and other Christian brothers and sisters!

Further cause for hope exists. Rome recognizes as valid the ordination of bishops in the Union of Utrecht, which numbers many churches. That means that their ordained priests who unite with Rome need not be re-ordained. Discussion between these two churches has resulted in a joint declaration signed in 1996 by Cardinal Edward Idris Cassidy, president of the Pontifical Council for Promoting Christian Unity, and by Archbishop Antonius Jan Glazemaker, president of the International Old Catholic Bishops' Conference of the Utrecht Union. It says:

> Both sides have the duty to cooperate if a member of the clergy is changing, to limit the pain for the parishes caused by such a changing, to prevent any kind of proselytism and to avoid impairing future ecumenical relations.

The document also established guidelines to be followed in such transfers.[7]

In 1993 Rome further ruled that a Polish National Catholic Church member who approaches a Roman Catholic priest for reception of Eucharist, penance, or anointing of the sick should be treated the same as members of the Orthodox Churches, who are granted access to those sacraments under certain conditions. (The Polish National Catholic Church is part of the Union of Utrecht.) These are historic milestones. With such gestures and declarations increasingly being made, can unity be far off? Perhaps Christians might yet remove the swinging door.

Chapter 9

Spirituality and Married Priests

P RIESTS HAVE BEEN called to be messengers of the Gospel, heralds of the Good News, sacramental ministers to God's Holy People. No one takes this honor to himself. To be worthy of that calling, they must give themselves knowingly, voluntarily, and wholeheartedly. This entails cultivating an inner life, an awareness of God's Word, a spirituality which alone sustains them.

The word "spirituality" engenders discomfort. It seems to imply disparagement of the world, a superior mode of existence, a dichotomy between matter and spirit. Spirituality can be found outside organized religion and even among nontheistic groups. Most frequently, however, the term is used by religious people to suggest an awareness of deeper realities, a sense of the divine. In Christian tradition, spirituality must be God-centered. Whether a personal being as mystics perceive, or the ground of being as some modern theologians contend, God is for the Christian believer the central reality.

One's orientation to that reality mirrors the tradition in which one is raised. Although those traditions vary, closer examination shows similarity in the quest for God and revealed truth. The Second Vatican Council recognized this when it observed:

> Throughout history even to the present day, there is found among different peoples a certain awareness of a hidden power, which lies behind the course of nature and the events of human life.... Thus, in Hinduism men explore the divine mystery and express it both in the limitless riches of myth and the accurately defined insights of philosophy.... Buddhism in its various forms testifies to the essential inadequacy of this changing world. It proposes a way of life by which men can, with confidence and

142

trust, attain a state of perfect liberation and reach supreme illumination either through their own efforts or by the aid of divine help.... The Church has also a high regard for the Muslims. They worship God, who is one, living and subsistent, merciful and almighty, the Creator of heaven and earth, who has also spoken to men.[1]

Spirituality, then, entails a prayerful pursuit of the divine. Spiritual exercises of religious groups show the asceticism entailed in that quest. It can be the five times a day turning to Mecca in obeisance to God, or the repeated chanting of religious lyrics in a frenzy of fervor. In each case, sublime mystery engulfs the worshiper, whose proper response is reverence and awe.

Christians have developed a variety of spiritual exercises, from the silent reflection of Quaker meeting rooms to the chanting solemnity of Orthodox liturgies. In Roman Catholic tradition, one also finds a range of religious practice, from the solitary lifestyle of the Carthusian hermit to the prayerful engagement of the Jesuit activist. Catholic spiritual exercises include the rosary, Stations of the Cross, hours of the divine office, benediction of the blessed sacrament, days of recollection, and much more.

All Catholic spirituality centers on Jesus. One's way of life, all one says and does, flows from that center. As the Epistle to the Romans declares, "neither death, nor life ... nor anything else in all creation, will be able to separate us from the love of God in Christ Jesus Our Lord" (Rom. 8:38–39). Accordingly, Catholics cultivate a personal relationship with Christ in the Eucharist. Honoring Christ's mother, Mary, and the saints who model Christ is a logical extension of that Christ-centeredness. Francis of Assisi in the thirteenth century and Mother Teresa in the twentieth exemplify that tradition.

But spirituality entails more than spiritual exercises. Protestant reformers correctly assert that one can do nothing to merit salvation; multiplying religious rituals cannot make one deserving of grace. Nevertheless, the discipline of regular prayer sensitizes one to eternal truths and opens the heart to God. As Ruben Habito has written, "Our human efforts do not *cause* the experience, but only enable us to dispose ourselves for that grace filled moment."[2] God summons all chosen followers to meditate on the Sacred Word and live by its teachings. God does the rest.

Historical Perspective

One can only surmise the devotional life of priests, bishops, and popes in the first centuries of the Church. The breaking of bread and scriptural reflection were the earliest religious exercises of the Christian community. Married clergy observed these practices and are honored as saints. Besides Peter and the Apostles, other married priests, bishops, and popes guided the Church. The Eastern Church later witnessed outstanding episcopal leaders like Gregory of Nyssa, Gregory of Nazianzen the Elder, and Gregory the Illuminator of Armenia. All were married. They stand in a long line of saintly married priests throughout two millennia.

Early Spirituality

Monasticism played an important role in Christian spirituality. Beginning with Athanasius's *Life of St. Anthony* in the fourth century, the deeds of men in eremitical and cenobitic life captured the imagination of all who tried to follow Christ. The *Rule of St. Benedict* in the fifth century became the preferred guidebook, influencing not only monks but also other faithful in responding to God's call.

In the following centuries, the Church increasingly recruited monks for the episcopacy. Their virtue and asceticism made them models for the Christian community; their celibate state saved the Church from an encroaching nepotism. These bishops exhorted priests to live like monks, under the evangelical counsels of poverty, chastity, and obedience. Unfortunately there arose also a disdain for clerical marriage.

During the Middle Ages, rapid increase in the number of priests, and their lack of education, created further problems. Simony became widespread. When the Council of Trent convened in the sixteenth century, it began addressing clerical abuses. The reforms of the Council led to development of a twelve-year program of priestly formation.

After being admitted at age eleven or twelve, a seminarian would spend six years in academic and spiritual training at a minor seminary, followed by six more years of philosophical and theological study at a major seminary. The prescribed way of life for seminarians mimicked the monastic model in removal from the world, observance of celibacy, and recitation of the Divine Office. Such practices, joined with meditation, daily liturgy, spiritual reading, and Marian devotions, set the pattern of clerical spirituality for centuries.

Traditional patterns of piety were at times ineffective. Priests in busy urban settings, like married persons generally, had to adjust their schedule of devotions. New methods were needed, involving not flight from the world, but fervor within it. Religious orders like the Jesuits, the Vincentians, and the Oblates led the way. For those caught up in the busy world, Ignatius Loyola's *Spiritual Exercises* outlined a vigorous new path, and Francis de Sales's *Introduction to the Devout Life* offered a balanced program of spirituality.

The Reformation of the sixteenth century affected all Christian communities, but in different ways. Catholic Christians reinforced the celibate ideal in priestly and religious life and presented models of heroic sanctity. Protestant Christians demonstrated a link between marriage and pastoral leadership; reformers and their followers gave exemplary witness to the devout life as married church leaders.

The virtue of married clergy in the Eastern Churches — Byzantine, Armenian, Coptic — through the centuries is also a matter of record. Besides universally recognized married saints in the early period, the Eastern Churches have continued to glorify the memory of married priests in succeeding generations, including many priest-martyrs during the communist period, like St. Maximus Sandovich, the father of eight children, and Alexander Validov, son of a priest and father of seven children. A glorious history of sanctity among married priests emerges.

Priestly Formation after Trent

Catholic seminarians in the post–Council of Trent Church were schooled in a common spirituality. It was built on a discipline of religious exercises and based in a theology of the priest as *alter Christus*, another Christ. This entailed formative years spent in a traditional seminary, combining study of philosophy and theology with guidance in the spiritual life. That spirituality centered on an imitation of Christ.

During the years of study, zeal for the Christian life inspired the seminarian to observe strictly the rules of the day. He remained faithful to a daily pattern of spiritual exercises, which included morning meditation, Mass, rosary, Stations of the Cross, visits to the Blessed Sacrament, spiritual reading, and evening prayers. During the last year in the seminary, the Church added recitation of the Breviary, requiring an hour spent daily reading in Latin the Hours of the Divine Office — Matins, Lauds, Prime, Terce, Sext, None, Vespers, and Compline.

By the time the ordained priest went out into the world, he was disciplined to turn his attention to the Living God throughout the day. Although he may have cultivated an intense prayer life, he received little help in adjusting the monastic schedule of spiritual exercises to the demands of ministry. Wise counselors were needed; not always were they found.

No one anticipated the profound reforms that would emerge from the Second Vatican Council. Its effect was cataclysmic, reaching into every facet of life and worship. Before the Council, the Sacred Liturgy was celebrated and the Divine Office was recited only in Latin. After the Council, that changed.

Other innovations occurred. Facing the faithful with gestures that communicated rather than standing before a wall in ritual rigidity, proclaiming the Sacred Words aloud in the vernacular so people could understand rather than mumbling them amid yawns and stares, using music in the idiom of the day with lyrics that touched the heart and instruments that moved the spirit — all these liturgical changes had a powerful effect. No longer did one participate in arcane rituals that were thought to produce their effect regardless of how sloppily one performed them or how ill preparedly one undertook them. The People of God, as the Second Vatican Council proclaimed, gathered joyously in Sacred Liturgy, the summit and source of the Christian life.[3]

The Influence of Merton in America

Other elements were at play in the evolving spirituality of priests and religious. These paralleled closely events in the life of Thomas Merton, one of the greatest spiritual guides of the day. Each stage of his development, as seen in his writings, echoed in the lives of priests, sisters, and laity.

Merton's early works, like *The Seven Storey Mountain* (1948), *Seeds of Contemplation* (1949), *The Waters of Siloe* (1949) and *The Sign of Jonas* (1953) guided many into a deeper intimacy with the Living God. These writings, which cultivated their spirituality and inflamed their zeal, led many to enter church ministry.

In the 1950s and 1960s, Merton became an advocate for racial justice and peace. He saw this as the natural fruition of prayer. *Seeds of Destruction* (1964) and *Faith and Violence* (1968) came from that period. To pray while ignoring the plight of brothers and sisters in pain, he asserted, reflected false piety. The liturgical movement proclaimed the same. This resulted in priests and sisters becoming more involved in the social work of the day. Laboring abroad with the poor and disenfranchised, American missionaries took that message to heart.

Merton's awakened love for a nurse during his hospital stay offered another poignant episode. He made no pretense about it. His journal for March 1967 records the "rainy evening when (S) came to say good-bye...and when I was so terribly lonely, lay awake half the night, tormented by the gradual realization that we were in love and I did not know I could live without her."[4] Although it was only a temporary interlude, the frankness of his admission endeared him to many clerics and religious who were going through the same. Merton abandoned the budding romance and, to the end, remained faithful to his monastic vows.

During his final years Merton explored Eastern religions. His dialogue with Buddhist monks resulted in one last journey, to Bangkok. In his last talk there, just two hours before he died, he said, "I believe that by openness to Buddhism, to Hinduism, and to those great Asian traditions, we stand a wonderful chance of learning more about the potentiality of our traditions."[5]

Each stage in Merton's life echoed in the lives of many priests and sisters. Like him, they struggled to read the signs of the times. In him, they found a wise and trustworthy guide. His Trappist Abbot, Flavian Burns, reminisced after Merton's death, "Those of us who had the privilege and the pleasure to deal with Father Louis on intimate terms, and submit our inner lives to his direction, know that in him we had the best of Spiritual Fathers."[6]

U.S. Bishops Study of the Priesthood

In the early 1970s, as described in chapter 3, the U.S. Conference of Catholic Bishops began a monumental study of the historical, psychological, sociological, and theological dimensions of priesthood in the United States. Among other findings, the study showed the American priest to be similar to other Americans in psychological growth. It also offered a sober, honest, and realistic image of the American priest, consistent with the biblical image, "Every high priest chosen from among men is appointed to act on behalf of men in relation to God, to offer gifts and sacrifices for sins" (Heb. 5:1).

Not satisfied with that research, the bishops in 1973 authorized one further study, on spiritual renewal of the American priesthood. This work presented Christian spirituality as "the living out in experience, throughout the whole course of our lives the death-resurrection of Christ that we have been caught up into by baptism."[7] All those baptized enter this paschal mystery, and priests are called to embrace it.

In their study, the U.S. Bishops observed "the apathetic, who are unconcerned with the plight of their neighbor and yet piously say their daily Mass, read their breviary and fulfill their celibate commitment in the ivory tower of an uninvolved existence, are often cop-outs from within."[8] Echoes of Merton abound. But the study also delineated the other extreme:

compulsive activists who are caught up in a ceaseless unreflective round of involvements and have no time for prayer, for moments of silence and solitude, for simple sharing with fellow priests or fellow human beings.[9]

The Trappist Dom Chautard's *The Soul of the Apostolate* articulated well the piety in which priests had been schooled.[10] This work urged them to pray regularly to fill up with grace, so they could then go out and spend that energy. If they did not keep going back, ministry would suffer. Formed in that discipline, busy celibate priests tried to balance the demands of ministry and the impulse to keep going back and filling up. Much frustration followed.

The bishops' study, in contrast, suggested that ministry was the ally of the spiritual life, not the enemy. In faith-filled ministry, one could find grace and nourishment from God. The study urged prayerful engagement with the world.

Contemporary Witness of Married Priest Couples

The disjunction between semi-monastic spiritual exercises of the seminary and a healthy prayer life needed in the active ministry demanded serious adjustment. Many faltered. Priests who married faced even more profound change and challenge to traditional practices. With priests in earlier centuries they shared the married state, but not canonical ministry. Although their new lifestyle was different, the reality of Christ in their lives remained the same. Consider the prayer experiences of Catholic married priest couples who took seriously their commitment to Christ.

Return to Traditional Practices of Piety

The journey of each priest who marries follows a different pattern. Some return in later years to the traditional patterns of piety that nourished them in their youth — daily Mass, praying the rosary, reciting the Divine Office, and similar practices. Two examples can be cited.

MICHAEL AND MARIA. Michael, a priest ordained in India, gained a doctorate in philosophy from Duquesne University and worked in the Pittsburgh Diocese. There he befriended Bishop (later Cardinal) Wright, with whom he had long discussions about the effect of the Church's ban on contraception. They regretted no plan was in place for educating the laity to accept this teaching.

After twenty-two years of priestly ministry, Michael became ill with internal bleeding and a low blood count. His doctor suggested diverting his energies to other projects, so he enrolled at a Goethe Institute in Doneaueschingen to study German. The last day of that school year coincided with the publication of *Humanae Vitae*. That night Michael had a severe bleeding spell and was rushed to the state hospital. His doctor recommended that he change his lifestyle. The archbishop, in agreement, helped him gain a dispensation from the law of celibacy.

During his hospital stay, Michael met Maria, a German nurse who cared for him. A Lutheran by birth, she later converted to Catholicism. They married in the Catholic Church and settled in Western Maryland, where Michael became head of the philosophy department at Frostburg State University and Maria a nurse at Sacred Heart Hospital.

In the early days of his marriage, Michael went through much soul searching. Despite his respect for the Petrine Office, his bleeding almost to the point of death after the issuance of *Humanae Vitae* raised troubling questions in conscience. Did one man, he asked, with the stroke of a pen have the right to throw the entire Church into turmoil?

While regularly attending services at St. Patrick's parish, Michael and Maria continued a rich prayer life. Michael taught scripture, chaired the parish council, served as Eucharistic minister and participated as leader in the parish renewal program. For sixteen years, he and Maria held weekly prayer meetings in their home. Besides his role in evangelization and outreach ministries in the parish, Michael was invited to preach in different Protestant Churches. He also maintained close friendships with married and celibate priests in the region.

Then, in 1993, Michael returned to Fatima, where he renewed the consecration to Mary he had first made forty-three years earlier. He was transformed. With his heart at peace, he came to look upon the Holy See as the last bastion of Catholic orthodoxy. He also perceived Mary as the focal point between the two testaments, representing

Israel in spousal relationship to God, and the Church in spousal relationship to Christ. Slowly he became convinced that Mary gave him back his priesthood and sent him on a journey to discover the richness of his Catholic faith.

Now in retirement after raising three children, Maria and Michael have turned their home into a cenacle of prayer. As part of their daily routine, in the morning and evening they pray the Divine Office and on their afternoon walks recite the rosary. Amid failing health, they find great consolation in the Lord.

WALT AND ANN traversed a similar path. Walt had worked as a priest in Charleston, South Carolina, with Joseph Bernardin, later cardinal archbishop of Chicago, and Horace Deets, later head of the American Association of Retired Persons (AARP). Ann, a School Sister of Notre Dame, taught in Catholic schools. Given to an intense prayer life, they continued, even after marriage, to lead prayer groups and share the fruit of their prayer life at gatherings of married priests and their wives.

After many years in the work force in Washington, they retired to Charleston, where Walt had been raised. Their continued involvement with religious groups led them one year to host in Charleston the national convention of the Federation of Christian Ministries. Then in 1991 Walt suffered a heart attack and underwent a near-death experience. He became convinced that God saved him and gave him added years to work for "end-time ministry." The apocalyptic struggle between the forces of good and evil, he was sure, had begun. He felt called to propagate that message throughout the world. With Ann he continues to do so.

The apparitions of Our Lady took on special meaning. Her appearances at Garabandal and Medjugorje reinforced for them past warnings through apparitions at Paris (1830), La Salette (1840), Lourdes (1858), and Fatima (1917). Walt and Ann maintain contact with a network of persons who report new apparitions, as they try to spread Our Lady's message to all who will listen. Walt also follows avidly the Marian Movement of Priests, who respond to the "interior locutions" of Father Stefano Gobbi. This mystic publishes messages addressed to priests by the Blessed Mother.

Ann works part-time as a librarian and supports Walt's end-time ministry. They were devoted to Pope John Paul II, whom they saw as encapsulating in his person the gargantuan struggles of these days. The terrorist attacks of September 11, 2001, confirmed their convictions regarding end times.

Spirituality in the Marketplace

While some married priests return to traditional spiritual exercises of earlier years and find there a renewed devotion, others take another route. The self-giving in marriage brings a new dimension to their religious life. Immersed in interpersonal relations with family, friends, and coworkers, these men and women cultivate, a spirituality no less profound. Although they do not resort as much to traditional practices of Catholic piety, they nevertheless reflect a spirituality in the marketplace.

BILL AND CINDY. A few married priests and their wives have tried to set up houses of prayer to which others can retreat from the busy world. They have done this in Canada and in the United States. By opening Mary's Fields, Cindy and Bill were able to fulfill such a dream in Connecticut. They began working with homeless, pregnant girls, sharing their home and providing counsel and care. This led to their setting up a retreat center. With the help of a board of directors, they bought a home with twenty-three acres for their ministry. The center contains sleeping quarters for twenty-eight, an indoor pool, tennis courts, a carriage house, and a pond.

Amid their many ministries, Cindy and Bill have raised six children. Aged thirteen to twenty-three, they all graduated from the local Catholic grammar school. Each child has chores at Mary's Fields and performs other jobs in the community. One cannot spend time with this family without perceiving their deep religious commitment.

Cynthia works full-time with what she calls her D.E. degree — Does Everything. Amazingly, she does many things well for her family and the house of prayer as planner, shopper, master cook, cleanup specialist, and manager of daily operations. To support themselves, Bill teaches Latin in the public high school, where he was recently designated Teacher of the Year. He performs the bulk of the counseling at Mary's Fields and, with his sons, manages most maintenance and repair work.

Bill served as a priest in the Allentown Diocese. While principal of a Catholic high school, he first met Cynthia, then a student. Eight years later they married and began the faith-filled ministry that has inspired them, their children, and countless others.

JEAN AND FRAN. For nineteen years, Jean taught and served as spiritual director at an archdiocesan seminary, then for nine more years pastored a seventeen-hundred-family parish. He offered spiritual guidance to young and old, married and single. Those skills were honed at the Seminaire St. Sulpice in Paris, France, and in graduate study at l'Université Laval, the University of Hartford, and North Carolina State University.

Upon marrying, Jean yearned to continue the work to which he was long dedicated, but found barriers within the Catholic community. He continued nevertheless his rich prayer life and spiritual counseling. Today Jean serves as chaplain and bereavement counselor at a hospice, as religion teacher at a community college, and as volunteer chaplain at a local hospital. When called upon, he also leads retreats and days of recollection for diverse groups.

Fran, a widow with grown children, proved to be his ideal partner. Originally an English teacher, she developed a passion for religious education, which became her life's work. With a master's degree in theology from St. Joseph's College after undergraduate studies at the College of New Rochelle, she served as director of religious education at parishes in Connecticut, Florida, and North Carolina. A gifted writer with the ability to apply scriptural texts to modern problems, Fran produces annually reflections on the Sunday Readings. These enjoy a wide circulation. She also has published articles in *National Catholic Reporter, Catechist, The American Catholic,* and the *Anthology of North Carolina Poets.*

Given to meditation and prayerful reflection, Jean and Fran remain busy, providing help to many. As Fran puts it, "I leave Jean free to spend his hour of prayer each morning, reflecting on the Scriptures and taking on the sufferings of the world. He leaves me free to 'word 'process' my prayers as I contemplate God." A delightful sense of humor is evident in all their human relations. In 2002 the Federation of Christian Ministries (FCM) presented them with the Anthony Soto Award for their spirit and vision in encouraging others to apply their talents to build up society.

On the Margins of Organized Religion

Under the influence of religious currents today, married priests and their wives have adopted other forms of spirituality. Some have become jaded by traditional religious practices, but still maintain a deep yearning for God. Robert E. Kennedy, S.J., described the experience in these terms:

> Many believers in God come up against the limits that their culture has imposed on their faith. They find they want to believe and hope and pray, but they can no longer accept faith that they perceive is based on untested authority, or on miracles, apparitions, private revelations, or a literal reading of Scripture that borders on the fantastic. Many adult Catholics sadly walk away from the Church because they have not found a vision of Catholicism that they can integrate into their mature experience of life. They are not interested in a new faith, or in watering down an old faith, or in arguing with authority figures about moral issues or old heresies.[11]

While some walk away under the strain of this reality, others continue their passionate quest for the Living God. Kennedy, who besides being chairman of the Theology Department at St. Peter's College is also a Zen teacher, writes, "In Zen they can find their own path, one that leads them to self-knowledge, deeper prayer, and lively service to others."[12] He views Zen Buddhism not as a religion, but as a way of seeing life that can enhance one's religious faith.

Many married priests and their wives have followed that route. Others have found renewal in Celtic spirituality, creation spirituality, or other approaches. These lead to a deeper prayer life, a greater self-awareness, and a more inspired giving of themselves to those in need.

Spirituality often is found at the margins of organized religion, moving its practitioners in the direction of the mystical and contemplative, where doctrine is less important and the experience of God all important. This awareness often leads to a renewed commitment to their traditional faith, as the example of the following two married priests and their wives shows.

FRANK AND MARIA. Throughout their history the Dominicans, the Order of Preachers, have tried to pass on the fruit of their contemplation (*contemplata aliis tradere*). That tradition is carried on even by those who no longer wear the garb of the Order. Frank was a Dominican priest and Maria, his wife, a religious and an educator. Although their marriage led them to different professional roles than before, elements of the Dominican training stayed with them.

Frank went on to spend thirty-one years in governmental relations in the transportation industry; Maria taught for forty years. As Frank explains, "Though the subject matter with which we dealt may not be spiritual . . . it is the manner in which one deals with it that shows what we are all about." They succeeded in their jobs, and continued to cultivate their inner life.

Eight years ago, Frank attended an intensive meditation retreat. Under the direction of a Jesuit, the retreat acquainted him with Zen Buddhist spiritual practices in the context of Christian spirituality. After that experience, Frank underwent training with Thomas G. Hand, S.J., at Mercy Center in Burlingame, California, and Robert E. Kennedy, S.J., in New York. Hand and Kennedy[13] studied Zen in Japan under the direction of the renowned Koun Yamada Roshi, and are recognized teachers of Christian and Buddhist meditation.

Frank has adopted a Zen Christian spiritual path that includes daily meditation, weekly communal meditation, and periodic interfaith Zen retreats. He does this as a member of the Zen Community of Baltimore/Clare Sangha, whose official Zen teachers are Sisters Janet Richardson, C.S.J.P., and Rosalie McQuaid, C.S.J.P. The experience has enriched him and his wife and resulted in greater involvement in their Catholic parish. They have learned to open their minds and hearts to the Living God and, as before, to give to others the fruit of their contemplation.

JIM AND DOROTHY. For many years, Jim was a well-known Sulpician seminary professor and administrator. He served as an adviser to the U.S. Catholic Conference of Bishops on spirituality and priestly life. In the turmoil that followed Vatican II, Jim resigned his canonical assignment for reasons personal and doctrinal. He found a job as a university administrator and, two years later, met and married Dorothy, a college professor.

Jim's long-standing interest in spirituality never left him. Today he is part-time leader and board member of an ecumenical institute for spiritual formation. He also serves as spiritual director to several, including a married priest and some Protestant ministers. Dorothy supports this ministry by accommodating a scattered calendar, identifying and procuring relevant books/readings, opening their home for spiritual direction sessions, and interacting with Jim about insights and practices of the spiritual life.

Jim remains a practicing Catholic lost in an urban parish where he prefers to obscure his background. Christian and Catholic at base, his spiritual bent is toward the contemplative, experiential, and psychological aspects of life in God, contrasted with a method more heavily doctrinal and conceptual. For him, the things of God and how God relates to us are far more fluid and amorphous than what is found in traditional Catholic spirituality. He thinks Meister Eckhart, the thirteenth-century Dominican mystic, was on to something when he prayed to God to "deliver me from God."

Summary

The anecdotal information given here is too thin to generalize. It would similarly be unfair to conclude about all celibate priests from the lives of John Vianney or Don Bosco, yet much can be learned from reflecting on the witness each has given. From the apostolic era to this day, married priests and their wives have given witness to the Christian message. They continue to do so. As with celibate clergy, deviations from their noble calling can be found. But also sanctity.

Few have articulated better the awakened spirituality of a married priest and his wife than my good friend Michael Machado. He wrote:

The spirituality of the priesthood has been enhanced by the spirituality of marriage. The union and communion of love between husband and wife, lived out each day with courage in the face of trials, can be a transforming union. It is a mutual self-giving that ends in a mutual self-recovery. In the mutual exchange of love each receives something they never had before. Progress in love involves the gradual disappearance of every form of deceit, dishonesty and selfishness that is detrimental to the union. At the same time it involves the acquisition of those qualities that bring greater harmony, peace and growth in holiness. As they learn to become less selfish, their capacity for self-giving is enhanced.... Seen in this light, marriage is not a second-order reality, inferior to the priesthood. It is the original matrix for the nurturing of a holy life, including a vocation to the priesthood.[14]

Most married priests and their wives are reticent to talk about their spirituality. Like most Christians, they pray without talking about it. While attending prayer groups and participating in liturgical celebrations, many prefer to take a back seat these days. They are more apt to pray at meals, observe Catholic feast days in the home, and devote spare time to a variety of services in the community. Theirs is a family spirituality.

Karl Rahner observed that the Christian of the future will be a mystic or nothing. The turmoil of contemporary life demands that. Married priests and their wives bear witness to that conviction.

Part Three

Personal Reflections

Chapter 10

My Journey

MY JOURNEY to the priesthood led me from a poor neighborhood in East Trenton, New Jersey, through study under the Felician Sisters in grammar school and the Franciscan Friars in high school, followed by philosophical studies at St. Mary's College in Orchard Lake, Michigan, and theological studies at Immaculate Conception Seminary in Darlington, New Jersey. A bout with tuberculosis interrupted my college work for one year (1954–5).

After ordination I served as an assistant pastor in a traditional Polish-American parish and part-time religion teacher at a nearby high school, then as a Latin teacher and rector at a seminary while doing weekend work for eleven years at a suburban parish. Intermingled was graduate study at Fordham University (M.A., 1966) and New York University (Ph.D., 1977).

After marriage I held various posts — research director at a trade association, branch chief at a state department of education, director of a university research center, education director at one trade association, executive director at another, dean of a business school in Poland, and executive director at a Christian social service agency. These activities rounded out my education.

God has guided me along diverse paths. In retirement I can now reflect on those experiences.

Preparation for Priesthood

The primary school where I spent my first nine years of formal education in the 1940s has closed. St. Hedwig's Parochial School, then run by over thirty Felician Sisters, numbered over a thousand students in kindergarten through grade nine, with each grade having two or three classes of about fifty students each.

The secondary school I attended in the late 1940s and early 1950s ended operation a generation ago. Trenton Catholic Boys High School, under the direction of more than twenty Conventual Franciscan priests, offered over eight hundred boys a good academic training and a challenging sports program. Forever closed.

The major seminary I entered in the late 1950s, Immaculate Conception in Darlington, New Jersey, surrendered its spacious grounds to a luxury housing development. In my day not only were all rooms filled but, with a projected doubling of enrollment, a new philosophy house was being planned. The neighboring Diocese of Trenton also held a successful financial drive to erect another major seminary. Everyone expected continued growth in vocations. No more so.

The high school where I first taught in the early 1960s, named after Pope Pius XII, was overcrowded. The new bishop started a drive to expand those school buildings and open two other high schools and a minor seminary. Then came the reversal. Pope Pius XII High School is no more, and even the new school named for Pope Paul VI was abandoned. Both closed.

A minor seminary opened in the diocese in 1965. For the first three years I served as Latin teacher, then for six years as rector. After I left, the school continued for another sixteen years. Then in 1990, after a quarter century, the experiment ended. Gone.

Those schools prepared many for life. Teachers and parents made sacrifices so that students could get a good education. Fond memories remain despite the sorrow at their closing.

Similarly my aspiration for the priesthood was almost derailed before it began. After two years as a seminarian, I contracted pulmonary tuberculosis and was banished for five months to a sanitarium. I spent my twentieth birthday at Donnelly Memorial Hospital in Trenton, New Jersey, followed by nine more months in recuperation at home. Noble figures preceded me. As seminarians, Pope Pius XII and Father Patrick Peyton of the Family Rosary Crusade endured the same long illness. My story, however, ended differently. With a plethora of vocations, bishops could afford to be selective. The bishop in Trenton,

New Jersey, my hometown, judged me a health risk and rejected me as a candidate for priesthood.

Bishop James McNulty of Paterson proved sympathetic to my plight. Not wanting to contradict the neighboring bishop, he recommended that I finish college studies on my own, and then apply to Paterson. If my health improved over the following two years, he promised to reconsider my candidacy. He kept his word. After graduating *magna cum laude,* I reminded him of his promise, and he authorized me to start the four-year theological program at Immaculate Conception Seminary in Darlington.

When a person earnestly wants something, he fights to overcome all obstacles. Once gained, he holds on even more. So it was, by the grace of God, with my priesthood.

Priestly Ministry

Not long after my ordination in 1961, the Second Vatican Council convened in Rome. It had a transforming effect on the entire church, not just its liturgy and ecumenical relations but also the structures of operation. The Church, and my life, would never be the same.

I spent the years of my clerical ministry in three locations: Passaic, Wayne, and Pompton Plains, all in New Jersey. First was the community of St. Joseph's in Passaic, where I served for three years as assistant pastor. This traditional Polish-American parish was formed at the turn of the twentieth century to serve immigrants from lands held by Russian, Prussian, and Austrian overlords. Their language and their faith bound them together.

The parish grew rapidly in the first half of the century, becoming the mother parish for five others. By the time I arrived in the early 1960s, it was a parish of mostly older people, with more funerals than weddings, and with diminishing enrollments in the elementary school as young people married and moved to more prosperous and mixed suburban neighborhoods. Polish remained the everyday language in sermons, in counseling, and in the confessional. I enjoyed working with the elderly, visiting them in their homes, bringing them the Eucharist, and sharing their pains and sorrows. They were a devout and long-suffering people.

A new bishop stormed into the diocese in 1963, intent on expanding Catholic education by setting up new high schools and a minor seminary. Before long he summoned me and told me to begin preparations to teach Latin in his planned minor seminary. This delighted me because, besides my love for Latin, this would give me the opportunity to further my education. I immediately enrolled at Fordham University in the Bronx and traveled back and forth for the next two years.

My second assignment took me as Latin teacher to Neumann Prep, the new diocesan minor seminary. The school opened in Wayne in 1965 at the close of the Second Vatican Council. Three years later a new bishop asked me to become rector. I accepted. To work with idealistic young men is an honor. They challenge you, frustrate you, and inspire you. For the next six years I headed Neumann, guiding its transition from seminary to prep school. When we opened, over a hundred seminary high schools dotted the land. In the following decade, all but a handful closed or changed their status. We were no different.

The third assignment, overlapping the second, was as weekend assistant at Our Lady of Good Counsel Parish in Pompton Plains. For the first year I lived in the rectory while the seminary buildings were under construction, then returned on weekends to help at liturgies and other celebrations for another ten years. I celebrated Masses, officiated at baptisms and weddings, and performed other sacramental rites in that community.

Barely a year passed after the close of the Vatican Council when in November 1966 Bishop Lawrence B. Casey of Paterson, New Jersey, announced his intention of organizing a senate of priests. He entrusted its formation to an ad hoc committee and over the next few months priests voted for a nineteen-member body. In January 1968, the first elected Senate of Priests for the Diocese of Paterson convened and chose Monsignor Joe Gallo as president and me as secretary. (I later served as vice-president.) All senators worked vigorously. In those first days, they installed a personnel board, started a priests' pension plan, set up training programs to educate priests on Council teachings, and aligned the clergy more closely with the struggles of the inner-city poor.

Some criticized the Senate for focusing too much on priests rather than the broader community. Of this valid criticism the senators were keenly aware. Father John Hill of Chicago recognized the same nationally when he wrote:

> We have not lost our sense of priority. We know that there are problems of more importance than whether or not there is a personnel board in the diocese. We have not forgotten Vietnam, Detroit, our decaying cities, the massive injustices meted out to black people in our day. But it will take a little time to get them in our sights.[1]

Bishop Casey welcomed these developments. Although senators felt awkward holding meetings without the bishop present, they kept him regularly informed about the results. A cordial partnership emerged. Casey always took pride in his relationship with priests, but he would readily intervene whenever he sensed the authority of Rome or of the bishops to be at stake.

In the next few years I served as one of two delegates from the diocese to the first gatherings of the National Federation of Priest Councils (NFPC). I attended the planning meeting in Des Plaines, Illinois, to discuss whether to have a federation, then the first two national conventions, first in Des Plaines, Illinois, followed by one in New Orleans. These events confirmed for me the necessity of reforms in the Catholic priesthood.

The issuance of *Humanae Vitae* in 1968 provoked consternation throughout the Catholic world, especially among clergy. The Diocese of Paterson was typical. In response to urgings by the apostolic delegate in Washington, Bishop Casey sent a letter to Rome indicating acceptance of this teaching by him and his priests. He gave no indication of the pastoral problems and the resultant turmoil. Younger clergy objected that it was dishonest to hide from Rome the true state of affairs at home. The climate in the diocese was different from that which the bishop had reported.

Because many priests were troubled over the proper approach in the confessional and in the pulpit, they gathered together privately to discuss the pastoral implications. Some had serious doubts about the wisdom of this teaching; others questioned its acceptance by the faithful; all were concerned about how to respond pastorally in this environment. A few urged rebellion. Younger clergy were disturbed that older pastors in the diocese proposed that a document of support for the pope be drawn up and that each priest be required to sign it. Such an action, younger priests were convinced, besides being damaging, would also be counterproductive.

The bishop responded cautiously. First he made known to the clergy his support for the encyclical; that explained his letter to Rome. Second, he recognized the anguish of married couples and the pastoral concerns of his priests, and respected the conscience of each. Third, he asserted nonetheless that if a priest publicly, through pulpit or press, taught the opposite of Rome's position, no option remained but to censure him; he did summon a few priests privately to discuss their public statements. Lastly, he prevailed on the older clergy to refrain from a signature-signing campaign; such actions would galvanize opposition and disrupt peace in the diocese. His approach averted public confrontation.

The year 1968 was memorable for me because of the formation of the NFPC, the assassination of Robert F. Kennedy, the accidental death of Thomas Merton, the chaotic Democratic Convention in Chicago, and the promulgation of *Humanae Vitae*. It also marked my appointment in June as rector of Neumann Prep, the Paterson diocesan minor seminary. For the next six years, I headed that school amid all the turbulence of the post–Vatican II era. My passion for the priesthood, moreover, resulted in continued involvement with the Federation, the diocesan senate, and all else that pertained to priests.

I joined the National Association for Pastoral Renewal (NAPR), the first of the reform groups after the Council, not because of a desire to marry. I was a happy and contented celibate with no yearning for marriage, but like Thomas Merton I realized that renewal of priestly life was needed, and that optional celibacy played a major role.

Upon becoming rector of Neumann Prep in 1968, I was eager to advance the religious and academic programs. Father Vincent Molloy as spiritual director promoted a healthy spirituality for young men and could be relied on to monitor that program well. I supported him fully. Knowing my desire to improve the science and math programs at the school, the Diocesan Superintendent of Schools recommended hiring a Presentation Sister who had an excellent reputation as a high school teacher of physics and calculus. Sr. Joan Sullivan proved a godsend. She challenged boys in the classroom and improved the academic program. Together we prepared the school for review by the Middle States Accrediting Commission, and gained full accreditation. In the course of those efforts, Joan and I fell in love.

Departure

When we realized our feelings for each other, Joan and I decided to depart as quietly and unobtrusively as possible. The pain of saying good-bye, the awkwardness of giving our reasons for leaving, and the reluctance to cause a public scene led us to this course of action. Church practice, moreover, urged priests to depart without fanfare and move to a distant region. We were prepared to do that.

The last Mass I celebrated publicly before leaving the Diocese of Paterson occurred on a Monday morning before a handful of people at Our Lady of Good Counsel Church in Pompton Plains. For eleven years I had worked in that community in good times and bad, through the assassinations of Martin Luther King and Robert F. Kennedy, through the ordeal of *Humanae Vitae* and its aftermath. Amid all the travails of the post–Vatican II era, I had grown to love those faithful parishioners.

Neither the bishop nor others in the diocese knew of my plans. On a Monday morning, my car was packed and ready for departure. But first the Mass. Strangely, I felt no worry, tension, or anxiety. I was at peace. As I gazed on the faithful that morning, an exhilarating joy came over me. I knew I would no longer see Joe and Eleanor, Paul and Jean, Bill and Barbara, the Filipino Sisters, and many stalwarts of that parish. But God had other plans.

The chapel where I had performed sacramental rites would be a memory. The confessional where I had absolved sins — mostly peccadilloes — no longer would hold me. Through the years, the Stations of the Cross, the Sacred Tabernacle against the wall, and the statue of Mary, all had been the focus of my attention.

I celebrated the Mass slowly, savoring each moment. After the Gospel I gave a short sermon — joyous, positive, and hope-filled — then lingered over the words of consecration. Communion with the parishioners enthralled me. In giving the final blessing and dismissing the congregation, I paused. They noticed nothing different as they hastily walked out of church. My thanksgiving after Mass was fervent. I divested, put on my coat, and departed for the last time.

I never said good-bye.

Arrival

Shortly after arriving in Washington, Joan and I met Holy Trinity's former pastor, Tom Gavigan. We told him that we were awaiting my dispensation from Rome, and wanted to marry at this Jesuit Church. He gave us papers to fill out and assured us that the moment we heard from Rome, the ceremony would follow. Six months later on a Monday, after my friend, the Chancellor in New Jersey, called to confirm that all was approved, I told Tom. He asked when we wanted the wedding. "This weekend," I blurted. "Sure enough," he said. And so, on Saturday, January 31, 1976, Joan and I married at the main altar of Holy Trinity Church, surrounded by sisters and brothers, family and friends.

A month after our wedding, I got a phone call from an official at the Washington Chancery. He requested that I stop by to sign papers. I made an appointment and, on the assigned date, appeared at the stately mansion next to the cathedral. An elderly monsignor greeted me and responded courteously. He said that he had a few papers from Rome related to my wedding, and suggested that I sign them.

Never having seen such documents, I read with care and reflection. The text in Latin was troubling. It treated me as a dishonorable person who was being disciplined because of immoral behavior. I recall at one time meeting a married priest in Minnesota who told me that when he went to get his dispensation, the chancery official related to him as though he were a first-class pervert unable to control his sexual appetite. He laughed at the absurdity but, to assuage Church officials, he signed the document. My treatment was not as gross, but I faced the prospect of acquiescing to a false depiction. I could not do that.

In preparing my petition for dispensation eight months earlier, I chose my words, rejecting disappointment in priesthood or denial of Christ and his teachings. I had fallen in love and asked for the Church's blessings. At no time did I consider my marriage immoral, nor my love for Joan perverse. I was willing to abide by the Church's discipline. But the documents presented a different version of events, and I was expected to endorse it.

I asked the monsignor, "What would happen if I did not sign this document?"

"Nothing," he answered. "I would simply note that you preferred not to sign this and file the document away."

"This does not affect the validity of my marriage, does it?"

"No, not at all."

"And what about Tom Gavigan, who performed the ceremony? Will he be called on the carpet or chastised for officiating at the wedding before securing my signature?"

"No. He won't even be aware."

I thought for a moment, and said, "Then I would rather not sign my name."

"Okay," he said, and put away the papers.

We shared pleasantries and I departed.

In succeeding months at Holy Trinity parish, Tom encouraged Joan and me to become active. In future years I became lector, minister to the sick, worship committee member and chairman; Joan a Eucharistic minister and instructor in the religious education program (CCD). Together one year, we led the convert training program (RCIA). I felt happy to minister once again.

When our son John arrived on St. Patrick's Day in 1978, the Holy Trinity community welcomed him at the waters of Baptism. Tom Gavigan officiated. Our birth announcement reflected our joy:

The Scriptures say that Elizabeth, in her later years, gave birth to a child whom Christ called the greatest born of woman. His name was John.

Neumann Prep, the school where we first met and labored together for five years, was named after a saintly bishop of Philadelphia. His name was John.

A good and holy pope opened the window onto the modern world and in so doing transformed our lives. His name was John.

In the 1960s, President Kennedy inspired us to a higher idealism and humanitarian concern. His name was John.

Joan's brother was the first to know of our commitment and be supportive of our plans. His name was John.

Tony's grandfathers on both sides were named John.

We rejoice in the birth of our son. HIS NAME SHALL BE JOHN.

In retrospect I recognize that I have been blessed with a beautiful wife — unfailingly kind, professionally competent, ever solicitous to the needs of our son. What more could I ask of God? Some priests marry and, either through choice or circumstance, never have children. That fate was almost ours. We were in our early forties when we married, and all but gave up hope of progeny. But two years later miraculously Joan gave birth at 45.

God blessed us. From the start, John showed himself to be intelligent and healthy. He excelled as a pianist, composing for the piano and playing trumpet in the school band. He was a good swimmer, competing successfully throughout his teen years. For the last three years of high school he gained honors as the school's top mathematician. He won early admission to Harvard, where he graduated with a concentration in philosophy in the year 2000. As proud father, I touted his accomplishments at every turn. One of my friends was led to ask one time, "Now how's that boy who walks on water?" Perhaps I did overdo it at times!

In later years, our son participated in the excellent catechetical programs at Holy Trinity parish, which prepared him for Penance, Eucharist, and Confirmation. I was especially delighted when among the catechists preparing him and us for those sacramental encounters were our friends — married priests and their wives.

Transitioning

In transitioning from clerical to secular life, the priest must get used to many things. No longer is he accorded the privileged place in the family, nor special deference in the community. It makes for awkward scenes.

One Sunday a short time after joining the parish, I engaged a young Jesuit priest in conversation in the back of the church. He was doing advanced study in theology. When I mentioned Hans Küng's name and his latest book, the cleric said, "Oh you shouldn't read stuff like that; it will only turn your mind." He did not know my background, so he related to me with clerical condescension. I quietly walked away.

Another incident involved my son. He took our status as normal and showed no awkwardness about it. In his high school religion class a Jesuit scholastic directed students to write a composition about a priest or nun they admired. My son raised his hand and asked if he could write about his mother and father. Speechless, the scholastic allowed it.

People occasionally are surprised to learn that I am an ordained and married Catholic priest, and that my wife is a former nun. Awareness of our past makes for amusing conversations. Not long ago, Joan and I talked with another couple at a party. The moment the woman discovered I was a priest who had married, she blurted out spontaneously, "How is it that you became disillusioned with the priesthood?"

I quickly responded, "I'm sorry, but I have never been disillusioned with the priesthood."

"Then . . . why?" she asked nervously.

"I fell in love," I said.

She smiled. Our conversation continued and, as time went on, we bridged her discomfort. She and her husband became our friends.

On another occasion, a staff member told a female worker that I was a married priest. She replied, "No. That can't be. Catholic priests don't marry. I know. I am a Catholic." She refused to accept what they were telling her. In succeeding days, we spoke together many times, and our friendship grew.

At meetings such as these, shock gives way to friendship. My respect for Catholic tradition and continued involvement in church activities destroyed negative stereotypes. Further conversations brought about a deeper religious understanding. On many occasions, I sensed a breakthrough.

Ministry of Married Priests

A passion for reform of priestly life led me even after marriage to continue my affiliation with priest movements. I became a member of the Fellowship [later Federation] of Christian Ministries (FCM), CORPUS — the Association for a Married [later Inclusive] Priesthood, and Celibacy Is The Issue (CITI). I was appointed to the first CORPUS board of directors, representing the D.C.-Maryland-Virginia region. In that capacity I co-chaired a task force to rewrite the organization's mission and objectives, and later chaired the search committee for a new executive director. Speaking for our region, I strongly urged holding annual conventions, and agreed to host the first, in Washington.

The new canon law of the Roman Catholic Church, issued in 1983, says in Canon 290, "Once validly received, sacred ordination never becomes invalid." And although the law forbids laicized priests from exercising sacramental ministry, it also recognizes occasions when they should minister. Canon 976, for example, says, "Even though he lacks the faculty to hear confessions, every priest validly and licitly absolves from every censure and sin any penitent who is in danger of death, even if an approved priest is present."

When the jet airliner crashed into the Pentagon on September 11, 2001, one of the first on the scene to minister was a married priest.

My friend Jack had been counseling in a neighboring prison when police told him about the tragedy. As they departed to the scene, the officers suggested that Jack accompany them. Grabbing the sacred oils that he kept in the glove compartment of his car for such emergencies, Jack hurried to minister to the dying. This conformed with Catholic Church law, which says in Canon 1003, "every priest is allowed to carry blessed oil with him so that in need he can administer the sacrament of the anointing of the sick."

On one occasion, I traveled to a distant state for a relative's baptism. When the family gathered for the celebration, the pastor was called away. Knowing my background and status, he authorized me to perform the baptism. I was delighted to do so, validly and licitly. Canon 230 says, "When the need of the Church warrants it and when ministers are lacking, lay persons, even if they are not lectors or acolytes, can also supply for some offices: exercising the ministry of the word, presiding over liturgical prayers, conferring baptism, and distributing Holy Communion in accord with the prescriptions of law."

There are other occasions in which I have been called upon to minister. My next door neighbor, Charlie, was a Brooklyn Jew, justly proud of his heritage. He married Dorotha, a Southern Baptist from Alabama, and enjoyed more than fifty years in a blessed marriage. They were good and solicitous neighbors. Today, in an unpredictable development, all their grandchildren are Roman Catholics. Nearing death, Charlie asked that I officiate at his burial. I rejoiced at the honor.

In response to his request, I visited the local synagogue and secured copies of the Jewish burial service. At the grave, I recited the Psalms of David, and Charlie's son, Gary, read in Hebrew a son's prayer for his father. Afterwards, we returned to my home where neighbors and friends gathered. There, I invited all to share with us their favorite "Charlie story," whereupon they recalled memories of his goodness, his friendliness, his unselfishness.

Opportunities like these arise without searching for them. I can only respond as I did when God first called: "*Adsum!* Here I am, Lord. I come to do your bidding."

For seven years I worked at a Christian social service agency that counseled women dealing with unplanned pregnancies and assisted couples in preparing for adoptions, domestic and international. The agency's views on the sanctity of life conform with the teachings of the Catholic Church. As executive director, I was often called upon to speak before church groups and business organizations in hope of gaining moral and financial support. My theme was always the same — the sanctity of life, the beauty of adoption. In churches, I would use a religious tone, employing scriptural passages and religious images; with business organizations, a secular tone, describing the plight of women, the innocence of children, and the joys of adoption.

One Sunday morning I was invited to speak before a small Baptist community. Never before had I even been inside a Baptist Church! When I arrived, the church custodian told me that the pastor was out of town and could not get back in time. Would I lead the services? Flabbergasted, I looked for the leader of music ministry and asked him to follow the usual schedule of service and I would preach at the designated time. The service went well. I was happy afterward to hear accolades from a warm and friendly congregation. They were aware neither of my background nor of my ignorance of the Baptist Church. I knew Christ, and that was all that mattered.

I have spoken before many congregations — Episcopal, Lutheran, Presbyterian, Methodist, nondenominational. The pulpits of my Catholic Church are closed to me, but the pulpits of other churches remain open. I am delighted to be able to preach the message of Christ to those who would hear it.

◆ ◆ ◆

At important moments on my journey, married priests fostered my career and enriched my life. I owe them much.

During doctoral studies in educational administration at New York University, I befriended a distinguished faculty member who counseled and encouraged me. He chaired my dissertation team and helped me gain a fellowship in Washington. Decades earlier, Paul had been a diocesan priest and assistant superintendent of schools in Steubenville, Ohio.

In one career move, I applied for an administrative position at George Washington University, and ended up among the four finalists. After the last set of interviews, the dean took me aside and told me that the search team had selected me. I then felt obliged to tell him that, although my resume gave no indication, I was a Catholic priest who had married. The dean stretched out his hand to me and said, "So am I." In earlier years, Gene had served as a diocesan priest in Charleston, South Carolina.

Marrying in our forties, Joan and I needed to save our pennies. We had no pensions, no accumulated savings, no family inheritances. We applied ourselves to our profession and the Lord blessed us. Through my good friend, Joe, we got sound financial advice. He guided us through insurance coverage, diversified investments, and long-term-care planning. Our retirement, as a result, will be more secure. Joe had served as a diocesan priest and high school principal in Allentown, Pennsylvania.

Without the help of Paul, Gene, and Joe, all happily married priests, life would have been different.

Family Relations

Joan and I come from staunchly Catholic families. For many generations as far back as we know, the Sullivan/Lynches and the Kowalski/Padykulas remained stalwart Roman Catholics. These two, the Irish and the Poles, have similar histories. From time immemorial, powerful neighbors tried to suppress their culture, their language, and their religion. Yet, neither the Irish nor the Polish would surrender what they held dear. The binding force for each as a nation has always been their Roman Catholicism. The more persecuted, the more they turned to their faith, which united them and made them strong.

Joan's mother and father, natives of the beautiful Dingle Bay area in County Kerry with its nearby Lakes of Killarney, cherished their Catholic heritage. Settling in New York City, they sent each of their four children to Catholic elementary and secondary schools. One son entered the minor seminary, and one daughter the convent. The two boys graduated from Notre Dame University. The other daughter married a Fordham graduate and raised five children. Michael Sullivan, deputy prison warden in New York and longtime daily communicant, and Hannah Lynch Sullivan, faithful and loving mother, provided well for their offspring. Each child married in the Catholic Church and keeps to this day his or her Roman Catholic identity.

My parents, similarly, set an example. Anthony T. Kowalski, a hard-working potter, and Mary Padykula Kowalski, devoted wife and daily communicant, guided their offspring in the faith. All six children were baptized and confirmed at St. Hedwig's Church in Trenton. Each child attended the parish grammar school and each has kept lifelong a commitment to Catholicism. Today, my oldest sister, Ronnie, is completing fifty-five years as a Felician nun. Other relatives have also devoted their lives to Church ministry: my first cousin Elvine, now a missionary in Africa, is completing fifty-four years as a Felician nun, and my first cousin Lou, forty-six years as a priest.

Against the background of these two families, the marriage of a Catholic nun from one and a Catholic priest from the other was alarming and unprecedented. Under similar circumstances, other families have disowned their offspring. Not so with the Sullivans, nor with the Kowalskis. I like to think they were too immersed in Christ to respond with anything but love. Joan and I were fortunate to sustain the affection and support of every family member. The arrival of our son, John, in our middle forties solidified that bond. He served as the catalyst that drew us together even more.

◆ ◆ ◆

When I come upon Catholics disturbed by rapid changes in the Church today, I am solicitous. These people must be respected. They remind me of my saintly mother — a good woman passionately dedicated to the Church. With little formal schooling, she had wisdom far beyond this world. My decision to marry was hard on her. She loved me dearly and took pride in my priestly work, but the marriage of a priest to her was unthinkable. She could not bring herself to attend my wedding. I understood. With my sister, Ronnie, she stayed at home and spent the entire day in prayer. Yet, never did she reject Joan nor me, never did she show harshness toward us, never did we experience from her anything but kindness. In succeeding years, my whole family embraced us with love and respect. They cultivated a special fondness for Joan and doted over our son.

For my mother, changes in the Church were troublesome. As with traditional Polish women, shaking hands in Church at the kiss of peace made her uncomfortable. A slight bow of the head to a neighbor is their custom. Nor would she touch the sacred chalice or take Communion in the hand. She considered herself unworthy. My explanations of theological matters satisfied her, and she remained always a faithful daughter of the Church.

My father too was a loyal Catholic. Church usher, parochial school supporter, member of the parish Holy Name Society — his commitment to the Roman Catholic Church endured to the end. He worked hard in the potteries and proudly maintained fidelity to God and country. He died of esophageal cancer when I was fifteen, so I didn't get to know him well enough.

Today, whenever I meet Catholics of strongly traditional bent, I recall my parents and my wife's parents. They were all loyal and conservative Catholics of another generation, attending novenas, praying the rosary, listening to Father Coughlin in the 1930s and Bishop Sheen in the 1950s. Changes in the Church surprised them, but in the end they acquiesced to everything.

Traditionalists these days can be obnoxious to progressives, but reformers in those days were at times insensitive to traditionalists. Today all must show increased tolerance and charity.

◆ ◆ ◆

A century ago my family split up over a conflict in the Polish Roman Catholic community in Scranton, Pennsylvania. That controversy resulted in the first major schism in the Catholic Church in America. During that melee, my grandfather Jan chose to remain Roman Catholic; his brother Walenty joined with Father, later Bishop, Francis Hodur to establish the Polish National Catholic Church. Our families, from that day forward, went their separate ways.

Knowing details of that controversy, I was heartened to hear Bishop James Timlin, head of the Roman Catholic Diocese of Scranton, speak in words reminiscent of Pope Paul VI. On the occasion of the centennial observance of the Polish National Catholic Church in Scranton, he met with Church leaders of that group and told them:

> I come to you, and with profound sorrow I beg your forgiveness for every offense, misunderstanding, unkind act, mistaken judgment or any other thought, word or deed ever committed against you through prejudice, thoughtlessness or suspicious misgivings on the part of anyone in the Roman Catholic community. And I pledge on the occasion of this meaningful anniversary that my desire, as long as I live, will be to ever strive to restore the unity that was once ours.[2]

Such sentiments give us great hope. They are too late to restore unity among relatives long gone, but the larger family of Christians can benefit from them. My labors among Christians of different denominations through the social service agency I headed has left me in awe. These Christians have preserved elements of the Gospel which at times are lost in my own community. Like Bishop Timlin, we must humbly acknowledge our faults and stretch out our hands in friendship.

◆ ◆ ◆

We have been on a unique journey. Joan, like me, departed from home at age seventeen to enter church ministry. If one counts from the time Joan entered the convent and I the seminary to the time we each left our canonical assignments to marry, one would count forty-eight years — beautiful, fruitful days during which, faithful to the call of Christ, we helped many. Peers and students bear witness to the success of those labors. We have no regrets. Those were happy and blessed times. We would do it all over again.

If those years had been spent in military service, each of us would be receiving pensions, education credits, and PX privileges. We would also bask in the respect of a grateful nation. But ours was religious, not military, service. Therefore nothing. Few former clerics and nuns receive pensions, and rarely do they request one; they enjoy no special privileges in the Church, nor do they seek after them. Even activities allowed to the average layperson, like teaching and ministering to the sick, are often denied. They may not, in the eyes of some, deserve gratitude, but rejection and discrimination from Church officials? Surely Christ would respond differently.

◆ ◆ ◆

The reality of my priesthood was brought home to me when my sister Jean lay dying of ovarian cancer at age fifty-six. Weak and emaciated, she could barely speak. Stumbling through words of comfort, I bent over her, when suddenly she grabbed my hands and whispered, "Tony, give me your blessing." I instinctively shrunk back, but she grasped me firmly. Where she mustered all that strength, I'll never know, but she held tightly and insisted, "Tony, you are a priest and will always be a priest. I am asking for your priestly blessing."

Tears came to my eyes as I stood stunned. From the start Jean had accepted my decision to marry; she also recognized how much priesthood meant to me. I recall how she smothered my son with kisses every time she saw him. I could only obey her request.

The words came haltingly to my lips, "May Almighty God bless you," I stammered, "the Father...and the Son...and the Holy Spirit." Feeling as though I was doing this for the first time, I made a large Sign of the Cross over her...then...we embraced. Shortly after that, she died.

Chapter 11

Priests in Transition

W HAT DOES our Gracious God ask of me? All my life I tried to be faithful, but now I faced a new world, a loving relationship, a challenging environment. After nine years as seminarian and fourteen as Catholic priest, I married the former Sister Joan Sullivan and began working at a trade association. Marriage and secular employment demanded no less fidelity to my God. The year was 1976.

Priests and nuns in transition travel varied, not always tranquil, paths. God, however, watches over them. Joan had taught in Catholic primary and secondary schools, and enjoyed broad respect as an educator. Her talents were obvious. After participating on visiting teams for the Middle States Accrediting Commission, she invariably was offered a job, usually by the chairman of the accreditation team. The same good fortune greeted her first interview in Arlington, Virginia, when the head of an educational research firm hired her. God also blessed me. Former head of a high school seminary, holding a fellowship in our nation's capital, and about to gain a doctorate from New York University, I had an easy transition.

We enjoyed job security, but yearned for more. This yearning has been described as "having a monkey on your back." I prefer to call it zeal for the ministry to which our Saving God summons us. The ceremony of ordination made that clear: "The Lord has sworn and will not change his mind. You are a priest forever according to the order of Melchizedek" (Ps. 110:4).

Priesthood was my life. Through prayer and reflection in those early days of marriage, I understood that something beyond my job impelled me. The plight of the poor, the sick, and the elderly had always been a chief concern. In time I recognized in married priests and their wives a special need. Some had an easier time in transition than others, but all faced problems of one kind or another: a job...a worshiping community...special circumstances of health and family. No two were the same. I tried, therefore, to help them in securing a livelihood, while staying faithful to the God who called them.

My avocation would be among those who had pledged their lives to the Gospel but found themselves outside canonically established church structures — women and men after years in Church service surviving apart from those surroundings. And survival was difficult. Deprived of a community with similar ideals and aspirations, they struggled to find their way. Their changed state of life challenged them to apply the Good News in a chaotic world, often without the support of family and friends, amid misunderstanding of loved ones who could not accept the decisions they made.

Finding the Resigned

A federally sponsored internship in Washington gave me access to governmental agencies. With access came the freedom to visit not only those offices, but also state, local, and private educational units. This became my passport to friendship. Hearing of a former clergyman at one of those offices, I discretely paid him a visit. There followed warm conversation and instant rapport. Lasting friendships were borne from such meetings.

On one of those travels I met Joe, formerly a monsignor and coordinator of Catholic education in New Jersey, now director of the federal agency responsible for outreach to private schools. He was just a name from the past, but we immediately connected because of mutual friends, New Jersey roots, and a common priesthood. In dozens of offices, other married priests appeared. At the Department of Education I found Jack and Joe in Elementary/Secondary, and another Joe in Higher Ed; then Ken at the U.S. Mint, Tony at the Pentagon, Carl and Shane at USAID, and Vic with the Social Security Administration.

Trade associations provided a vast network of contacts — Ted with trucking, Arnie serving the blind, Joe with Independent Testing Labs,

Mick and Horace serving the elderly, and many more. At neighboring school systems I met Jim in Fairfax County, John in Baltimore City, and George in Montgomery County. At universities there was Michael in Frostburg, Girard at George Mason, and two Tonys at Georgetown. Outside the government and academia they also were found — Maury in housing, Bob with hospitals, and Sean at the United Nations. Wherever I turned, ex-clergymen abounded.

Counseling the Ex-Cleric

Early on I learned about the extraordinary work of Warren Barker, a former Jesuit who wed in the late forties, when married priests were not well received either in the job market or in the church community. Securing a job was difficult for him because religious leaders refused to provide a transcript of credits or documentation of academic degrees. Nevertheless Warren persevered, took a job with the federal government, and rose to positions of prominence. That proved fortuitous. When the exodus from clerical and religious life began in the 1960s, he was positioned to counsel others. At his retirement celebration years later, the auditorium was filled with dozens of grateful former clergy and former nuns.

In the 1960s and 1970s, Bearings for Reestablishment played an important role. Funded with a contribution from Chicago insurance magnate Clement Stone, the agency helped men and women leaving ministry to get their bearings in secular society. From its main office in New York and through a series of offices across the country, Bearings made a difference in the lives of many. John Mulholland aided those in the Washington area, giving regular weekend workshops that at their height averaged forty or fifty participants. This dedicated layman taught Catholic and Protestant clergy and nuns the basic skills needed to get a job. He was a master at it.

George Spellman became another prime mover in the counseling of those in transition. As executive director of Joint Action for Community Service (JACS), he hired some and counseled many more. To carry on the work more broadly, George set up the Warren Barker Foundation. In the course of twenty years, he and the foundation helped countless men and women, including provincials of religious orders, principals of Catholic schools, and an array of priests and nuns at every level. I was privileged to serve on that board.

Counselors of those in transition followed a similar pattern. When reached by phone, they would invite the person out for lunch or to their office. Listening to their plight and sharing one's own resulted in a bond of trust. The stories varied. Some had endured painful assignments under cruel pastors or administrators, and bore psychological scars. Many were happy with their ministry but fell in love; they would have liked to continue their pastoral work, but came up against the reality of Church law. Some flew in to Washington to check the job market before making their final departure; others arrived with everything they owned and with meager prospects of work. Each had different needs.

By the time board members met them, most priests had made up their minds to leave. Dissuading or discouraging them was not an option. They had already decided to move from their canonical assignment and asked only for help in making that transition. At times one felt compelled to describe the weak job market, but even then one tried to be positive and helpful. Those transitioning needed to realize that they would neither profit themselves nor promote their happiness if they wallowed in self-pity or bitterness. They had to put aside hurts if they were to be truly happy. Most learned quickly.

Board members advised them about assessing their talent, preparing a resume, meeting employers, and responding in an interview. Usually counselors gave them names and phone numbers of three other married priests working in fields where they might apply their talents. The rest was up to them. Each contact could lead to other introductions. As the network expanded, a job offer would come along, frequently from the most unlikely source.

Some never returned. After securing a job, they began a new life and wanted to break with the past. But others maintained a close friendship that has endured. They still show up at annual days of prayer or social gatherings for former clergy and wives.

Starting New Ministry

Not only priests came to our doors, but also sisters. Once a modest nun from a conservative religious community visited me after changing into lay clothes at a friend's house. A gifted linguist, Pat had good interpersonal skill and exuded warmth and professionalism. With the help of a married priest friend, she gained a job with the U.S. State Department, where language fluency served her well.

Pat was later stationed at the U.S. embassy in El Salvador during the savage slaying of four American Church women. One of the first to come upon that grizzly scene, she knew each woman and had entertained them at her apartment a few days earlier. When U.S. officials heard further death threats, they whisked Pat away and reassigned her to Germany. Serving at the U.S. embassy when the Berlin Wall fell, she took part in that grand celebration. Hers was an exciting and distinguished career with the State Department.

Another competent and professional nun similarly impressed me. After an interview at the American Bankers Association (ABA), I hired her, only to have her stolen away in a short time by the executive director of another trade association. Angela became administrative assistant and then personnel director at the American Association for Retired Persons (AARP). Later she assumed a similar position at another trade organization. Her talents were put to good use.

Not all faced success and excitement. Although a few rose to the top of their profession as executive directors, TV commentators, and university administrators, others spent years in drudgery work, with little chance of advancement. Often they had given up respected positions as pastors and administrators to undertake jobs at clerical and secretarial levels. Some endured staff cutbacks and walked unemployment lines. When children came along, the pressure to succeed added to their burdens. A few went through hard times.

On one occasion, my neighbor invited Joan and me for supper. She was hosting a married priest and wanted to share with us his story. Jim had been a missionary in South America and in the course of his ministry fell in love with a native woman. After marrying, he tried to gain a job in the same community but was prevented by the archbishop, who sent out word that no one should hire him. This left them destitute. After a few months, Jim's family in America came to the rescue by sending money, enabling him to return with his wife to the States. When I met him, he and his family were living comfortably — he as assistant superintendent of a public school system and his wife as a medical school student.

What followed made his story even more poignant. He said that the local pastor in Southern Virginia once paid them a visit. Jim responded to the knock on his door and, when he opened, the priest said, "I want to invite you to our Church. With your Irish name and your wife's Hispanic features, you two must surely be Catholics." "No, we're not," replied Jim, as he closed the door. He was unable to shake the bitterness of those long days in poverty. Neither he nor his wife would acknowledge their past; they wanted nothing more to do with the Catholic Church.

Another priest phoned me for help. In his late fifties, he had long worked as a Jesuit high school teacher, but now as a married man faced unemployment. He secured a part-time job, but in the market of the day was unable to gain enough income to support his family. Try as I might, I could not find him a job. Each time he phoned, his voice sounded more desperate. He later moved away and I never heard from him again.

Fortune favored others. To go from assistant professor of Sacred Scripture at the Church's national pontifical university to senior cataloguer of Hebrew language books at the Library of Congress might appear a logical step, but the transition of my friend Peter was not immediate. Before coming to Washington he trained at Rome's Pontifical Biblical Institute and taught Scripture at the New York Archdiocesan Seminary. His marriage to Clare, a former Benedictine sister, foreclosed further work for the Church. He explored a wide variety of opportunities. At last he found a job where his knowledge of Semitic languages and skills honed in scholarly research could sustain him.

Nat too had a good transition. A former Jesuit, he took a crash course in diplomacy at the State Department. His first assignment landed him in Teheran as the Ayatollah Khomenei took charge of the revolution. Nat settled in as Moslem militants periodically strafed the embassy. He endured for nine months amid sieges and constant stress. Later assignments at embassies in Rome, Antwerp, and Tokyo provided more peaceful surroundings. He briefly came out of retirement to help at the American Embassy in Australia.

Not all transitions were that exciting. A few men, after starting a job, faced cutbacks or downsizing. If in their fifties and sixties, they found such actions troublesome, because opportunities for a job at that age are vastly diminished. The blow to one's self-esteem cannot be adequately described. Yet many survived and experienced what the rest of the world does — self-doubt, uncertainty, instability. As in every family, moreover, their children often had growing pains, religious doubts, and ethical lapses. God did not spare them.

One evening I got a phone call from Brazil. My old friend and classmate, Arthur, whom I had not seen in thirty years, was on the line. We had grown up together in Trenton, New Jersey, attended the same Catholic grammar and high schools, and then headed off for priestly study — he to the Franciscan and I to the diocesan seminary. Even before ordination, Arthur volunteered as a missionary to South America. A few years later he met and married Vilma, a native Brazilian, with whom he had two sons named after his Franciscan heroes, Francis, and Elias. In our telephone conversation he asked about returning to the States with his family so that his boys could get a good education and he could more adequately support them. Would I help? Joan and I eagerly said yes.

Despite the poor job market, we were determined to help them. They arrived — Vilma, Arthur, Francis, and Elias — and we welcomed them warmly. At first, speaking English was a problem. Even Arthur had difficulty with some phrases, for he had been away too long. But the boys were young and in two years were speaking like native Americans. Vilma too progressed rapidly, taking a job as nurse's aid in a rest home, then at a university hospital where she hoped to start studying nursing. After a few months they moved to their own apartment and were able to support themselves.

Because of his fluency with Portuguese, Spanish, and English, Arthur secured a job at the Brazilian bank in Washington. When financial reversals occurred in Brazil, he lost his job. He then worked as a clerk in a drug store, but never got what he had hoped for in salary and prestige. In sadness, the family returned to Brazil and Arthur resumed the hospital administration job he had earlier held. The boys vowed they would return. Today, Francis and Elias live in the States, one with a successful career in computers and the other completing college. Arthur and Vilma remain in Brazil.

My journeys with priests in transition acquainted me with many missionaries who had married abroad and returned with their brides. Some were biracial couples; many spoke diverse languages. They faced added burdens brought about by cultural and linguistic differences. Most adjusted well.

Organizing the Dispersed

In the late 1970s married priest couples came together on a larger scale in the Greater Washington, D.C., area when they discovered the plight of David. A former religious education director in a Midwestern diocese, Dave married a nurse and moved to Northern Virginia. Because of a scarcity of jobs, he began working with a roofing construction firm. As fate would have it, on one of those assignments he fell off the roof and ruptured his spine, causing permanent injury. His wife was in her seventh month of pregnancy. When married priests heard about this misfortune, they organized a benefit social event. Some also agreed to give monthly support until Dave and Peg could get on their feet. Peg was a nurse and, not long after delivering their son, went back to work.

At about the same time I became aware of a community in the Washington, D.C., area called the Sunday Bunch. Two former Jesuits and their wives — Joe and Kathy, Carl and Pat (see chapter 6) — gathered together in each other's homes every Sunday for prayer. Soon they attracted others, mostly married priests and their wives. As attendance grew, they continued to cultivate a warm friendship and camaraderie. Joyous music and stimulating theological reflections bound them together. They created a wholesome environment for those disenfranchised from their Church community.

Experiences like these motivated married priests and their wives in Maryland, Virginia and the District of Columbia to organize. Three of us — George in the District of Columbia, Vic in Maryland, and I in Virginia — met, pooled mailing lists, and sent out invitations for a day of prayer and reflection. The response was immediate and encouraging. The success of that gathering reinforced the resolve to do more. Parties, summer picnics, and meetings with prominent theologians followed.

An early supporter was Bishop Frank Murphy of the Baltimore Archdiocese. At first, I felt apprehensive about his attending our meetings. Knowing that some married priests harbored bitter memories of bishops, I feared that anger or disrespect might break out. My anxieties were groundless. Frank showed up in turtleneck shirt and jacket, and blended with the group. When called upon to say a few words, he spoke softly and disarmed everyone. He began by expressing gratitude to each person for the years of service given to the Church, and then he encouraged them in their prayer life. All loved him for it. He was a giant among men.

Much has occurred in the years since those first meetings. The gatherings for annual days of prayer continued. Participants found inspiration from one another and from friends who joined in discussion and reflection. These included F. X. Murphy, C.S.S.R., of Xavier Rynne fame; Sr. Theresa Kane, a leader of women religious; Gino Baroni, the inner-city social worker and priest; Walter Burghardt, S.J., famed preacher and Jesuit theologian; Eugene Walsh, S.S., distinguished liturgist and seminary professor; Gerard Sloyan, national leader in liturgy and religious education; and many more. Their presence gave comfort on the journey.

In 1988, this Maryland-D.C.-Virginia group hosted the first national conference for married priests under the auspices of CORPUS, the newly restructured national association for a married priesthood. The historic gathering met at American University. Hearts were moved, old friendships revived, and new acquaintances made as priests and wives renewed their commitment to the Lord. About four hundred attended. CORPUS continued to hold annual conferences in different regions of the country. After six more years, the

Washington area group volunteered to run another conference, this time in Northern Virginia. The same camaraderie prevailed.

For twenty-five years, married priests and wives in the Maryland-D.C.-Virginia region have been meeting together. Sometimes pastors and religious superiors hosted them, sometimes the Knights of Columbus or CARA (The Center for Research in the Apostolate) rented them their auditoriums, at other times different Christian churches welcomed them. Each event has been a blessing. These gatherings refreshed spirits and renewed a commitment to Christ, to the Church, and to priesthood.

Predicting the Future

Since the early days of our gatherings, many brethren have died. Several stalwarts of the movement were added to the roll call of deceased — including Joe Sere, who wore sandwich boards in front of the first CORPUS Convention; F. X. Murphy, who supported and entertained married priests at many of their meetings; and Bob Flanagan, always affable and faithful to those gatherings.

What will the future hold? Resigned priests and their wives are increasingly graying and moving around less sure-footed than before. Their numbers are dwindling. Not that priests are no longer leaving the clerical state. They are. But most who leave today no longer wish to be associated with any organized group of priests.

Tom Brokaw called those who fought in the Second World War "the greatest generation." I feel similarly about those who caught the spark of the Second Vatican Council and, under the influence of the Holy Spirit, made life choices undreamed of. They still live with that dream. For them the Second Vatican Council remains a vital source of strength. Its documents awakened them to the beauty of God's creation and aroused in them a renewed commitment to Christ.

They concur with Cardinal Bernardin, who said, "I find it very helpful — and at times, simply necessary — to return again and again to the Council's teachings. There is such richness and breadth in their vision and perspective that I never tire of the task." And they concur with John Paul II, who called Vatican II "the great grace bestowed on the Church of the twentieth century; there we find a sure compass by which to take our bearings in the century now beginning."

Bert Peeters of Belgium summed it up best when he wrote:

> Within a few years the present generation of married priests will have gone. They have to transmit to the priests of tomorrow, most of whom will be married, a new type of secularized priesthood, continuing the dream of the worker-priests, men and women, married and celibate, active in a parish or in the hard world of today where Christians have to implement the Kingdom of God.[1]

We may never see the day of change. That is not important. What is important is that we prepare the way with joy, with hope, with love.

Chapter 12

A Nurturing Parish

I N TRANSITIONING to secular life, priests and nuns yearn for a vibrant parish where they can continue to grow, interact, and be
nourished. As Paul A. Janowiak has written almost poetically:

> Liturgical memory and practice cradle our immediate reality and
> invite its transformation and consecration, and (out of the con-
> text of our faithful gathering) orient the future hopes and dreams
> of a waiting world.[1]

At seminaries and formation houses, they had learned to esteem the
liturgy in all its majesty and, despite their changed status, they still
crave those treasures. Yet few Catholic parishes offer them.

For devout followers of Christ, such deprivation can be devastat-
ing. Search as they might in churches, colleges, and chapels, those
transitioning fail too often in their quest for good liturgy and sound
preaching. The parish that supplies these in a de-clericalized climate
of brothers and sisters in Christ is an exception. That community becomes a magnet for the masses, an oasis in an arid wasteland, and a
threat to uneasy diocesan officials.

To be members of a Catholic community where sermons are well
prepared and liturgies tastefully celebrated, where laity and clergy
interact with one another as sisters and brothers respectful of each
other's gifts, is a great blessing. Few experience it. Yet for three
decades, since arriving in the D.C. area in June 1975, Joan and I
have known such a community, the Jesuit-led Holy Trinity Parish in
Georgetown.

This parish nurtures the lives of good and talented members. Its
liturgies, especially the Family Masses, are always festive, with tasteful music and full participation of the faithful. Preaching especially

191

stands out. Through the years superb homilists like Regis Duffy, O.F.M., Walter Burghardt, S.J., William McFadden, S.J., Robert Waznak, S.S., and James Greenfield, O.S.F.S., regularly manned the pulpit. Nor has the homiletic skill of resident clergy been lacking.

Having the professional staff of the Georgetown University Liturgy Center nearby helped. These gifted liturgists guided the parish to a renewal consistent with the reforms of Vatican II. Without them, the community could not have sustained its spirited and tasteful mode of worship, making Trinity a mecca for thousands in the Greater Washington, D.C., area.

Many former seminarians and former nuns are found in the congregation. Their backgrounds in religious education, liturgy, and counseling prepared them well for ministry. Some of them are also natural leaders, heading committees, organizing social services, and serving on the parish council. Their talents are put to good use.

Pastoral Leadership

Throughout my thirty years of membership in the community, I have witnessed outstanding pastoral leadership at Holy Trinity. Loyal sons of Loyola, these Jesuits brought Ignatian spirituality to the forefront of parish life. Each pastor fostered lay involvement, encouraging to ministry talented parishioners, female and male. Serving normally six-year terms, these remarkable Jesuits — Jim English, Jim Connor, Jim Maier, Larry Madden, and William Byron — committed themselves to the reforms of the Second Vatican Council. In doing so, they followed the inspiring example of their predecessor and trailblazer, Tom Gavigan.

Tom was pastor of Holy Trinity in the tumultuous post–Vatican II era. He studied the Council decrees, began liturgical reform, and established educational programs that prepared the community for change. He did this in a collegial manner that his successors emulated.

Holy Trinity had its share of controversy. Most notable was the protest conducted in the late 1970s by Mitch Snyder of the Community for Creative Nonviolence (CCNV). This well-known champion of the homeless conducted a fast-to-the-death on the grounds of Holy

Trinity unless the parish diverted to the poor at least part of its planned funding for a new organ and interior renovations. His fasting alarmed the pastoral leadership and challenged the entire community. A few years later the parish began tithing its income, giving annually ten percent to the poor and the needy. The practice continues to this day.

The second controversy, centering on the role of women, was even more painful. For many years, the Holy Trinity community had advocated women's rights in the Church. Before other parishes had female altar servers, Trinity started the practice. Women, moreover, shared equal status as lectors, parish council members, Eucharistic ministers, liturgy coordinators, social work coordinators, and religious education directors. Some parishioners wore blue ribbons on their lapels each Sunday and gathered together in Church after the Family Mass to pray for greater justice toward women. More boldly, every Sunday morning one brave man, Ray McGovern, stood throughout the liturgy to protest the denial of women's rights in the Church. At times, others joined him.

Archdiocesan officials were well aware of this advocacy. They heard reports that at different times women (well-educated theologically and well-formed spiritually) spoke at services in church. They became alarmed. All came to a boil when officials got word that, at an ecumenical service in the church, female ministers from neighboring churches preached and distributed communion. That crossed the line. Cardinal Hickey summoned the pastor and demanded that he apologize publicly.

Activities like those sparked a broader investigation. One day three prominent clerics including an auxiliary bishop arrived at the parish to conduct an inquisition, interrogating separately behind closed doors every member of the staff. The hierarchs suspected heresy. Although they used tape recorders, the trio of examiners forbade the interviewees to tape the sessions, or to bring witnesses as support. This twentieth-century witch hunt engendered anguish among staff, and mistrust among parishioners.

During those clerical machinations the pastor, Larry Madden, showed remarkable leadership. He remained calm, comforted the staff and guided the community with patience and courage. A weaker man would have caved, under such pressure. In the end, the inquisitors found no heretics. Parishioners and staff stood together and were strengthened by this misguided ecclesiastical charade.

Such controversies reflect a vibrant, living community trying to follow Christ. The Second Vatican Council heightened the faithful's awareness of Gospel teachings. Pope John XXIII, furthermore, had urged people to read "the signs of the times," among which he mentioned the role of women in Church and society. Acknowledging those signs can put a community at odds with Church leaders. Conflict is unavoidable. The path will always be uneasy for those who faithfully follow the words and actions of Christ.

Married Priests at Trinity

Holy Trinity gave my family a home. Other married priests and former nuns also joined the parish and offered their talents. Although ordained, none of the married priests tried to violate Church regulations or perform sacramental actions like celebrating Mass, hearing confessions, or preaching a homily. They did not seek that, nor was the opportunity offered. But other activities of the laity — lectoring, teaching, Eucharistic ministry, ministry to the sick — were also open to them. Tom Gavigan and other pastors encouraged it. The result was a welcoming climate that fostered talent and benefited the entire community.

Let me recall the stories of married priest families at Holy Trinity. Their lives bear witness to their devotion to Christ and to the Catholic tradition. The unique atmosphere of this parish enabled them to grow spiritually and minister faithfully as lay men and women.

Marvin and Barbara

To go from urban pastor and chancery official to the staff of the national conference of bishops and member of the papal Peace Commission is a remarkable achievement. But then to marry, become active at a local Catholic parish, and serve on its parish council, well, only at Holy Trinity. Marvin did it all.

In earlier years, he had served as pastor in the Baton Rouge Diocese, first at a small parish in Simmesport, then at one of the largest, in Shreveport. His championing of desegregation and fostering of community decision making led to appointment as vice-chancellor and secretary to the bishop. He also founded and edited the diocesan newspaper. In demand as a public speaker, Marvin gave conferences and professional development seminars to groups around the country, from Air Force chaplains to diocesan leaders.

His growing reputation for getting things done and for empowering broader coalitions brought Marvin to the attention of the National Conference of Catholic Bishops (NCCB) in Washington, which hired him to organize and spearhead nationwide efforts for justice and peace. For six years, he directed the NCCB office of international affairs, first under Bishop Paul Tanner, then under Bishop Joseph Bernardin. In heading that office he created a network of constituent organizations centering on world development.

During that period, Marvin co-founded the Center for Concern in Washington, co-founded the Overseas Development Council, and served on Pope Paul VI's international eighteen-member Peace Commission. With each assignment he gained fame. One dubious distinction, however, was his role as carrier of the official Latin text of *Humanae Vitae* from Rome to Washington for translation in the United States!

Marvin's passion for social justice did not end with marriage; he found an outlet in organizations like UNICEF, the Population Resource Center, and the American Conference on Religious Movements, and still found time to work in his local community. For three years he filled an elective post on the Holy Trinity Parish Council, and his wife, Barbara, became active with the school programs. Their two children received religious instruction and sacramental preparation at Trinity, then succeeded at Catholic prep schools and colleges. One is a doctor; the other a social worker. While Barbara worked at a governmental agency, Marvin founded and presided over the American Conference on Religious Movements. Outspoken on issues of social justice and deployment of parish resources, Marvin's passions betray a lifetime of commitment to those causes.

Ed and Kathleen

Social justice is important at Holy Trinity. Besides a Gospel mandate, this parish priority arises also from the Jesuit oft-proclaimed preferential option for the poor. Although one of the wealthiest parishes in the Washington area, Trinity attracts those concerned about the needy and the disenfranchised. Few parishioners show that concern more than Ed and Kathleen.

When I first met them in the 1970s, they lived in offices of the Community for Creative Nonviolence (CCNV), which Ed had founded in Washington. Their lifestyle mirrored their profound convictions. Living in poverty with a growing family, they were later able to buy a home in northwest Washington. Their four children were born during the struggles for civil rights and peace, and attended Holy Trinity School, Catholic high schools, and Catholic colleges.

Ed manages homes for the disabled and advocates for their welfare. For over twenty years he also has guided part-time a soup kitchen in Washington. He serves as its director, problem solver, and principal fundraiser. Kathleen works in a similar role for an agency that offers "education, support services and housing to at-risk, single parent families striving against homelessness, poverty and abuse." Under her guidance this agency transformed an abandoned elementary school in Kensington, Maryland, into one of the area's only community-based programs offering integrated family services and helping people to develop self-sufficiency, resiliency, competency, and self-respect.

Before their marriage, Ed was a Paulist priest in Washington. During the turbulent Vietnam War era he worked as university chaplain and community organizer with the full support of the Paulists. Friends of the Berrigan brothers and other stalwarts of the peace movement, Ed and Kathleen took in Mitch Snyder, the radical champion of the poor, after his release from prison and helped him settle in the Washington area. Their commitment to the poor and needy has endured throughout a lifetime together.

Donald and Ann Marie

The functioning of a Catholic parish today demands the harmonizing of diverse talents of the laity. Empowering them and enabling them to work together in ministry reflects good pastoral leadership. Holy Trinity was blessed with pastors who encouraged such activism. Hundreds of talented people were attracted to the parish and invited to a variety of ministries.

Donald and Ann Marie are among them. As a couple they founded the marriage preparation program at Trinity and served on its board. For five years they also coordinated the baptismal preparation program at another parish. Devoted lifelong Catholics, they sent their two children to Catholic elementary and high schools and took a prominent role in activities at each school. They held the first joint presidency of Holy Trinity's school board.

Donald's passion for the Church springs from his earlier training. After theological studies at the Louvain Seminary in Belgium, he gained a masters degree in religious education, and later a masters degree in counseling. Shortly after ordination he was named director of Washington's Archdiocesan Family Life Program.

Donald married and spent many years working in governmental agencies. He now heads training programs for the Veterans Administration. As a licensed clinical counselor, he supplements his main work with counseling as needed. He has always tried to apply his talents to help the Church fulfill its mission. Like other married priests, he wrote to offer his services to the archdiocese, but received no response.

Joe and Carol

Offering one's talents to the Church in its varied ministries is, among married priests, a constant refrain. Because of their training, experience, and passionate commitment to Christ, they can be a resource in the Christian community. But seldom do church officials tap those talents. Holy Trinity was an exception.

Each year on a weekend before Christmas, the entire Holy Trinity community observes Toy Sunday. In preparation for this season of giving, parishioners are invited to give their used but first-class toys to the poor. They respond with hundreds of toys of all sizes — bicycles, dolls, computer games, sports equipment, and more. Watching the endless parade of children bringing their gifts to the altar, among them quizzical tots unsure about parting with their favorite toys, is always heartwarming. It has become an eagerly anticipated annual event. For several years Joe and Carol orchestrated that production.

Despite their busy schedules, they always found time to volunteer for church activities. Carol served on the Liturgy Planning Committee, coordinating altar servers, ushers, lectors, announcers, musical ministers, and others. Joe became Eucharistic minister and helped for ten years as a member of the Communications Committee.

As a cleric years earlier, Joe edited the diocesan newspaper in his native Springfield Diocese in Massachusetts. In that role, he hired Carol. When Joe was appointed chaplain of the state university, she succeeded him as editor. Gradually they realized their love for each other, moved to Washington, and married. There they gave themselves as much as permitted to religious activities in the Church.

Today Carol is assistant dean at Georgetown University Law School. Joe worked over twenty years at a trade association, retiring as executive director. He serves as consultant to different organizations. Their daughter Ann graduated from Georgetown University. They now apply their efforts to So Others May Eat (SOME), a project sponsored by the Church, providing food for the poor in the Washington area.

Al and Renee

Trinity draws Catholics from forty miles in every direction, lured by the preaching, the liturgies, and the brotherhood/sisterhood that binds them together in Christ. By encouraging small prayer groups to meet in their neighborhoods during Lent and Advent, the parish nurtures the piety of all its members, even those in remote areas. These gather together weekly far from the Church complex to reflect on next Sunday's scriptural passages and share the Good News. Al and Renee have long been regulars at these weekly gatherings in Fairfax, Virginia.

Both participate in a variety of parish activities. On Saturday mornings Al joins with a group of Trinity men who, with no fixed agenda, share their Christian reflections on issues of the day. A profound piety inspires them. Renee assists the Catholic chaplain a full day each week at a local hospital. Then on Sunday mornings, she and Al bring the Eucharist to homebound Trinity parishioners.

These behaviors reflect a lifetime of Christian service. Years earlier, Al was pastor in a small Midwestern town. He also served as secretary to the bishop, with whom he attended one session of the Second Vatican Council. His clerical responsibilities included head of religious education, secretary to the marriage tribunal, and assistant manager of the diocesan newspaper. When he returned recently with Renee to the parish he once shepherded, members of the community joyously welcomed them. He sensed that, if permitted, these parishioners would accept him again as pastor, married or not.

Renee, a former Dominican nun, spent fruitful years as a teacher and school administrator. After marriage, she became lay administrator in an all-girls Catholic school in Washington until it closed. They raised a daughter, and Renee returned to the classroom, teaching in public schools. By the time of retirement, she had spent over forty years as an educator.

Renee's former community of Dominican sisters maintains close relations with them, reflecting a pattern of solicitude found in many female religious congregations. Despite the departure of many sisters, the remaining nuns invariably regard highly, remember prayerfully, and cultivate warmly their former companions in ministry. They manifest Christian community par excellence.

Viewing their joyous disposition, one could not suspect the unique crosses Al and Renee have borne. After five weeks of marriage, Al had suffered a debilitating heart attack. He spent twenty-two days in the hospital and many months in recuperation without salary. After returning to work, he had two more heart attacks and operations. Today Al plays golf, walks three miles a day, and cultivates with pride his rose-filled garden. Renee has also had many illnesses in recent years. Together in Christ, they share the burdens of life.

Rich and Jean

The Sunday nine o'clock liturgical community at Holy Trinity has grown so much that it needs two simultaneous Masses — one in the church, the other in Trinity Theater. With combined seating for over twelve hundred, these buildings are regularly filled to overflow. After the liturgies, all are invited to meet over coffee and donuts — a simple event but, given the volume of food and the size of the crowds, requiring detailed planning. That's where Jean and Rich went to work.

Setting up beforehand and cleaning up afterwards, ordering the donuts and plugging in the coffee pots, they accurately planned everything. Their smiling faces and cheerful demeanor created a climate of friendliness that proved welcoming to everyone. For many years they served the community with grace and charm. Observing them, one would not have suspected their background.

Rich was a former Sulpician priest; Jean, a Franciscan Sister. They met while teaching in Argentina — Jean on a Fulbright Scholarship, Rich on a mission assignment. Later they worked for the federal government until retirement. Returning only occasionally to the parish, Jean and Rich now live in Costa Rica, where they continue to minister to the poor and foster the expatriate community's liturgical life.

Anthony and Joan

One benefit of membership in Holy Trinity parish is the superb adult religious education program. Current religious topics are treated by experts, resulting in stimulating presentations that enrich one's faith. A stalwart of the parish lecture series through the years has been Anthony, chairman of the Theology Department at Georgetown University. He has regularly shared with the community the fruit of his scholarship.

With advanced degrees from the Catholic Institute of Paris, the Pontifical Biblical Institute, and Union Theological Seminary, Anthony can handle with clarity and inspiration diverse topics covering the entire field of liturgy, scripture, and theology. He never disappoints. Always orthodox and respectful of the Catholic tradition, he holds one's interest every time. Because of these talents, he has become a favorite lecturer in the Smithsonian Lecture Series and an able tour guide on pilgrimages to the Holy Land.

Before coming to Trinity and Georgetown, Anthony was a priest with the Montfort Missionaries. His wife, Joan, belonged to the Daughters of Wisdom, a congregation established by the same founder. They have devoted their lives to Catholic education — Joan as a teacher of religion and history in a Catholic girls' school, Anthony as theologian and professor at a Catholic university. In those roles they have served the Church faithfully for many years.

Bob and Patricia

For a parish as large as Trinity — close to four thousand families — running the annual parish picnic becomes a major production. Food distribution, entertainment, games, all organized with an outdoor liturgy as the centerpiece, calls for planning, collaboration, and attention to detail. Bob and Patricia were equal to the task. Patricia held a senior administrative post at the Pentagon and, with her organizational ability, added much to the success of the event. And Bob, with his sense of humor and hard work, supplemented her work in every way. As co-chairs of the parish picnic for two years, they benefited the Holy Trinity community through their winning partnership.

Their parish activities did not stop there. Each participated as Eucharistic minister. Bob also assisted in the needed but unheralded job of counting the Sunday collections. Until their retirement in Pennsylvania, they regularly attended the adult education lectures and the Lenten neighborhood discussion groups.

Their earlier years, however, were different. Bob served as pastor in the Madison, Wisconsin Diocese. He also spent years as a military chaplain in Europe and in the States before meeting Patricia. They raised one daughter, who recently gave birth to their first grandchild.

During his final years, Bob responded readily to requests of young couples to officiate at their weddings. He also served as chaplain on a cruise ship when they were unable to find a Catholic priest. In his opening service to those on the cruise, he explained his true status and was given a standing ovation. He celebrated Mass daily, including once for the Italian crew. His humor and charm inspired everyone.

Bob was a passionate fan of the Fighting Irish, with an equally firm commitment to his Catholic Faith. He used every opportunity to assuage disturbed Catholics and bring them back to their Faith. In May 2002, he died of cancer. His final e-mail message to me was typical: "A couple from Argentina came to a Catholic Church nearby to have their baby baptized. The local church community found that the intended godmother was slow turning in her envelopes, so they are 'uninterested' in baptizing. Of course I'm baptizing."

Carl and Janaan

Transitioning to secular life can be a troubling time. Married priests and nuns often search in vain for a way to continue their Christ-centered ministry. Most are forced to give up entirely the work to which they had long dedicated themselves. Few are permitted to carry on their labors under Catholic auspices. Fortunately for the faithful, Janaan and Carl were able to do so. Their story is unique.

Carl was a Jesuit priest; Janaan, a Franciscan sister. They worked as associate directors of the National Center for Religious Education, set up by the U.S. Catholic bishops. As one might expect, their departure from the national center to marry caused grave concerns.

Though they waited for a dispensation from Rome before marrying, their work in catechetics was almost curtailed by well-meaning people unable to accept their marriage. But God works in strange ways. When dioceses withdrew invitations for Carl to speak, Archbishop William D. Borders of Baltimore welcomed him. At the publishing company where Carl and Janaan's major publication was in progress, a staunch Catholic wanted their names removed from all books that they authored. But cooler heads prevailed. Through judicious interventions by the vice-president of the company, a black Baptist woman, their names remained on their books. Today they enjoy the respect and esteem of Catholics and other Christians across the land. Deservedly so.

Educating children in the Catholic faith is their special talent. For many years Janaan and Carl published one of the standard Catholic religion textbook series in the United States. To help catechists, they give workshops and run training programs in different parts of the country. Their fidelity to the Church in all their writings and presentations has never been questioned. They glow with the warmth of their Christian faith. Fittingly they were honored at the 2001 Convention of the National Catholic Educational Association (NCEA) for many years of dedicated work in the catechetical field.

Whether preparing children for First Communion or First Confession or Confirmation, Janaan and Carl have been willing to work with members of the Holy Trinity community. They can always be relied on to convey the essence of the Christian message with understanding and love. Having them as regular parishioners has been a blessing.

Assistant Pastors

Two of the most popular assistant pastors at Holy Trinity in recent years were Ed and Ned. Good preachers and catechists, they each showed warmth and charity in dealing with people of all ages. They provided exemplary priestly ministry. After marriage, they continued to participate in liturgies at Trinity, but as laymen. Ed and his wife, Ellen, with their daughters, Elizabeth and Molly, attended services regularly. Ned and his wife, Cathi, also joined the community, assisting as much as permitted. Both families gather with parishioners at the Eucharistic Table.

Recently the death of another former assistant pastor, Peter, was announced in the parish bulletin. He left behind a wife and two children. These three married priests, all former Jesuits and assistant pastors at Trinity, are remembered fondly and welcomed warmly in this beloved community of Christ's followers.

A Model Parish

I share all these stories not to pretend that married priests played major roles in the running of this parish. They did not. In a church community of over thirty-eight hundred families with talented and well-educated parishioners, their role was insignificant. Of greater significance was the acceptance given to married priests and their families. More than most Catholic parishes, this community has welcomed them and made them feel at home.

In earlier centuries, the Church forcibly separated married priests from their families. Wives were banished to a convent to do penance and, on occasion, sold into slavery. In more recent times, the Church urged former clergy to move far away from the site of their ministry, lest they give scandal. They called it *scandalum pusillorum,* meaning scandal of the faint-hearted. Contact with married priests was thought to demoralize the young or the weak, who had to be protected from them.

A new day is dawning. An educated laity — well-versed in the teachings of Christ, committed to the Gospel message, and trained for many years in Catholic institutions — no longer needs such coddling, if they ever did. These faithful welcome married priests and their families into the Christian community. Such behaviors demonstrate a major advance in Church practice in this day.

On February 27, 2001, Holy Trinity in Georgetown was designated one of three hundred outstanding Catholic parishes in the country. A team of researchers from the Parish/Congregation Study at the University of North Carolina in Wilmington conducted a two-year nationwide investigation that tried to identify "parishes that nurture the human spirit, draw people closer to God, bring them into loving service, and exemplify what is best in local churches throughout America."[2] That study verified what parishioners already knew. Holy Trinity is a model of Church renewal and reform, a beacon of light in a darkening world, a source of strength for all its members. And married priests and their wives had a hand in that ministry.

Chapter 13

The Cultural Revolution

DURING THE CULTURAL REVOLUTION in China a generation ago, communist zealots demanded loyalty to Chairman Mao. They spouted his words by memory from the "little red book" containing his sayings for all occasions. Waving the book high in the air, they urged others to memorize and repeat those dictums. Coupled with a code of propriety came a cult of personality. Mao loomed larger than life. Adulation verged on idolatry, and no one dared speak or write a word against him; to do so put one's life in jeopardy. The chairman and his teachings reigned supreme.

Truth squads sprang up across China searching for any deviation from Mao's teachings. Those in prominent positions were especially susceptible to attack. Truth squads branded some as heretics, derided them in public, and brought about their removal from office. Paraded publicly, such victims were scorned, pelted with stones, and forced to wear dunce caps. Kangaroo courts quickly decreed guilt, imprisonment, and death.

Truth squad members were promoted to positions of honor. By making charges and rooting out suspected opponents, they endeared themselves to Mao and his henchmen. By rewarding such loyalists, the government blatantly fostered their reprehensible conduct. A climate of fear and mistrust gripped the nation.

In 1956, Chairman Mao launched the "Let One Hundred Flowers Bloom" campaign, in which he encouraged Chinese citizens to discuss freely their reactions to his regime. It was a ruse. Those who criticized the regime were slaughtered or imprisoned.

What folly! To consider the utterances of one person superior to all others, to harass and punish divergence from his teaching, and to reward subservience with honors, titles, and added power!

205

Revolution in the Church

Unfortunately, cultural revolution can also creep into the Catholic Church. Self-styled truth squads roaming the churches, fomenting discord and hatred against bishops, theologians, and rank-and-file Catholics — these can and do occur. They result from enforced codes of conduct and idolatrous cults of persons. Paul Wilkes describes them well: "These are the orthodoxy police who make hell for any progressive, innovative priest and parish reporting real or imagined breaches of Catholic practice. They are spirit killers."[1]

Many such groups thrive within the Catholic Church today. They repeatedly allege heresy before the apostolic delegate in Washington and Curial officials in Rome, where their charges are listened to and acted upon. Bishops fear them. Victims have no recourse. Married priests in particular feel their wrath.

When Joe sought to teach theology in a Midwestern college, a wealthy layman threatened to resign from the board and sabotage the fund drive unless the school dismissed him. Joe had to leave. When Bob and Ann sought to work as religious education coordinators in parishes, despite their dispensations and sterling references, they were hounded by members of Catholics United for the Faith (CUF). They too had to leave. Many more unsavory stories could be told.

Such behaviors would be less heinous if church officials recognized and repudiated the hate-mongers. Instead, pastors and bishops take their allegations seriously and allow the witch-hunters to intimidate them. Unwittingly they encourage repeated slander and calumny. Innocent souls, including bishops and theologians, see their names besmirched, their livelihood curtailed, and their role in the assembly overthrown.

My first exposure to unscrupulous attacks came from people I had never met. They accused me of lying and opposing papal teachings. They cynically mocked and ridiculed me. But I am ahead of the story. Let me give the background to these events.

The Gatherings

For a quarter century, we have gathered together periodically in prayer at days of recollection. By "we" I mean married priests and their wives in the greater Washington area, accompanied by friends and supporters. Some have passed away and surviving partners continue to join with us. From as far away as North and South Carolina, some have traveled to participate in these events. All are welcome.

The purpose of these gatherings is to pray together, strengthen faith convictions, and renew bonds of friendship. These couples are aware that they share a common calling and are bound together as brothers and sisters in Christ. In prayer and reflection they come together. The day begins with a prayer service — scripture reading, commentaries, and song — and ends with a prayerful remembrance of departed companions. In between, a guest speaker offers food for thought. Against the background of common experiences, participants reflect on those messages. Invariably, they find a refreshing atmosphere among friends and renew their faith.

Many prominent Catholics have joined with them and taken a lead in these days of prayer. Presenters include not only notable clergy and religious, male and female, but also talented members of the married priest community, who have given inspiring presentations.

Pastors and Church leaders have supported these efforts. On one occasion, Father Carl Lyon, pastor of St. John the Baptist Church in Silver Spring, allowed the use of his church hall and participated in the day's events. Another time, Father Jim Young, C.S.P., not only welcomed the group into the Paulist House that he headed, but also donned an apron and served lunch. The Center for Applied Research in the Apostolate (CARA) permitted the use of its auditorium near Catholic University. And a few times the Knights of Columbus in Arlington and the Missionhurst community in Arlington enabled them to come together on their grounds to pray. The group always paid a modest stipend and received a warm welcome. Recently, however, everything changed.

The Intervention

On a spring morning, a phone call came to me from a man who identified himself as Grand Knight of the Knights of Columbus in Arlington. He asked about the group that was renting their hall. As with everyone who asked, I responded openly that we are married priests and wives who meet in prayer and reflection, as we have been doing for years in this region.

He then said, "This is CORPUS, isn't it?"

I answered, "No. This is not a CORPUS-planned event. We in this metropolitan region have been holding these gatherings by ourselves for many years." To assure him of the propriety of our gathering, I gave him the name of a participant from the Grand Knight's community. I also suggested getting in touch with my Georgetown pastor. The Knight told me he would get back to me.

Next day he called to say that all was proper. He had spoken with my friend Bill, who had confirmed the truth. I felt relieved. Twenty-four hours later he phoned again and said he had changed his mind. Our group could not use the K of C building. From the conversation and other sources I learned that some people, including a few Arlington clerics, had convinced him that this group was opposed to papal teachings and was engaging in underground liturgies. As a loyal Catholic, he felt impelled to deny us the use of the K of C hall. I was unable to convince him otherwise. Written notice, he said, would follow.

I waited a week. The only item to arrive in the mail was a multi-xeroxed memo dated six years earlier and sent by the Arlington Diocesan Chancellor to "Pastors and All Administrators of Church Properties." It stated:

In response to repeated recommendations made by a number of priests during our Presbyteral Meeting on March 29th, we are making explicit what is already implicit in Canon Law; that pastors and other administrators of church properties are not to allow use of their facilities to groups which advocate against church teachings or legitimate church practices.

No other correspondence came. The message was clear enough. Although the local K of C hall is not a "church property" in the canonical sense, the Grand Knight judged participants at the proposed Day of Recollection to be those who "advocate against church teachings or legitimate church practices." Clear also was the outside pressure exerted on the Grand Knight. He did not identify the informants who pestered him until he acted against us, but I learned that the State Deputy of the K of C had alerted him and some local clergy encouraged the action. Gracious in his refusal, the Grand Knight nevertheless said he had no other choice.

I then caucused with friends. One suggested going public, letting the world know all that happened. Others demurred. In the end, unwilling to provoke scandal with charges and countercharges in local newspapers, I decided not to publicize the decision but simply to alter our plans.

When my good neighbor, a member of the Congregational Church a block away from the K of C Hall, learned about our predicament just a few weeks before the scheduled Day of Prayer, she urged her community to come to our aid. They welcomed the group happily and, though accustomed to higher rental charges, would not accept a larger fee than the K of C. They gave me keys to the building and graciously hosted the gathering.

I sent another mailing to those previously invited, calling attention to the change of location, but not giving the reason. I also phoned the local manager of the K of C Hall to thank him for past assistance and to let him know I bore him no malice. He assured me that the rejection did not come from him or his staff. Powers above him intervened and he was unable to override them. At the Day of Recollection, participants asked why we changed the location. I explained as honestly and charitably as I could what had happened. It was not clear then who was prodding behind the scenes. I soon found out.

The Attack

A month after our prayerful gathering, my friend Joe sent me a newsletter titled "The Truth." It came from a self-styled truth squad, called Les Femmes, which took clergy and laity to task for deviating from official church teachings. I recognized in full force the Cultural Revolution.

The eight-page newsletter contained a two-and-a-half-page diatribe against Sr. Joan Chittister, denouncing her remarks at the recent NCEA Convention and highlighting her role as keynote speaker at the next three Call to Action regional conferences. It described her as "a longtime dissenter from core Church teachings and a staunch advocate of women's ordination" who speaks "radical feminine nonsense." In reporting Chittister's NCEA talk, the newsletter observed, "Like a teenager in a T-shirt. . . . Chittister urged her audience to throw out 'old maps,' and teach their students to question everything."

The same newsletter chided local pastors — one for financial irregularity, another for "seeing a married woman in his parish." It attacked Archbishop Alexander Brunett of Seattle for allowing a Northwest Women's Convocation to advertise in his diocesan newspaper, and Cardinal Edward Egan "for permitting pro-abortion politicians like Al Gore to attend the Al Smith dinner in New York." It also roasted Seton Hall University for awarding an honorary degree to a person the newsletter termed an abortion advocate.

My eyes drifted to another article that centered on me. I realized that was why Joe had sent the newsletter. I repeat the text in its entirety — italicized comments, bold print, and all — as it appeared in the 2001 spring edition of "The Truth":

Dissenters Deceitful Day Dumped: Tony Kowalski thought he'd put one over on the Knights of Columbus by scheduling the CORPUS Region 5 Day of Recollection at the Andrew Douglas White Council Hall in Arlington. CORPUS, the National Association for a Married Priesthood, is a support/dissent group of ex-priests who have abandoned their vows, many to enter invalid marriages. They lobby for reinstatement to the active priesthood, approval of married priests, ordination of women, etc. We discovered the plan when a Texas femme e-mailed us the Region 5 web page describing the event: 'Arlington Virginia.

Tony Kowalski, working from his home in Arlington, Virginia has just finalized arrangements for the next annual Day of Recollection, which will be held on Saturday, April 28 **at the same location as last year** (*our emphasis*), the Knights of Columbus Hall at 5115 Little Falls Road in Arlington, Virginia. Father Gerard Sloyan, one of the great intellectual leaders in the post–Vatican II Church, has agreed to lead the participants for the day.'

We immediately notified the Grand Knight of the Council ... and several priests in the diocese, and sent a letter to the club manager with details about CORPUS and Fr. Sloyan, a founder and board member of ARCC (Association for the Rights of Catholics in the Church). ARCC is one of the most malicious groups attacking the faith. *The Grand Knight* called Kowalski who said the meeting had nothing to do with CORPUS, a direct lie. (*Dissenters and the truth often part company.*) Happily, the Knights canceled the event and CORPUS had to take their dissenting corpses (*oops ... corpora: third declension neuter, accusative case, plural*) to another location. For future reference we suggest the creedless Unitarian church where members may believe any insanity they wish as long as they smile and play nice. We extend our sincere appreciation to the Knights of Columbus for their swift and decisive response. Please pray for the members of CORPUS, their families and their lay brothers and sisters in invalid marriages who work in vain to change Church doctrine to accommodate their sin.[2]

How does one begin to respond to such cynical broadsides? I appreciate them praying for us, but "a support/dissent group of ex-priests who have abandoned their vows"? "one of the most malicious groups attacking the faith"? "a direct lie"? "their dissenting corpses"? and "accommodate their sin"? Slander and cynicism gush from their pen.

I was honored to be lumped with such distinguished Catholic leaders as Cardinal Egan, Archbishop Brunett, Sr. Joan Chittister, and Father Gerard Sloyan. *Domine non sum dignus!* (Lord, I am unworthy!) All these attacks were found in just one edition of the newsletter. Imagine the many innocent bishops, priests, sisters, and lay people attacked in earlier editions! And in later editions!

When Pilate accused him of crimes, Jesus "gave no answer, not even to a single charge" (Matt. 27:14). Christ, moreover, warned that scorn would also be heaped on us. "Blessed are you when men revile you and persecute you and utter all kinds of evil against you falsely on my account. Rejoice and be glad, for your reward is great in heaven, for so men persecuted the prophets who were before you" (Matt. 5:11). But should one remain silent?

The Response

I prayed over this. I had heard of such groups attacking bishops, priests, and nuns, but for the first time I saw it up close, and was startled to find that the accused and condemned was none other than myself. At no time did the author of the article get in touch with me. Never did she verify matters with me or ask my opinion. She gave no opportunity for response, or rebuttal. Les Femmes gloated over its success in getting the Grand Knight to deter us.

Upon further reflection, I sat down and penned a note, not to the writer of the slanders, but to the Grand Knight of the Knights of Columbus who had succumbed to their intimidation. To him I sent the following letter, dated June 5, 2001:

Dear [Grand Knight]

I am grateful for your attempt to treat us with fairness last month when confronted with accusations against us. You are in a position requiring prudence and sound judgment in responding to charges of that type. I recognize your effort to act responsibly. Recently, however, a friend shared with me the enclosed article, taken from the publication of Alexandria-based *Les Femmes*. This group labeled me a liar and dissenter apparently after conversations with you. In the light of that, I feel I must respond.

When you first informed me that K of C facilities would not be available to us, I caucused with my friends. We decided not to go to the press and publicize this. It would only lead to charges and countercharges, with grave public scandal. So we remained silent. But now that these women have chosen to give their own slanderous interpretation of these events, I must clarify matters for the record.

For over twenty years we have gathered together, married priests and their wives, for a day of prayer and recollection. As I indicated in previous correspondence, we have been honored through the years with the support of many distinguished Catholic leaders — bishops, priests, sisters, and laity who joined with us in prayer. Many Catholic organizations, including the K of C, have hosted us. One of the former Grand Knights from Maryland attends every year. Our objective has always been simply to renew the priestly bonds that unite us in Christ and to share our experiences on life's journey. These gatherings have provided inspiring religious moments for each of us. They have given support to many and have engendered for all a renewed commitment to Christ.

"The Women of Truth" prefer to paint us in the most pejorative light. They resort to slander and calumny with no opportunity for us to defend ourselves. They wreak hatred. Is this the Body of Christ? Is this the spirit of Our Lord Jesus? Let me try to respond to some charges.

1. To state that I "put one over on the Knights of Columbus" is furthest from the truth. Each time I reserved the K of C Hall I made clear who we were and for what purpose we were using the facilities. Even you must attest that I was similarly open and honest with you. Let me add that the local officials always treated us kindly and with respect. They deserve to be praised, not censured, for the kindness they have shown us.

2. To define this event as "the CORPUS Region 5 Day of Recollection" is disingenuous. That region includes all the states between Maryland and Texas — the entire Southern region of the country. One need only read the letterhead of our mailing to

realize that this was an independent effort sent to people in MD, DC, VA, and DE. Our mailing list furthermore goes far beyond CORPUS membership. It numbers well over 200.

3. To state that I gave "a direct lie" is clear calumny, as you surely can attest. I indicated to you that this event was neither sponsored nor planned by CORPUS. That organization chose to publicize our gathering and we welcome it. If we could get more married priests through *Les Femmes* publicizing it, we would welcome that too. Our goal is to attract all married priests and their spouses in the area to these days of prayer.

4. Cynically referring to what they call a "creedless Unitarian church where members may believe any insanity they wish as long as they smile and play nice" is hardly in the spirit of ecumenism that Pope John Paul is advocating. Nor is this of Christ. It is an affront to those of other religions.

Thanks be to God we held our Day of Recollection again this year and once again experienced inspiring, Christ-centered reflections together. Frankly, I am honored to have been placed in the company of Sr. Joan Chittister and Fr. Gerard Sloyan — suffering slanders and calumnies at the hands of those who choose to be our enemies. Christ warned us that it would be so. May the same Lord Jesus guide us all in these days of renewal and reform, so that we his followers may proceed in charity and in peace.

Sincerely in Christ,
Anthony P. Kowalski

The Grand Knight never responded.

Cultural Revolutionaries Today

Perhaps we should let such incidents pass without comment. I am not sure. The masthead of the Les Femmes newsletter identified it as being "in the Catholic Diocese of Arlington." This shows the residence of the group, yet it suggests much more. The women of Les Femmes, I came to learn, work closely with some conservative clergy in the diocese who encourage them to act against married priests. The publication furthermore purports to be a defender of the Holy Father, and a watchdog of orthodoxy. Similar groups are found in other dioceses, fostered by right-wing bishops and priests.

One subversive group that investigates bishops for doctrinal orthodoxy, harassing them and reporting them to the apostolic delegate, is called the Roman Catholic Faithful (RCF). Their Web site declares that their sole purpose is "to actively (and prayerfully) restore the Roman Catholic Church." It points out that investigations are under way by them in the dioceses of Albany, New York; Joliet, Illinois; and Rochester, New York. Also, it "is actively pursuing leads" in other dioceses and archdioceses, including Detroit, Michigan; Joliet, Illinois; Los Angeles, California; Milwaukee, Wisconsin; Pittsburgh, Pennsylvania; Saginaw, Michigan; and Santa Fe, New Mexico. The Web site identifies the bishop of each. It further boasts, "RCF has had great success in its efforts to remove Bishop Daniel Ryan from his office as Bishop of Springfield in Illinois."

Such viciousness undertaken in the name of Christ continues to blight the Church, slandering innocent bishops, priests, nuns, and lay people. Complicating the matter further are clerical supporters who frequently hold senior positions in the diocese. They encourage muckrakers behind the scenes. Because of their friendship with highly placed clerics in Rome and in the apostolic delegate's office in Washington, they are feared at the local level. They bring scurrilous charges before bishops and lay leaders, who become intimidated and then try to please and appease the attackers. Bishops fear reaction from Rome. By acquiescing, they encourage these outrageous behaviors.

Inspired Leaders of Tomorrow

Cultural revolutions are not limited to China and the communist world. They flourish in organized churches. Less likely to go unchallenged in a democracy, they thrive wherever people regard one person as a Delphic oracle, and denounce, ridicule, and persecute those whom they judge to be deviating from his pronouncements. The results are always the same — slander, ridicule, and persecution.

When the Chinese woke up to the atrocities perpetrated against their citizens, they rebelled. In the aftermath of the Cultural Revolution, they seized its ringleaders and imprisoned them. Those who perpetrated the vilest barbarities paid for their crimes. Victims earlier reviled and taunted assumed new positions of prominence.

This calls to mind Angelo Roncalli. During the Modernist Controversy at the start of the twentieth century, some accused him of modernist leanings. Documents containing charges against him were on file at the Vatican and, after his election as John XXIII, were brought to his attention. He found these records amusing, but took no action. He tolerated his detractors.

In the same way some traditionalists censured and silenced Catholic theologians in the 1940s and 1950s, only to see them restored and honored in the 1960s and 1970s. Many of the latter played prominent roles at the Second Vatican Council. A long list could be made. Without their wise guidance, the outcome of the Council would have been far different.

The cycle goes on. Self-styled champions of orthodoxy wreak havoc in the Church by imposing their code of conduct and pursuing their cult of persons. They hold up to ridicule churchgoers with whom they disagree. Their days are numbered.

In this new millennium, the Holy Spirit will raise up new leaders — women and men, married and celibate — to guide and inspire the Church. They will gain the respect of the faithful not by imperial mandates or public ridicule, but through humble service. They will comfort the weak and the needy and will protect the powerless from the onslaughts of the powerful. Their hallmark will be charity and peace.

Chapter 14

Married Priesthood Today

R EVELATIONS OF clerical abuse and episcopal cover-up continue unabated. The press has removed the veil of secrecy, uncovering problems long concealed. The Church must show honesty and transparency in dealing not only with financial matters, but also with sexuality, marriage, and priesthood. The Church will be the stronger for it. These reflections are offered humbly and respectfully against that background.

The Family Dimension

The Scriptures depict Jesus in the context of family. He took flesh of Mary, under the protection of Joseph. After eight days, his parents had him circumcised and named him Jesus (Luke 2:21). When the time for purification came, they brought him to Jerusalem and presented him to God (Luke 2:22). These are the rituals of a devout Jewish family.

Jesus' first miracle occurred at a wedding feast, a ceremony honoring a man and a woman committed in love (John 2:1–11). He wanted the joy of that ceremony to continue, so he multiplied wine and made merry. This was a Jewish wedding celebration with family and friends.

While observing the Passover, Jesus took bread, broke, ate, and shared it; he raised the cup, drank, and passed it around; then he ordered his disciples in memory of him to do the same (Luke 22:19). He acted like a father presiding over the family meal.

Paul bore witness to the earliest Christian practice: "For I received from the Lord what I also delivered to you, that the Lord Jesus on the night when he was betrayed took bread..." (1 Cor. 11:23–26).

In weekly gatherings, the community of his followers continued to do as the Lord commanded, "breaking bread in their homes" (Acts 2:46) and listening to the Good News. Again, "On the first day of the week, when we gathered together to break bread, Paul talked with them" (Acts 20:7). These were family celebrations.

Paul greeted "Aquila and Prisca, with the church in their house" (1 Cor. 16:19; Rom. 16:3–5). And he exhorted the Galatians to "do good to all men, and especially to those who are of the household of faith" (Gal. 5:10). These texts depict families gathering in a home and celebrating the Eucharist.

With the dwindling number of celibate priests in our day, the Eucharist is celebrated more and more amid throngs gathered in large churches, stadiums, and auditoriums. The Word of God is barely heard and the rituals are viewed from afar. If that is the only Eucharistic celebration people know, they fail to perceive the essential family dimension of such gatherings. *What a high price to pay for the retention of an all-male, all-celibate, priesthood!*

Marriage and Celibacy

Bert Peeters observed, "Twice in history the unity in the Catholic Church was broken: in 1054 and in 1517, and each time mandatory celibacy of the clergy and the hard position of Rome played an important role in this painful process."[1] Although not central to either of these ruptures in the Church, clerical celibacy constitutes a defining disciplinary difference among the resultant bodies.

Because of these fractures, Christianity today is fragmented into three main groups: Catholic, Orthodox, and Protestant. With each, the discipline of celibacy varies. Catholics maintain the rule of clerical celibacy, and enforce it. The Orthodox allow priests to marry, but demand celibacy of bishops. Protestants, in contrast, abolished the law of celibacy; most of their Church officials are married.

In our day, ecumenical relations among these different Christian bodies have grown. Churches engage in dialogue and reach agreement on important issues. In this irenic ecumenical climate, is it too much to expect them to reflect on their common experiences and review the laws of celibacy and marriage?

Despite differing disciplines, each of the three traditions manifests fidelity to Christ. Protestants witness to a link between marriage and ministry in all leadership positions. The Orthodox combine celibate dedication of bishops and monks with local leadership of married and celibate clergy. Catholics have advocated a celibate lifestyle for priests, sisters, brothers, monks, and friars.

All Christians can learn from one another.

Loss of Ministry

During the communist upheaval in Central Europe in the 1940s, many abandoned their professional careers. They had labored for years as doctors, lawyers, and university professors, but suddenly everything changed. Because of their sympathies with previous regimes they had to give up their practices. Communist officials deprived them of the exercise of their professional talents and forced them to undertake other work to support their families. They became cab drivers, gravediggers, and secretaries. What a loss to society!

Consider the concert pianist who from earliest years developed technique and mastery in his art, and who through many concerts gave great pleasure to audiences, but later was denied the right to play the piano. If then the government forbade the public from participating in his performances, the pianist's frustration would be enormous. Imagine the lost symphonies, the unplayed concerts, the resultant cultural poverty! What a loss to the music world!

So is it often with married priests. In pursuit of an ideal, they studied, developed professional skills, and engaged in sacramental ministry. Then all was curtailed because of marriage. If they try as married persons to exercise their talents, institutional leaders ban them or excommunicate them. To survive, they take jobs far removed from their world of experience. Imagine the unpreached sermons, the uncelebrated liturgies, and the sacramental deprivation at a time most needed! *What a loss to the Church!*

The Vernacular Movement

In the late 1950s and early 1960s, National Liturgical Conferences grew in artistry and swelled in numbers. After each Conference, several attendees stayed on. They were committed to a reform many considered too radical. Seminarians dared not remain after the Conference to join them because seminary officials were known to have evicted students from the seminary for attending those meetings. The group was called the Vernacular Society. Its members advocated sacramental celebrations in the people's language.

The Roman Catholic Church had long conducted all liturgical services in Latin. Then in 1963, the Second Vatican Council issued its Constitution on the Liturgy and introduced the people's language into liturgical worship. Members of the Vernacular Society were exhilarated. In an extraordinary move, they voted to disband.

The Vernacular Society became probably the only organization to hold one final meeting, a victory celebration, and unanimously agree to end their work. Beyond their wildest dreams, they achieved every goal. Nothing more was needed. *The movement for an expanded priesthood, male and female, married and single, in the Roman Catholic Church will follow a similar pattern.*

Use of Words

Words are important. When growing up in a poor multiethnic neighborhood in East Trenton, New Jersey, I heard many called micks, spicks, dagos, polaks, and niggers. We no longer use such terms because we know they are offensive. More appropriately people today speak about the Irish, Spanish, Italians, Poles, and African-Americans. Offensive labels must not be used.

In the same neighborhood, one also heard references to morons, cripples, deaf and dumb. Such words no longer pass a person's lips because they have diminish the dignity of others. One speaks instead about the intellectually challenged, the disabled, the speech and hearing impaired. The other terms are to be avoided.

Today, however, we continue to hear about ex-priests and former priests. These terms belittle and insult. Priesthood is forever. More properly can one speak of the ex-clergy or ex-religious, the former clergy or former religious. Clerical or religious status does not remain, but priesthood endures. *Words are important.*

Violation of Vows?

Have priests who marry violated a solemn vow? Have they abandoned a sacred commitment to the Living God? Are they disobedient men who do not deserve to be trusted with ministry because they betrayed it? Are they selfish men who preferred their pleasure to the needs of the community for which they were ordained? Married priests at times hear such accusations.

Leaving aside the difference between a vow taken by religious priests and a promise made by diocesan priests, one must admit that all priests pledge fidelity to the celibate state. Every priest made such a vow or promise as a condition for ordination to the Roman Catholic priesthood. There is no getting around that.

In his famous speech "Broken Promises,"[2] Anthony Padovano dealt with this issue perceptively by invoking the story of Jephthah (Judg. 11:29–40), whom the Lord God blessed in battle. To gain God's favor and successfully conquer the Ammonites, Jephthah made a vow to the Lord, "If you will give the Ammonites into my hand, then whoever comes forth from the doors of my house to meet me, when I return victorious from the Ammonites, shall be the Lord's, and I will offer him up for a burnt offering" (vv. 30–31). So Jephthah went into battle, and the Lord "gave them into his hand" (v. 32). A great slaughter occurred and Jephthah returned victorious.

As he neared his home, who ran out from the doors of his house to greet him joyously but his beloved only child, his daughter. "And when he saw her, he rent his clothes, and said . . . I have opened my mouth to the Lord, and I cannot take back my vow" (v. 35). She replied, "My father, if you have opened your mouth to the Lord, do to me according to what has gone forth from your mouth" (v. 36). But she first begged, "let me alone two months, that I may go and wander on the mountains, and bewail my virginity, I and my companions" (v. 7). He said, "Go." And after two months she returned and Jephthah slew her according to his vow.

Is the God of Jephthah the same as the God made known by Jesus of Nazareth? Is the vow of Jephthah the same as the vow taken by Catholic priests today? Does the Living God demand that vows be observed with absolute rigor? From all that has been taught about God by Jesus of Nazareth, I find it hard to believe that Our Loving Father would delight in Jephthah's murdering his only daughter. Nor can I imagine that the same God would prefer that priests' children not exist, that their marriage vows not be made, and that their promise of celibacy be maintained at all cost.

Looking upon these children, how can anyone think that they resulted from sin? They are the fruit of love. And looking upon these wives, how can anyone associate them with evil? The beauty and joy of marriage has been theirs.

And yet, like Jephthah of old, church officials insist that priests must obey the law and keep their vows or promises. Rome permits few exceptions. There may be grounds in the Old Testament for such thinking, but those same texts also regard marriage very highly. And what of the message of love that Jesus proclaimed and the dignity of marriage which Jesus honored? *How far have Christians strayed from Christ's teaching and example!*

Return to Ministry

At times one hears the argument that, if the Church changes its discipline and allows married priests back into ministry, it will be unfair to those who gave up love of wife and family. Some have suggested that celibate priests might respond with jealousy, like the brother of the prodigal son who resented the father's lavish celebration of his son's return (Luke 15:28–30). That may be true of some.

The analogy, however, limps. First, priests who marry are not prodigal sons; by and large, they are not immoral persons who have lived profligate lives. Second, celibate priests should not be compared with the brother of the prodigal son; they respond far differently.

Surveys consistently show that most celibate priests would welcome married priests back to ministry. I sense that attitude with my closest celibate priest friends. And the laity in even larger percentages welcome that return.

One part of the prodigal son story holds true. The father loves the son who stood at home and the son who went away. He prepares a banquet feast, a joyous celebration, to which he eagerly invites them. *It is clear that God lavishes his love on them all.*

Sanctity in Marriage

A cultivated mystique in the Catholic Church exalts clergy and nuns above others. The greatest saints, the true heroes in the Church, those perceived to have surrendered themselves fully to Christ, are priests, sisters, bishops, and popes — all celibates. At a lower class within the Church, one finds a secondary group consisting of mothers and fathers, sisters and brothers, relatives and friends — the married. Good people these, but lacking heroism, and dedication to Christ. Or so it seems.

The Church's practice of canonization, by proclaiming as saints virtually only celibates, reinforces that mystique. Lay people are rarely canonized. Yet among relatives and parishioners many true saints can be found; every vibrant Christian community has them.

On October 21, 2001, Pope John Paul II hailed a husband and wife for leading an exemplary life. Luigi Beltrame Quattrocchi, who died in 1951, and Maria Corsini, who died in 1965, became the first married couple in modern times to be beatified, that is, recognized in the preliminary stage for canonization as saints. Luigi was a lawyer for the Italian government and an activist with Catholic groups; Maria studied nursing and accompanied invalids on pilgrimage to shrines. In the ceremony of beatification, the pontiff said, "Today we have singular confirmation that the path to holiness, followed together as a couple, is possible, is beautiful and is fundamental for the good of the family, of the church and of society."[3]

Rome recognized sanctity in marriage. That is cause for joy. But it is also well known that this married couple gave up their marriage bed for the last twenty years of their lives. Is that the main reason for their canonization? Does this not convey a wrong and long discredited message, that to engage in sexual relations, even in marriage, is less pure and holy than sexual abstention?

A new day dawns. The Holy Spirit is leading the faithful to a greater awareness. *Virtue, heroism, and holiness can emerge from a celibate life; virtue, heroism and holiness can also be found in a happy, sexually fulfilled married life.*

The Chaff and the Wheat

The media have reported many cases of pedophilia, ephebophilia, and other sexual misconduct among clerics. Such reporting ignores the heroic virtue and defiles the good name of exemplary celibate priests. The same media also highlight from time to time the outstanding virtue, goodness, and competency of married priests and their families. These portrayals shatter Catholic stereotypes. They discourage traditionalists.

A few years ago, I attended a play called *The Durango Kid*, which depicted a man who relived the cowboy past. He dreamed about those glorious days when heroes wore white hats and villains black ones. He thrilled to the noble tales of yesteryear. Everything went well for him until the hero began showing deplorable traits, and the arch-villain virtuous behavior. In a climactic scene, he cries out, "I can't stand to live in a world in which the good guys...and the bad guys...are the same guys."

The anguish of that man is echoed in the lives of countless Catholics today. Faced with heinous scandals in high places, and noble virtue in low places, average churchgoers are stunned. They cannot fathom this. Their refrain is the same, "I can't stand to live in a world in which the good guys...and the bad guys...are the same guys." And many leave the Church.

Faithful Christians are bound to see virtue and vice. They must be content with the promises made in the parable of the wheat and the chaff. At harvest time, God "will clear the threshing floor and gather

his wheat into the granary, but the chaff he will burn with unquench-
able fire" (Matt. 3:12). In the meantime, *a mature faith commitment
is needed, one not discouraged by sexual scandal among highly placed
clerics, nor surprised by heroic virtue among lowly placed laypersons.*

Accountability for Actions

God gifted humankind with conscience, intelligence, and common
sense. This means that a person is to use his/her intelligence to study
scientific advances and follow common sense in discerning between
conflicting wisdoms of this world. Upon reflection and guided by
faith, a person will follow his/her conscience in making decisions.
The same applies to every aspect of life.

In dealing with health, a person studies medical advances, recognizing that doctors in this day have gained exceptional knowledge
of the human organism, have cultivated refined methods of diagno-
sis and cure, and have learned the principles for maintaining good
health. It would be foolish to ignore that. And yet, there are conflicting research findings and contradictory medical advice. One must not
reject outright the advice of doctors, nor slavishly follow it. Using intelligence, following conscience, and guided by faith, one must act
accordingly.

In dealing with the world of economics, the same holds true. Financial advisers and planners have access to knowledge far beyond
the layperson. They have studied the market and understand its va-
garies. They also have advised others in similar straits. So people
wisely seek their counsel. But financial advisors at times give contradictory advice. Once again, a person must use his or her intelligence
to weigh such counsel and use common sense to decide the proper
course of action. One's faith-inspired conscience also leads to good
management of the earth's resources.

Religious matters are not much different. One would be foolish
to ignore scholars who have dedicated their lives to the pursuit of
revealed wisdom, and Church leaders, whose pastoral roles demand
respect. One should turn to them for counsel, but also apply common
sense. Not all scholars and church leaders give the same advice, even

within the same religious group. After consulting with theological experts and spiritual guides, one must follow one's properly formed conscience.

God will hold everyone accountable for their actions. This means that doctors, financial advisers, religious leaders and others are responsible for advice given and coercion exerted. In the end, each stands accountable before God. As shown in the Scriptures, God is not a stern judge impervious to human frailties, but a merciful shepherd, filled with kindness and mercy. *Awareness of the Loving and Forgiving God provides much consolation.*

Honorable Celibates

Serious study of priests who marry has yet to be undertaken. These men are by no means less intelligent than celibates; a disproportionate number have either studied in Rome or taken advanced degrees. As seminarians or clerics they were not immoral or dissolute; frequently they ranked among the most respected and admired. But just as it is wrong to caricature priests who marry, it is also improper to belittle priests who remain celibate.

I have met outstanding men in the celibate priesthood. They live dedicated lives under immense pressure and deserve to be respected, especially in these days. Several celibate priests among my contemporaries come to mind.

Jack would stand out in any assembly for his intelligence and genuine charity. As head of the diocesan matrimonial bureau for many years, he brought wisdom and compassion to family ministry. As director of priestly personnel, he showed understanding and gave wise counsel to brother priests. As a Catholic spokesman in the public media, he performed brilliantly. To this day, Christ permeates his every word and action.

Dick came from the same mettle. With consummate skill, he directed diocesan religious education programs. In shifting from the pre– to the post–Vatican II Church, prudence and vision were needed. Dick had them in great measure. He caught the spirit of the Second

Vatican Council and set up training programs that resulted in a profound renewal across the entire diocese. His joy, his intelligence, and his indomitable spirit enabled him to overcome countless obstacles.

My classmate Gerry showed the same qualities. He played football at the Catholic high school where Vince Lombardi began his coaching career. A muscular and heavy lineman, Gerry showed the fierce aggressive spirit that Lombardi engendered. Yet as priest he showed the opposite — a warm, gentle, Christ-centered ministry. His dialogue homilies as he wanders up the aisles in church today engage parishioners in their faith. He is a true pastor to his people, tirelessly responding to their needs. He ministers faithfully to the Gospel in these trying times.

Bob is another. No one could ever accuse him of rudeness or lack of charity. The spirit of Christ took hold of his soul. Gentleness and kindness have long permeated all his relationships. Bob's pastoral response to all who call on him today marks him as a man of prayer, a man of God.

All these priests, my friends and contemporaries, give strong celibate witness to Christ and his message. I admire each. Their virtue, piety, and intelligence are a credit to the Church. They demonstrate that *celibate witness is a treasure.*

The True Follower of Christ

Who is the true follower of Christ? Is it the person who acknowledges Jesus as Lord and Savior and invokes his Name regularly, as our evangelical friends affirm? Is it the person who gives assent to every doctrine and discipline that church authorities propound, as traditional Catholics today insist? Is it the person who privately studies the Word of God and tries to live according to its teachings, as independent Christians profess?

We all know preachers like Elmer Gantry who profusely invoke the Name of Jesus, but privately resort to all sorts of wickedness. We all have met church leaders who support every church doctrine and discipline, but whose pride, arrogance, and hypocrisy contradict the Christian message. And we've seen others who maintain that they live according to Christ's teachings, but want nothing to do with Christians, seemingly placing themselves above others.

So who is the true follower of Christ? We must let God be the judge. The course for Catholics is clear. Despite occasional doubts, Catholics are called to embrace wholeheartedly Christ's message as it has come down through legitimate teachers in the Christian community. And so, the Catholic professes faith in the traditional creed and seeks to abide by Church discipline. He or she continually invokes the Name of Jesus, realizing that Christ alone is Our Salvation. And he or she unites with fellow believers in striving to live out the Gospel in daily life. *The rest lies in the Hands of God.*

Ordained and Married

Priests who marry travel with their wives along an arduous path. At times they stumble; at times they are hurt; and at times they scandalize others. In their frailty, they fail more than once. All can strike their breasts and utter a profound *mea culpa.* They are not always sure where the path leads, but the Living God blesses them. During this journey, they stretch out their hands in friendship to celibate priests and bishops, and to faithful women and men everywhere, as they respond to God's call. But time is growing short.

The noted sociologist Richard Schoenherr, in his posthumously published work *Goodbye Father,* notes that the Church is running out of time. He argues that:

> unless a married priesthood soon breaks the status quo, many sectors of this ancient organization will regress to prerational religion. The demand for blind obedience will replace the demand for the Mass and sacraments. Superstitious magic will displace mystical transcendence. Unbending patriarchy will suffocate the equality and dignity of women. If the Catholic Church cannot say goodbye Father, many faithful Catholics will have no choice but to say Goodbye Church.[4]

Will the Roman Catholic Church adopt once again a married priesthood? Look at the record. First, from the days of the apostles to this day a married priesthood has endured, especially in Eastern Rite Churches. Second, married formerly Protestant clergymen are being ordained as Roman Catholic priests and their number is growing. Third, the ranks of married deacons are expanding in America and around the world. Fourth, thousands of validly ordained and then validly married Roman Catholic priests flourish in the Church, albeit as laymen. Adding all this up, one can conclude that *more than half the men who have validly received Sacred Orders in the Catholic Church are today married!*

The Sanctity of Life

I wholeheartedly endorse the Catholic bishops' position on the sanctity of human life. It seems to me that a consistent ethic of life reflects the basic and essential teaching of Christ. That consistent ethic, among other things, entails opposition to war, opposition to abortion, opposition to capital punishment, opposition to ready access to guns, and opposition to the proliferation of nuclear weapons. Reverence for the sacredness of life requires this.

At the same time I find myself uncomfortable with those who, while allowing no exception whatsoever to the ban on abortions, simultaneously introduce all sorts of distinctions to justify their strong advocacy of war. That is inconsistent.

I am also uncomfortable with church leaders who on the one hand refuse to stand next to politicians who have expressed support for abortion and even threaten to excommunicate them, while at the same time they are eager to stand next to the politician who has never seen a capital punishment sentence he did not like, and who eagerly initiates unprovoked war. That is hypocrisy.

Perhaps more importantly, I cannot support the mentality of those who in macho fashion tell military men "It's okay to strafe that village or drop bombs on that population even though there might be 'collateral damage,' " while at the same time they sternly tell raped and abused young women, "Under no circumstances are you to have an abortion." Such macho arrogance and insensitivity appalls me.

We must be consistent in our commitment to the sanctity of life and faithful to the Jesus who told us, "I have come that they may have life, and have it abundantly" (John 10:10).

The Plight of Our Bishops

I take no delight in the current plight of our bishops — the loss of trust, the lack of respect, the absence of leadership. It would be presumptuous of me to tell the bishops what they must do. At an earlier time in my life I would have considered it arrogant to offer advice to bishops. Yet seven decades of uninterrupted communion with our Roman Catholic sisters and brothers, and the current malaise throughout our Church, emboldens me to respond.

I do not agree with Cardinal Oscar Rodríguez Mariadaga — this is not the fault of the press, nor of the media. They have acted responsibly and professionally. Nor can this be blamed on the faithful, who are unbelievably tolerant. They and their children have been the prime victims of these crimes. Nor can blame be apportioned to all priests, many of whom live heroic lives. Blame for this must be placed squarely at the feet of the bishops, from whom the faithful have every right to expect a profound *mea culpa, mea culpa, mea maxima culpa.* And, according to the bishops' teachings, such confession must be accompanied by a firm purpose of amendment and an act of penance. What kind of penance?

Richard John Neuhaus has written correctly that what is needed is "fidelity, fidelity, fidelity."[5] That means fidelity to Christ and his teachings. Particularly relevant in this regard are the words Christ addressed directly to the Twelve, whom we recognize as predecessors to our bishops, cardinals, and popes. Matthew 20:17–28 records that "As Jesus was going up to Jerusalem he took the twelve disciples aside ... and said 'You know that the rulers of the Gentiles lord it over them, and their great men exercise authority over them. It shall not be so among you; but whoever would be great among you must be your servant, and whoever would be first among you must be your slave; even as the Son of man came not to be served but to serve, and to give his life as a ransom for many.' " These words I have never heard proclaimed in our churches. They should be.

In keeping with those admonitions, I make the following suggestions as a way of restoring trust, respect, and leadership to our bishops:

First, put aside those pretentious titles with which you address one another — Your Excellency, Your Eminence, Your Grace, Most Reverend, Right Reverend, and Very Reverend. Instead, become once again Peter and Andrew, James and John.

Second, put aside the pretentious, expensive, and effeminate attire, the red buttoned dresses with which you flit about. Instead, dress like men of our day, in imitation of Christ and the apostles, who dressed like men of their day.

Third, put aside what appears to be an eagerness to hurl censures, excommunications, and penalties of all types. Instead, learn to serve and wash the feet of Christ's faithful.

These actions, in fidelity to Christ, would go far to restoring trust, respect, and leadership in our Church.

The Non-Clerical Jesus

We are called to follow the non-clerical Jesus of Nazareth:

- a Jesus who wore no distinctive garments that set him apart from others, only the normal garb of Jewish men of His day;

- a Jesus not addressed with titles of nobility, like "Your Eminence," "Your Excellency," or "Your Grace," but known to all brothers and sisters simply as Jesus;

- a Jesus who welcomed women into his presence, and chose them as disciples; they in turn stood by him to the end, even as his male apostles abandoned him;

- a Jesus who spoke little about sexual sins and readily forgave the woman taken in adultery, but reserved his strongest condemnation for hypocrisy, slander, and violence;

- a Jesus who taught his followers how they were to guide his flock, saying, "You know that the rulers of the Gentiles lord it over them, and their great men exercise authority over them. *It shall not be so among you.*"

That is the Jesus I live for; that is the Jesus I die for.

Conclusion

IN HIS BOOK on the changing face of the Catholic priesthood, Donald Cozzens writes:

> Priests still sense that they are members of a mysterious brotherhood that continues to shape their lives and world view. Not only is their pastoral identity grounded in the covenant of ordination, they experience a spiritual bond linking them to priests the world over, indeed to priests from ages past and to the priests yet to come.[1]

Awareness of that identity endures with Roman Catholic priests, celibate and married. God called them to priesthood. As if that were not enough, God also blessed some with wives and children. Through these sacramental actions of ordination and marriage, priests have benefited from extraordinary divine largess. All priests, nevertheless, face the escalating turmoil engulfing the Church. Scandalous sexual behavior of priests and secret payoffs by bishops add to the ferment. Each day brings new revelations. Robert J. Silva, president of the priests' federation, notes perceptively:

> it is growing more certain with each passing day that there is something "of God" in what is taking place...it is for us to trust the movement of the Life-giving Spirit to bring the Church to a new moment in its history.[2]

Like Gamaliel of old (Acts 5:34–39), Silva suggests that this development may be "a God-given grace," by which the Church can be renewed and ministry can once again flourish.

Yet the frustration of Catholics continues. Many cite with despair the appointment of nothing but staunchly conservative bishops and cardinals, who seem chosen mainly for their subservience to senior

Roman officials, with little accountability to the local Church. Can these men adequately lead the faithful? Edward Stourton dismisses such pessimism, pointing out that to think this way

> is to ignore the Holy Spirit, and His recent track record. An ecumenical council from a Pope expected to be no more than a caretaker, a devastatingly reactionary encyclical from his most modern-minded successor, a pontificate that lasted for a month and the first non-Italian pope for four hundred and fifty years — the Church has thrown up so many surprises during the last four decades that we have come almost to expect the unexpected.[3]

Bernard Häring expressed the same sentiment in the introduction to his final book, where he wrote, "I think I have solid reasons for expressing hope: a powerful turnaround is taking place. Old models of the church are on the decline; new ones are coming to view."[4] In this third millennium, who can predict the new structures, and new modes of operation?

Priesthood is in transition; the entire Catholic Church is in transition. As Karl Rahner has noted:

> If we honestly admit that we are in a period of transition, if we are convinced that what is to remain of the old can be salvaged only by being resolutely accepted as we accept the new situation, must we — and particularly authority — not think more of the future than of the present and past? Must we not adopt a spirit of self-criticism and resist a very dubious conservatism, which is becoming virulent as the euphoria of Vatican II is fading and the ordinary routine begins again, when we must set to work seriously and some confusion cannot be avoided?[5]

Rahner's message rings true. We must, first, look more to the future than to the present or past; second, we must adopt a spirit of self-criticism, which everyone finds difficult; and third, we must work seriously amid unavoidable confusion.

In this period of transition, the urgent need for a married priesthood is beginning to be recognized. Vatican Council II took preliminary steps to prepare the Church for the changes that are to come. This is seen particularly in its treatment of marriage. Unlike past proclamations, the Council in its "Pastoral Constitution on the Church in the Modern World" in 1963 extolled "The intimate partnership of life and love that constitutes the married state."[6] The document spoke of marriage not as a concession to human weakness, but as "an image and a sharing in the partnership of love between Christ and the Church; it will show forth to all men Christ's living presence in the world and the authentic nature of the Church."[7] Furthermore, in its Decree on the Ministry and Life of Priests in 1965, the same Council acknowledged that celibacy was "not demanded by the priesthood by its nature" and praised the "many excellent married priests" in the Eastern Churches.[8]

Five years later, in a letter to Cardinal Villot, his Secretary of State, Pope Paul VI admitted that he was prepared to accept married men as canonical priests if most bishops approved and if requests for such a dispensation were limited to mission countries. In principle, then, he accepted a married priesthood for the Latin Rite. Recently the ordination of dozens of married Protestant ministers as Catholic priests (not just for mission territories) under John Paul II confirmed that principle.

Recommendations for the ordination of married men have come from Cardinals Hume of Britain, Suenens of Belgium, Malula of Zaire, Pellegrino of Italy, Darmojuwono of Indonesia, and Arns and Lorscheider of Brazil. National conferences of priests in Zaire, England, and South Africa, the European Colloquium of Parochial Clergy, and the Assembly of Provincials of the Oblates in Asia proposed the same.

Priests in the United States have consistently advocated for a married priesthood. The first American bishop, John Carroll, recommended to Rome the ordination of married men. Surveys by Joseph Fichter, S.J., in 1968 showed that 62 percent of priests under thirty-five approved of a married clergy. In an unpublished study in 2001, Hoge and Wenger of Catholic University recorded that 52 percent of Catholic priests believed that "Priests who have resigned from the priesthood should be invited to reapply for permission to function as priests again, whether they are married or single;" and 56 percent agreed that "Celibacy should be a matter of personal choice for diocesan priests." Religious priests registered more positive responses than diocesan priests, but most in each group supported the measures.[9]

The laity also are expressing themselves strongly on this matter, as reflected in a survey[10] conducted by sociologists at Catholic University in 2001. It showed that, when faced with varying options to meet the priest shortage, 53 percent of Catholics favored ordaining married women, 62 percent celibate women, and 71 percent married men. In that same survey, a majority of Catholics in every generation, at every level of education, and in every range of family income, including 75 percent of Catholic men and 79 percent of Catholic women, favored a return of married priests to ministry.

Anthony Padovano summarizes the data most cogently:

> By every standard of measurement, it is clear that the hour for a married priesthood has come. Scripture calls for it as does the tradition of the Church. Indeed we are not asking for an innovation but for a restoration, the restoration of a married priesthood which has been an option for most of church history.... The desire for a married priesthood has been expressed in overwhelming majorities by women as well as men, by clergy as well as laity, by religious as well as diocesan priests, by old as well as young, by the entire world, in every country, on every level of economic and social life. *The time has come.*[11]

Epilogue

The New Pontificate

A S THIS BOOK goes to press with the Crossroad Publishing Company, we face the extraordinary events of 2005, culminating in the death of John Paul II and the election of Benedict XVI. These occurrences have captured the attention of the public at large, and understandably of Catholics in particular. Because the role of pope is of central importance to Catholicism, and because the hopes of a multitude of Catholics for the reform and renewal of the Church as promised by Vatican II remain, we must approach these events with sober, faith-filled reflection and with hope-filled confidence. Let me share with the reader my reflections on these two personages of critical significance to the Church. It is too early for anyone to give conclusive judgment on these men. We must nevertheless face up to their central role in the drama of our times. In doing so, we cannot ignore our hopes and our dreams.

Pope John Paul II

I approach the legacy of John Paul II with mixed feelings. This arises on the one hand from pride in my Polish heritage and on the other hand from pride in my married priesthood.

I was not quite five years old when the Nazis invaded Poland. My earliest recollections are of my mother in tears receiving letters from her family in Poland, from which she had departed at age thirteen. First she learned that her older brother, Joseph, her closest friend, had been tortured and killed while his wife was expecting their seventh child. Then she read about the horrors endured by her sisters and the death of her youngest brother, Michael, in a Gestapo torture cell. Throughout that period, Nazis treated Poles as slaves. They closed all Polish colleges, universities, and seminaries and permitted no more than a trade school education. Unlike in France, no puppet government was allowed. By the thousands Nazis killed, terrorized, or carried away to work in German war factories the helpless Polish people. Barely nineteen when the invasion occurred, Karol Wojtyla was forced to curtail his formal studies and work in a nearby stone quarry.

After Nazi barbarism came communist domination with its atheistic agenda imposed on a deeply religious people. For fifty years my relatives were denied freedom, education, democracy, self-determination. I identified very much with their plight. For them Karol Wojtyla became a savior. He kept hope alive throughout years of terror. He guided their destiny and inspired the peaceful overthrow of a system of gargantuan evil. Poles will always and justifiably be grateful to John Paul II for his leadership. In all these labors, he was Christ to his people.

We need, however, to recognize another aspect of Karol Wojtyla's life. He was not God. He was a human being like us, subject to the same human frailties, inclined to the same selfishness and pride, unwilling like the rest of us to give up any semblance of power. And though I praise him for the good he did for so many, I also must identify with those he overlooked.

First among them by reason of their pain are the survivors of clerical abuse and their families. A bishop in Christlike fashion should hasten to these people and offer help, not work through lawyers to limit scandal and pay for a coverup. Second and perhaps more important are women, 51 percent of the faithful, who need more than just words of affirmation; we must formally and respectfully incorporate them into the decision making structure of our Church. Third are our gay brothers and sisters, whose dignity has been violated; we must accord them the respect they deserve. And last but by no means least are my married priest brothers and their wives and children. Though John Paul II fostered dialogue with the Orthodox, Protestants, Jews, Muslims, and others, and while he met with Fidel Castro, Tariq Assiz, Augusto Pinochet, and others, he never dialogued with any of these Christ-centered people. Not only did he refuse personally to meet with them; he also would not allow bishops to do so. In all this, he was *not* Christ to his people.

And so, as a man who identifies with his Polish heritage, I extol John Paul II for his role in the overthrow of communism and for giving hope to so many terrorized people, especially his countrymen. By the same token, as a priest who has married, I also recognize the neglect of so many others during his reign — women, survivors, theologians, the poor in need of liberation, priests who have married and their families. We must give them cause for hope. We must re-address the injustices perpetrated against them, frequently in the very name of the Gospel.

Pope Benedict XVI

Joseph Ratzinger now sits on the throne of Peter as Pope Benedict XVI. At the outset of the recent Conclave, he identified the greatest threat to the modern world as relativism and the foremost need as the affirmation of absolute truth. The cardinal-electors accepted that assessment and chose him to lead the Church in that direction.

Returning from the Conclave, our American cardinals sought to put a positive spin on the selection of the man called Panzerkardinal by his countrymen and God's Rottweiler by other Western critics. These cardinals shared with us their personal dealings with the new Pope, whom they uniformly described as warm, kind, and caring. They were certainly sincere. But there is another side. The list of talented journalists, accomplished theologians, committed women religious, and inspiring episcopal leaders who have suffered at the hands of the Congregation for the Doctrine of the Faith in the last two decades is long. We cannot easily forget them. Nor should we.

Today, however, even progressives like Hans Küng and Richard McBrien have urged caution. They insist that we give the pope the benefit of any doubt, suspend our judgment, and render respect to the papacy. As many have noted, every person entering public office must be allotted a honeymoon period. So also with the pope. Some have also called attention to a potential "Nixon in China" scenario.

According to that thinking, only a person of such unquestionably conservative background as Nixon could have pulled off a monumental breakthrough in relations with a major communist nation. Such transformations are always possible. Pope Benedict XVI may yet surpass all expectations. We earnestly hope and pray for that.

The Future

What then does the future hold? We must proceed with prophetic faith and Christian hope. As Jim Wallis has said, "Prophetic faith does not see the primary battle as the struggle between belief and secularism. It understands that the real battle, the big struggle of our times, is the fundamental choice between cynicism and hope."[1] Our hope is in the Living God, and no one else. We trust not in any bishop or pope, but in the saving message of Jesus Christ. He remains the way, the truth, and the life (John 14:6). Let there be no doubt that the reassessment of priestly ministry and its openness to men and women, married and single, is inevitable, necessary, and just a matter of time. May God hasten the day!

Notes

Abbreviations for Collections of Classical Church Writings

CSEL   *Corpus Scriptorum Ecclesiasticorum Latinorum,* 91 vols. Vindobonae: Hoelder-Pichler-Tempsky, 1866–1998.

ES   Henricus Denzinger/Adolfus Schonmetzer, eds. *Enchiridion Symbolorum.* Freiburg: Herder, 1976.

PG   Migne, J. P., ed. *Patrologiae Cursu Completo: Series Graeca,* 161 vols. Paris, 1857–66.

PL   Migne, J. P., ed. *Patrologiae Cursu Completo: Series Latina,* 221 vols. Paris, 1857–66.

Preface

1. Bernard Häring, *My Hope for the Church* (Liguori, Mo.: Liguori/Triumph, 1999), 121.

1. The Other Tradition

1. Raymond E. Brown, S.S., Joseph A. Fitzmyer, S.J., and Roland E. Murphy, O. Carm., eds. *The Jerome Biblical Commentary* (Englewood Cliffs, N.J.: Prentice Hall, 1968), 267.

2. Raymond E. Brown, S.S., *An Introduction to the New Testament* (New York: Doubleday, 1997), 521.

3. Brown, Fitzmyer, Murphy, *The Jerome Biblical Commentary,* 267.

4. John L. McKenzie, *Dictionary of the Bible* (Milwaukee: Bruce, 1965), 663.

5. "Of course, the Church knows that in the NT celibacy was not demanded of all who follow Jesus or even of the Twelve, but it was held up as an ideal to those who were able to bear it." Raymond E. Brown, S.S., *Priest and Bishop: Biblical Reflections* (New York: Paulist Press, 1970), 25.

6. Jean-Paul Audet, *Structures of Christian Priesthood* (New York: Macmillan, 1968), 70–71.

7. Eusebius, *Ecclesiasticae Historiae* V, 24 (*PG* 20, 295).

8. Hippolytus, *Philosophomena* IX, 12, 22 (*PG* 16, 3388).

9. *Vita Cypriani,* 4 (*PL* 4, 78).

10. Clement of Alexandria, *Stromata* III, 6, 53 (*PG* 8, 1158).

11. Ibid., 12, 90 (*PG* 8, 1191).

12. Eusebius, VI, 42 (*PG* 26, 614).

13. Ibid., VIII, 9 (*PG* 20, 762).

14. *Apostolic Constitutions,* II, 2 (*PG* 1, 598).

15. *Didascalia Apostolorum,* IV.

16. John W. O'Malley, "Some Basics about Celibacy," *America* 177, no. 13 (October 28, 2002): 9.

17. Jerome, *Adversus Jovinianum,* 1, 20 (*PL* 23, 258).

18. John Chrysostom, *De Virginitate,* 19 (*PG* 48, 547).

19. Edward Schillebeeckx, *The Church with a Human Face* (New York: Crossroad, 1985), 241.

20. Edward H. Landon, *A Manual of Councils of the Holy Catholic Church* (London: Gilbert and Rivington, 1846), 24.

21. Ibid., 256.

22. Ibid., 258.

23. Socrates, *Ecclesiastical History,* Bk. I, Ch. 11 (*PG* 66, 1485).

24. Petro B. T. Bilaniuk, "Celibacy and Eastern Tradition," in *Celibacy: The Necessary Option,* ed. George H. Frein (New York: Herder and Herder, 1968), 40.

25. Schillebeeckx, *Human Face,* 241.

26. Jerome, Letter to Oceanus, LXIX, 2 (*PL* 22, 654).

27. See the Internet Medieval Sourcebook organized by the Fordham University Center for Medieval Studies, "The Canons of the Council of Trullo": *www.fordham.edu/halsall/basis/trullo.html.*

28. Uta Ranke-Heinemann, *Eunuchs for the Kingdom of Heaven* (New York: Doubleday, 1990), 107.

29. Anne Llewellyn Barstow, *Married Priests and the Reforming Papacy* (Lewiston, N.Y.: Mellen, 1982), 142.

30. Ibid., 107.

31. Schillebeeckx, *Human Face,* 243.

32. Bert Peeters, *The Story of the Married Priest* (Mequon, Wis.: Word Working, 2000), 13–14.

33. Richard P. McBrien, *Lives of the Popes* (San Francisco: Harper, 1997).

34. Ludwig Freihere von Pastor, *The History of the Popes from the Close of the Middle Ages,* ed. Ralph Francis Kerr (St. Louis: Herder, 1930), 15:74.

35. Ibid., 19:17.

36. *ES,* 1809.

37. Ibid., 1810.

38. Ibid., 1812–16.

39. A review of the *vota* from the worldwide episcopate during the preparatory phase of Vatican II reveals that the only suggestion of a relaxation of priestly celibacy came from eight African bishops. This aroused the pope's interest. See Etienne Fouilloux, "The Antepreparatory Phase: The Slow Emergence from Inertia (January 1959–October 1962)," in *History of Vatican II,* vol. 1, ed. Giuseppe Alberigo and Joseph A. Komonchak (Maryknoll, N.Y.: Orbis Books, 1995), 130, n. 179.

40. Heinz Vogels, *The Church and Married Priests* (Paris: International Federation of Married Catholic Priests, 1993), 31.

41. Peeters, *The Story of the Married Priest,* 27.

42. Henri Fesquet, *The Drama of Vatican II,* trans. Bernard Murchland (New York: Random House, 1967), 696.

43. Vogels, *The Church and Married Priests,* 32.

44. *Vatican Council II,* vol. 1, ed. Austin Flannery, O.P. (New York: Costello, 1998), 892.

45. Ibid., 296.

46. Bernard Häring, *Priesthood Imperiled* (Liguori, Mo: Triumph Books, 1989), 104.

47. Leo Cardinal Suenens, *Memories and Hopes,* trans. Elena French (Dublin: Veritas, 1992), 920.

48. Peeters, *The Story of the Married Priest,* 29.

49. Ibid., 47.

50. Suenens, *Memories and Hopes,* 251.

51. Schillebeeckx, *Human Face,* 211–32.

52. Peeters, *The Story of the Married Priest,* 90.

53. Vogels, *The Church and Married Priests,* 33.

54. Ibid.

55. Ibid.

56. Ibid., 33–34.

57. Ibid., 34.

58. Ibid.

59. Ibid., 36.

60. Ibid., 32.

61. *The Australian,* May 1996, cited by James E. Biechler, "A Question of Rights: Catholic Justice Fails Married Priests," *http://astro.temple.edu/~arcc/rights17.htm.*

62. Jim McBeth, "Sex Scandal Bishop Loses Cancer Battle," *The Scotsman*, May 25, 2005.

63. Bishop Francis Murphy, letter to Allen Moore, president of CORPUS U.S.A., published in *CORPUS Canada: The Journal* 2, no. 5 (September–October 1999), online at *http://corpuscanada.org/995bishop.html*.

2. Beloved Wives

1. *The Inclusive New Testament* (Brentwood, Md.: Priests for Equality, 1996), 336–37.

2. As the outstanding New Testament scholar John Meier noted, "Did the historical Jesus have women disciples? In name, no; in reality — putting aside the question of an implicit as opposed to an explicit call — yes. Certainly the reality rather than the label would have been what caught most people's attention.... Whatever the problem of vocabulary, the most probable conclusion is that Jesus viewed and treated these women as disciples." John P. Meier, *A Marginal Jew: Companions and Competitors* (New York: Doubleday, 2001), 3:79–80.

3. Meier notes that Luke was the only scriptural author to use the Greek feminine form of disciple — to describe Tabitha, a devout Christian woman in the early Church (Acts 9:36). See ibid., 79.

4. Tertullian, *De Cultu Feminarum*, I.1 (*PL* 1, 1304).

5. Origen, *Selecta in Exodum* (*PG* 12, 298).

6. Ambrosiaster, *On 1 Corinthians 14, 34* (*CSEL* 81, 160).

7. Anne Llewellyn Barstow, *Married Priests and the Reforming Papacy* (Lewiston, N.Y.: Mellen, 1982), 43.

8. Bernard Verkamp, "Cultic Purity and the Law of Celibacy," *Review for Religious* 3 (March 1971): 206–7.

9. Barstow, *Married Priests*, 83.

10. Peter Damian, *Contra Imperantes Clericos* (*PL* 145, 410 ff.).

11. Heinrich Kramer and Jakob Sprenger, *Malleus Maleficarum*, Part I, Question 6, trans. Rev. Montague Sommers (Suffolk: John Rodker, 1928), 41–47.

12. Uta Ranke-Heinemann, *Eunuchs for the Kingdom of Heaven* (New York: Doubleday, 1990), 100.

13. *Codex Juris Canonici* (Roma: Typis Polyglottis Vaticanis, 1917), 32.

14. John Lynch, commenting on the rights and obligations of clerics in James A. Coriden, Thomas J. Green, and Donald E. Hentschel, eds., *The Code of Canon Law: A Text and Commentary* (Mahwah, N.J.: Paulist Press, 1985), 211.

15. Ibid., 139.

16. *Catechism of the Catholic Church* (New York: Doubleday, 1995), no. 370.

17. John Paul II, "Letter to Women," *Origins: CNS Documentary Service* 25, no. 9 (July 27, 1995): 139.

18. A. W. Sipe, "The Future of the Priesthood: Celibacy, Sex, and the Place of Women," in *Shaping the Future Priesthood*, CORPUS Research I (Minneapolis: CORPUS, 1988), 15.

19. *The Poems of St. Paulinus of Nola,* trans. P. G. Walsh (New York: Newman Press, 1975).

20. Donald E. Ericson, *Abelard and Heloise: Their Lives, Their Love, Their Letters* (New York: Bennett-Edwards, 1990), 73–95.

21. Ranke-Heinemann, *Eunuchs for the Kingdom of Heaven,* 169.

· 22. *What Luther Says: An Anthology,* comp. Edward M. Plass (St. Louis: Concordia, 1959), 888.

23. Linda and Phil Marcin, "Chronicles from Vineyard," *CORPUS Reports* (September–October 2001): 26–28.

24. Jan Currie, "If Only, Sean ... " *The Tablet,* June 9, 2003.

25. *Council Daybook — Vatican II, Session 4* (Washington, D.C.: National Welfare Conference, 1965), 365.

26. Joan Chittister, address to the 2001 Call to Action meeting, Los Angeles, cited in Arthur Jones, "Looking through Vatican II's Prism," online at *www.beliefnet.com/story/86/story_8695_1.html.*

3. Organizing Priests

1. *Vatican Council II,* vol. 1, ed. Austin Flannery, O.P. (New York: Costello Publishing, 1998), 580.

2. Ibid., 600.

3. Robert Kennedy, "A Review of Priests' Councils," in *The Time to Build* (Huntington, Ind.: Our Sunday Visitor, 1968), 6.

4. Cited in the monthly newsletter of the National Association for Pastoral Renewal, January 1969, 4.

5. William F. Powers, *Free Priests: The Movement for Ministerial Reform in the American Catholic Church* (Chicago: Loyola University Press, 1992), 19.

6. *The Catholic Priest in the United States: Sociological Investigations,* NORC Study directed by Andrew Greeley (Washington, D.C.: USCC, 1972), vi.

7. From edited transcript of presentation by Bishop Thomas Gumbleton on May 25, 2002, in Lexington, Massachusetts.

8. William F. Powers, *Free Priests: The Movement for Ministerial Reform in the American Catholic Church* (Chicago: Loyola University Press, 1992).

9. Anthony Padovano, "Broken Promises," *Shaping the Future Priesthood* (Minneapolis: CORPUS, 1988), 6.

10. Anthony Padovano, "A North Atlantic Federation," *CORPUS Reports* 29, no. 3 (May–June 2003): 42–43.

4. *The* Humanae Vitae *Debacle*

1. See Charles E. Curran, Robert E. Hunt, et al., *Dissent in and for the Church: Theologians and Humane Vitae* (New York: Sheed & Ward, 1969), 26.

2. Statement sent to Cardinal O'Boyle on August 4, 1968. Cited in "Theologians on Birth Control: Spouse May Decide," *Washington Post,* July 31, 1968, p. A18.

3. "Vatican Edict Fails to Silence Critics," *Washington Post,* July 30, 1968, p. A11.

4. James Patrick Shannon, *Reluctant Dissenter* (New York: Crossroad, 1998), 148.

5. Ibid.

6. Ibid., 147.

7. CELAM: Consejo Episcopal Latinoamericano, the Latin American Episcopal Council.

8. Shannon, *Reluctant Dissenter,* 153.

9. Ibid., 150.

10. *National Catholic Reporter,* December 31, 1999, 23–24.

11. *Council Daybook, Vatican II, Session 3* (Washington, D.C.: National Welfare Conference, 1965), 201.

12. Charles R. Morris, *American Catholics* (New York: Vintage Books, 1997), 306.

13. George Gallup Jr. and Jim Castelli, *The American Catholic People* (New York: Doubleday, 1987), 50.

14. James A. Coriden, *The Canonical Doctrine of Reception* (Delran, N.J.: ARCC, 1998), 1.

15. Yves M. Congar, "Reception as an Ecclesiastical Reality," *Concilium* 77 (New York: Herder and Herder, 1972), 57–66.

16. Bernard Häring, *My Hope for the Church* (Liguori: Liguori/Triumph, 1999), 136.

5. Working for the Church

1. George Anderson, "Of Many Things," *America,* November 11, 2002, 22.

2. Raymond E. Brown, *The Critical Meaning of the Bible* (New York: Paulist Press, 1981), 102.

7. Prominent Former Clerics

1. Javan Kienzle, *Judged by Love: A Biography of William X. Kienzle* (Kansas, Mo.: Andrews McMeel Publishing, 2004).

2. John Dominic Crossan, "Almost the Whole Truth," *The Fourth R* (bi-monthly magazine of the Westar Institute) 65 (September–October 1993).

8. The Swinging Door

1. Joseph Fichter, *The Pastoral Provisions* (Kansas City, Mo.: Sheed & Ward, 1989), 69.

2. Mary Vincent Dally, *Married to a Catholic Priest* (Chicago: Loyola Press, 1988), 220–21.

3. Frederick J. Luhmann, *Call and Response* (Berryville, Va.: Dialogue Press, 2001), 98–100.

4. Ibid., 154–55.

5. Fichter, *The Pastoral Provisions,* 123.

6. *The Ecumenical Movement: An Anthology of Key Texts and Voices,* ed. Michael Kinnamon and Brian E. Cope (Grand Rapids, Mich.: Eerdmans, 1997), 146.

7. *Origins: CNS Documentary Service* 26, no. 41 (April 13, 1997).

9. Spirituality and Married Priests

1. "Declaration on the Relations of the Church to Non-Christian Religions," *Vatican Council II,* vol. 1, ed. Austin Flannery, O.P. (New York: Costello Publishing, 1998), 738–40.

2. Ruben L. F. Habito, *Total Liberation* (Maryknoll, N.Y.: Orbis Books, 1984), 3.

3. "The Constitution on the Sacred Liturgy," *Vatican Council II,* 6.

4. From Thomas Merton's personal journal, dated March 23, 1967. Found in Michael Mott, *The Seven Mountains of Thomas Merton* (Boston: Houghton Mifflin, 1984), 437.

5. Patrick Hart, ed., *Thomas Merton, Monk: A Monastic Tribute* (New York: Sheed & Ward, 1974), 216–17.

6. Ibid., 219–20.

7. *Spiritual Renewal of the American Priesthood* (Washington, D.C.: U.S. Catholic Conference, 1973), 3.

8. Ibid., 4.

9. Ibid.

10. Dom Jean-Baptist Chautard, O.C.S.O. *The Soul of the Apostolate* (Trappist, Ky.: Abbey of Gethsemani, 1946).

11. Robert E. Kennedy, *Zen Spirit, Christian Spirit* (New York: Continuum, 1999), 14.

12. Ibid., 15.

13. Each has written extensively on the subject. See: Chwen Jiuan A. Lee and Thomas G. Hand, *A Taste of Water: Christianity through Taoist-Buddhist Eyes* (New York: Paulist Press, 1990) and Kennedy, *Zen Spirit, Christian Spirit.*

14. Personal letter to the author; printed with permission.

10. My Journey

1. John J. Hill, "Rationale for a National Organization," in *The Time to Build* (Huntington, Ind.: Our Sunday Visitor, 1968), 29.

2. *Origins: CNS Documentary Service* 26, no. 41 (April 13, 1997).

11. Priests in Transition

1. Bert Peeters, *The Story of the Married Priest* (Mequon, Wis.: Word Working, 2000), 90.

12. A Nurturing Parish

1. Paul A. Janowiak, "Running to Communion," *America* 189, no. 13 (October 27, 2003).

2. Paul Wilkes, *Excellent Catholic Parishes* (Mahwah, N.J.: Paulist Press, 2001).

13. The Cultural Revolution

1. Paul Wilkes, "Ten Commandments of Church Renewal," *CORPUS Reports* (July–August 2002): 5.

2. *The Truth* 6, no. 2 (Spring 2001): 3.

14. Married Priesthood Today

1. Bert Peeters, *The Story of the Married Priest* (Mequon, Wis.: Word Working, 2000), 16.

2. Anthony Padovano, "Broken Promises," in *Shaping the Future Priesthood* (Minneapolis: CORPUS, 1988), 1.

3. From the homily of John Paul II on Sunday, October 21, 2001, on the occasion of the Beatification of Luigi Beltrame Quattrocchi and Maria Corsini (see *www.vatican.va/holyfather/john_paul_ii/homilies*).

4. Richard A. Schoenherr, *Goodbye Father* (New York: Oxford University Press, 2002), 216.

5. Richard John Neuhaus, "The Public Square," *First Things* (January 2003).

Conclusion

1. Donald B. Cozzens, *The Changing Face of the Priesthood* (Collegeville, Minn.: Liturgical Press, 2000), 48.

2. Robert J. Silva, "Between Promise and Fulfillment," *Touchstone* 17, no. 3 (Spring 2002): 26–27.

3. Edward Stourton, *Absolute Truth* (New York: TV Books, 2000), 248.

4. Bernard Häring, *My Hope for the Church* (Liguori, Mo.: Liguori/ Triumph, 1999), xv.

5. Karl Rahner, *The Shape of the Church to Come* (New York: Crossroad, 1983), 27.

6. *Vatican Council II*, vol. 1, ed. Austin Flannery, O.P. (New York: Costello Publishing, 1998), 950.

7. Ibid., 951.

8. Ibid., 892.

9. Dean Hoge and Jacqueline Wenger, "Survey of Priests, 2001" (unpublished report, Catholic University, 2001).

10. William V. D'Antonio, James D. Davidson, Dean R. Hoge, and Katherine Meyer, *American Catholics* (Walnut Creek, Calif.: Alta Mira Press, 2001), 110.

11. Anthony Padovano, "Broken Promises," in *Shaping the Future Priesthood* (Minneapolis: CORPUS, 1988), 4.

Epilogue: The New Pontificate

1. Jim Wallis, *God's Politics* (San Francisco: HarperSanFrancisco, 2005), 346.

Bibliography

Audet, Jean Paul. *Structures of Christian Priesthood*. New York: Macmillan, 1967.

Barstow, Anne Llewellyn. *Married Priests and the Reforming Papacy*. Lewiston, N.Y.: Mellen, 1982.

Bilaniuk, Petro B. T. "Celibacy and Eastern Tradition." In *Celibacy: The Necessary Option,* ed. George H. Frein. New York: Herder and Herder, 1968.

Brodrick, James. *St. Ignatius Loyola: The Pilgrim Years*. New York: Farrar, Strauss & Cudahy, 1956.

Brown, Raymond E. *The Critical Meaning of the Bible*. New York: Paulist Press, 1981.

———. *An Introduction to the New Testament*. New York: Doubleday, 1997.

———. *Priest and Bishop: Biblical Reflections*. New York: Paulist Press, 1970.

———, Fitzmyer, Joseph A., and Roland E. Murphy, eds. *The Jerome Biblical Commentary*. Englewood Cliffs, N.J.: Prentice Hall, 1968.

Butler's Lives of the Saints. Edited by Herbert Thurston, S.J., and Donald Attwater. New York: P. J. Kenedy & Sons, 1956.

Catechism of the Catholic Church. New York: Doubleday, 1995.

The Catholic Priest in the United States: Historical Investigations. Ed. John Tracy Ellis. Collegeville, Minn.: St. John's University Press, 1971.

The Catholic Priest in the United States: Psychological Investigations. Directed by Eugene C. Kennedy and Victor J. Heckler. Washington, D.C.: Publications Office, USCC, 1972.

The Catholic Priest in the United States: Sociological Investigations. NORC Study directed by Andrew M. Greeley. Washington, D.C.: Publications Office, USCC, 1972.

Chautard, Dom Jean-Baptist. *The Soul of the Apostolate*. Trappist, Ky.: Abbey of Gethsemani, Inc., 1946.

The Church and Married Priests. Paris: IFMCP, 1993.

Congar, Yves M. "Reception as an Ecclesiastical Reality." *Concilium* 77. New York: Herder and Herder, 1972.

Coriden, James A. *The Canonical Doctrine of Reception.* Delran, N.J.: The Association for the Rights of Catholics in the Church, 1998.

———, Thomas J. Green, and Donald E. Hentschel, eds. *The Code of Canon Law: A Text and Commentary.* Mahwah, N.J.: Paulist Press, 1985.

CORPUS Research I: Shaping the Future Priesthood. Proceedings of First National Conference on a Married Priesthood. CORPUS, 1988.

Council Daybook, Vatican II. 3 vols. Washington, D.C.: National Catholic Welfare Conference, 1965.

Cozzens, Donald B. *The Changing Face of the Priesthood.* Collegeville, Minn.: Liturgical Press, 2000.

Crossan, John Dominic. "Almost the Whole Truth." *The Fourth R* 7, no. 5 (September–October 1993).

———. *A Long Way to Tipperary.* San Francisco: HarperSanFrancisco, 2000.

Dally, Mary Vincent. *Married to a Catholic Priest.* Chicago: Loyola Press, 1988.

D'Antonio, William V., James D. Davidson, Dean R. Hoge, and Katherine Meyer. *American Catholics.* Walnut Creek, Calif.: Alta Mira Press, 2001.

Didascalia Apostolorum. The Syriac Version Translated and Accompanied by the Verona Latin Fragments with an Introduction and Notes by R. Hugh Connolly. Oxford: Clarendon Press, 1929.

The Ecumenical Movement: An Anthology of Key Texts and Voices. Ed. Michael Kinnamon and Brian E. Cope. Grand Rapids: Eerdmans, 1997.

Ericson, Donald E. *Abelard and Heloise: Their Lives, Their Love, Their Letters.* New York: Bennett-Edwards, 1990.

Fesquet, Henri. *The Drama of Vatican II.* Trans. Bernard Murchland. New York: Random House, 1967.

Fichter, Joseph H. *The Pastoral Provisions.* Kansas City, Mo.: Sheed & Ward, 1989.

———. *Wives of Catholic Clergy.* Kansas City, Mo.: Sheed & Ward, 1992.

Fiedler, Maureen, and Linda Rabben, eds. *Rome Has Spoken.* New York: Crossroad, 1998.

Fouilloux, Etienne. "The Antepreparatory Phase: The Slow Emergence from Inertia (January 1959–October 1962)." In *History of Vatican II,* vol. 1, ed. Giuseppe Alberigo and Joseph A. Komonchak. Maryknoll, N.Y.: Orbis Books, 1995.

Frein, George H., ed. *Celibacy: The Necessary Option.* New York: Herder & Herder, 1968.

Gallup, George Jr., and Jim Castelli. *The American Catholic People.* New York: Doubleday, 1987.

Gibson, David. *The Coming Catholic Church.* San Francisco: HarperSan-Francisco, 2003.

Habito, Ruben L. F. *Total Liberation.* Maryknoll, N.Y.: Orbis Books, 1984.

Häring, Bernard. *Priesthood Imperiled.* Liguori, Mo.: Triumph Books, 1989.

———. *My Hope for the Church.* Liguori, Mo.: Liguori/Triumph, 1999.

Hart, Patrick, ed. *Thomas Merton, Monk: A Monastic Tribute.* New York: Sheed & Ward, 1974.

Hill, John J. "Rationale for a National Organization." In *The Time to Build.* Huntington, Ind.: Our Sunday Visitor, 1968.

The Inclusive New Testament. Brentwood, Md.: Priests for Equality, 1996.

John Paul II. *Wisdom of John Paul II.* Compiled by Nick Bakalar and Richard Balkin. New York: Vintage Books, 2001.

Kennedy, Robert. "A Review of Priests' Councils." In *The Time to Build.* Huntington, Ind.: Our Sunday Visitor, 1968.

Kennedy, Robert E. *Zen Spirit, Christian Spirit.* New York: Continuum, 1999.

Kramer, Heinrich, and Jakob Sprenger. *Malleus Maleficarum.* Trans. Rev. Montague Sommers. Suffolk: John Rodker Publishers, 1928.

Landon, Edward H. *A Manual of Councils of the Holy Roman Church.* London: Gilbert and Rivington, 1846.

Lea, Henry C. *An Historical Sketch of Sacerdotal Celibacy in the Christian Church.* Boston: Houghton Mifflin, 1881.

Lee, Chwen Jiuan A. and Thomas G. Hand. *A Taste of Water: Christianity Through Taoist-Buddhist Eyes.* New York: Paulist Press, 1990.

Luhmann, Frederick J. *Call and Response.* Berryville, Va.: Dialogue Press, 2002.

Luther, Martin. *What Luther Says: An Anthology.* Compiled by Ewald M. Plass. St. Louis: Concordia, 1959.

Marcin, Linda and Phil. "Chronicles from Vineyard." *Corpus Reports* (September–October, 2001): 26–28.

McBrien, Richard P. *Lives of the Popes.* San Francisco: Harper, 1997.

McKenzie, John L. *Dictionary of the Bible.* Milwaukee: Bruce, 1965.

Meier, John P. *A Marginal Jew: Companions and Competitors.* New York: Doubleday, 2001.

Morris, Charles R. *American Catholic.* New York: Vintage Books, 1997.

Mott, Michael. *The Seven Mountains of Thomas Merton.* Boston: Houghton Mifflin, 1984.

Naughton, Jim. *Catholics in Crisis.* Reading, Mass: Addison-Wesley, 1996.

Padovano, Anthony T. "Broken Promises." In *Shaping the Future Priesthood.* Minneapolis: CORPUS, 1988.

———. *Hope Is a Dialogue.* Mequon, Wis.: Caritas Communications, 1998.

———. "A North Atlantic Federation." *CORPUS Reports* (May–June 2003): 42–43.

Pastor, Ludwig Freihere von. *The History of the Popes from the Close of the Middle Ages.* Ed. Ralph Francis Kerr. St. Louis: Herder, 1930.

Peeters, Bert. *The Story of the Married Priest.* Mequon, Wis.: Word Working, 2000.

The Poems of St. Paulinus of Nola. Trans. P. G. Walsh. New York: Newman Press, 1975.

Powers, William F. *Free Priests: The Movement for Ministerial Reform in the American Catholic Church.* Chicago: Loyola University Press, 1992.

Rahner, Karl. *The Shape of the Church to Come.* New York: Crossroad, 1983.

Ranke-Heinemann, Uta. *Eunuchs for the Kingdom of Heaven.* New York: Doubleday, 1990.

Rice, David. *Shattered Vows.* New York: William Morrow, 1990.

Schillebeeckx, Edward. *Ministry.* New York: Crossroad, 1981.

———. *The Church with a Human Face.* New York: Crossroad, 1985.

Schoenherr, Richard A. *Goodbye Father.* New York: Oxford University Press, 2002.

Schüssler Fiorenza, Elisabeth. *In Memory of Her.* New York: Crossroad, 1987.

Shannon, James Patrick. *Reluctant Dissenter.* New York: Crossroad, 1998.

Silva, Robert J. "Between Promise and Fulfillment." *Touchstone* 17, no. 3 (Spring 2002): 14–15.

Sipe, A. W. "The Future of the Priesthood: Celibacy, Sex, and the Place of Women," *Shaping the Future Priesthood.* Minneapolis: CORPUS, 1988.

Spiritual Direction for Priests in the U.S.A. Washington, D.C.: U.S. Catholic Conference, 1977.

Spiritual Renewal of the American Priesthood. Washington, D.C.: U.S. Catholic Conference, 1973.

Steinfels, Peter. *A People Adrift.* New York: Simon & Schuster, 2003.

Stourton, Edward. *Absolute Truth.* New York: TV Books, 2000.

Suenens, Leo Cardinal. *Memories and Hopes.* Trans. Elena French. Dublin: Veritas, 1992.

Vatican Council II. Ed. Austin Flannery, O.P. Vol. 1. New York: Costello Publishing, 1998.

Verkamp, Bernard. "Cultic Purity and the Law of Celibacy." *Review for Religious* 3 (March 1971): 206–7.

Vogels, Heinz. *The Church and Married Priests.* Paris: International Federation of Married Catholic Priests, 1993.

Wallis, Jim. *God's Politics.* San Francisco: HarperSanFrancisco, 2005.

Webber, Christopher L. *Finding Home.* Boston: Cowley Publications, 1997.

Wilkes, Paul. "Ten Commandments of Church Renewal." *CORPUS Reports* (July–August 2002): 4–7.

Index

Of Related Interest

John Wijngaards
WOMEN DEACONS IN THE EARLY CHURCH
Historical Texts and Contemporary Debates

One of the most common arguments against the ordination
of women deacons is that it represents a break with tradition. As John Wijngaards beautifully demonstrates through
the English translation of new historical evidence, tens of
thousands of women deacons served in early Catholic communities, and there is no reason not to ordain women to
such orders today.

0-8245-2393-0, $19.95, paperback

Phyllis Zagano
HOLY SATURDAY
*An Argument for the Restoration
of the Female Diaconate
in the Catholic Church*

A serious effort to faithfully investigate the history and
canonical viability of the female diaconate. Based on thor-
ough research, as well as sound historical and theological
analysis and reflection, this book makes a significant contribution to the discussion and development of women's
roles in the modern church.

0-8245-1832-2, $16.95, paperback

crossroad

Of Related Interest

Deborah Halter
THE PAPAL "NO"
*A Comprehensive Guide
to the Vatican's Rejection of Women's Ordination*

Growing out of the author's experience as head of the Women's Ordination Conference, this book is the complete resource on the question of women's ordination. This definitive work includes all source text regarding Vatican pronouncements on women's ordination, as well as a close examination of these sources documenting the Vatican's inconsistent response.

0-8245-2271-0, $24.95, paperback

Please support your local bookstore,
or call 1-800-707-0670 for Customer Service.

For a free catalog, write us at

THE CROSSROAD PUBLISHING COMPANY
16 Penn Plaza – 481 Eighth Avenue, Suite 1550
New York, NY 10001

Visit our website at
www.crossroadpublishing.com
All prices subject to change.

crossroad